REAL PIGS

REAL PIGS

SHIFTING VALUES *in the*
FIELD *of* LOCAL PORK

BRAD WEISS

Duke University Press
DURHAM AND LONDON 2016

Designed by Heather Hensley
Typeset in Chaparral Pro by Westchester Publishing
Services

Library of Congress Cataloging-in-Publication Data
Names: Weiss, Brad, author.
Title: Real pigs : shifting values in the field of local pork /
Brad Weiss.
Description: Durham : Duke University Press, 2016. |
Includes bibliographical references and index.
Identifiers: LCCN 2015049624
ISBN 9780822361381 (hardcover : alk. paper)
ISBN 9780822361572 (pbk. : alk. paper)
ISBN 9780822374237 (e-book)
Subjects: LCSH: Pork industry and trade—North Carolina. |
Cooking (Pork)—North Carolina.
Classification: LCC HD9435.U63 N68 2016 | DDC
338.1/736400922756—dc23
LC record available at http://lccn.loc.gov/2015049624

Cover: Farmer's Hybrid pigs eating. Photo by Brad Weiss.

CONTENTS

PREFACE

This project began quite differently from most of my ethnographic work. I was on vacation. It was the summer of 2007, and I was in the midst of fine-tuning the final draft of my last book, a work that looked at popular culture in the tourist town of Arusha, in Tanzania. My wife and I had driven up to Sonoma County from my parents' home in Southern California, and we stayed on the Russian River, which I liked to think of as my regular getaway, or as much of one as it could be for someone who lives 2,900 miles away. I was also enthusiastically anticipating becoming the chair of my department in about a month. All of these circumstances conduced to my pondering what kind of research I might do next. I know—just the kind of guy you want to take on your next vacation. In any case, as I was pretty sure I would not have the opportunity to pop over to Tanzania in the near future, and as my work in Arusha was all but finished, I took a look around in Sonoma. Gravenstein apples in Sebastopol caught my eye. Yeah, I had eaten those as a kid. Now these sweet crisp apples with origins in Denmark were touted as part of Sebastopol's local heritage. Every little town—Forestville, Occidental, Monte Rio, Guerneville—had a string of artisanal food products for sale. Amid the wineries I saw an array of goat farms, some offering pygmy goats for sale as pets and livestock, others raising dairy goats for California *chèvres*.

My interest was piqued, but I was not sure quite what I was looking at. I recall idling about in a bookstore (I believe it was in Calistoga) that had what seemed like an enormous display of books dedicated to local foods. I skimmed through the most recent issue of *Gastronomica* on its shelves. When I talked to my wife over dinner, I told her that I had an idea for a research project. Taking advantage of her indulgence, I said that there was something called Slow Food, and I thought it could be looked at as a social movement in the United States. Even better, I said we could spend our summers up in Sonoma while I did the research, since the stuff seemed to be everywhere. How hard could that be?

I tucked the thought away for a while. We flew back to our home in North Carolina. I took up my ungodly commute to my newfound administrative tasks at the College of William and Mary, and I thought about those goat farms. One Saturday morning in 2008, I went shopping at the Carrboro Farmers' Market, about a mile and a half from my house. Until that point, although I had lived in the area for five years and had done some shopping at the market, I had not been a regular there; I usually went to the market only for seasonal fruit—strawberries in May, or watermelon in the summer. I certainly did not know any of the vendors by name, or even by sight. On this Saturday, though, it suddenly dawned on me that I really did not need to go anywhere to investigate the questions I had become interested in out in California. Local food, as the term suggests, is everywhere and, as it happens, quite prominently so in North Carolina's Triangle (the area that lies between the three cities of Raleigh, Durham, and Chapel Hill), where I lived.

I was enlivened by the prospect of doing this work almost literally in my own backyard, albeit a little wistful that I might not have to go to Sonoma to do it. In looking around the Carrboro Farmers' Market on that fateful Saturday, I also realized something rather obvious: it would not be possible for any one person to study the Slow Food movement, at least not in the ethnographic fashion that is typical of the kind of anthropological research I have usually done. In part as a happy accident of the cultural geography of central North Carolina, I saw a number of vendors offering pork products for sale, and I realized that I might be able to look more closely at pigs and pork as a lens through which to examine the wider questions posed by contemporary efforts to transform American food systems. The fact that pigs are iconic of North Carolina's preferred cuisine made the case for choosing matters porcine even stronger. Moreover, the pig as a culinary form and a lively creature is, as I knew even before I thought of this as research, highly thought of by devotees of Slow Food and high cuisine. "The pig has powerful mojo in the world of cooking," as Sara Dickerman noted in her essay on the gastronomic lyricism that pigs and pork inspire (2006). Of course any ethnographer worth his Maldon sea salt knows that human-porcine relations are the stuff of legendary anthropological theorizing, from the abominations of Leviticus (Douglas 2012; Soler 1997) to English forms of linguistic abuse (Leach 1964), and from Bakhtinian revels (Stallybrass and White 1986) to Melanesian ritual (Rappaport 1968). All this, coupled with their ironic gustatory appeal to an otherwise nice Jewish boy, made an ethnography focused on the array of values generated by the (re)production, transformation, distribution, and consumption of pigs and their pork seem like just the thing for me to do.

Before I really began my research efforts in earnest, I was struck again with the particularity of the language that I heard and read being used to describe foods, like pigs and pork, by advocates for these innovations in the food system. What made a food local? Could it be just a matter of regulation and certification of the kind carried out by a number of markets—including the Carrboro Farmers' Market—that assured their customers that all of the products purveyed at the market were "local" because they came from less than fifty (or thirty, or a hundred, or however many) miles from the market? Is something local simply by virtue of its proximity in geometric space? Similarly, how did some food become recognized as part of a regional "heritage"? And what made some kinds of foods part of a "foodway," while others were recognized as "heritage" and still others were noted as "heirloom" varieties? How did some kinds of foods become one thing and not another? The slipperiness and unreliability of these terms is, of course, notorious, as this book demonstrates. It is not always clear whether they are intended to convey information to consumers; certify the presence of some distinctive property in the designated foods; brand the farmer, producer, or purveyor of the product being sold; or purposefully delude potential customers with a marketing ploy. Did this complex lexicon actually index any reliable content?

Moreover, I was especially intrigued by what semioticians would call the iconic function of these terms (Fehérváry 2013; Manning 2012; Munn 1986)—that is, the particular kinds of qualities that are evoked by the use of specific terms. "Heritage," for example, is a particularly complex term to use, perhaps especially with respect to food. In a few instances it might be the product of a certification process that labels foods meeting specific criteria that have been agreed on, either by experts in a particular field (for example, by animal scientists trying to protect the biological profile of a particular "heritage" breed) or by producers who want to regulate their markets so as to create premium value for their "heritage" good. Just as often it is simply a term that is used willy-nilly to suggest quality to potential consumers.

But why—and how—does "heritage" suggest quality? It implies a certain temporal depth to a product, one that suggests a legacy of usage or production over many generations (but how many? and where?). Even advocates for Slow Food in the United States recognize that "heritage" means something very different in Europe, where Slow Food began, than it does in the United States (Petrini 2006). While European producers often seek protection for products and practices that are held to have a long, recognized legacy in a particular region, most American farmers and artisans are less committed to this notion of "heritage" (Paxson 2012). Nonetheless, "heritage" flourishes as a term in the production or sale of particular foods in the United States. What can it mean, for example, that an apple like the Gravenstein, which is known to come from South Jutland in Denmark, could be declared a heritage variety in Sonoma County and be included in the U.S. Slow Food's "Ark of Taste" (Local Harvest n.d.)? Or that pigs celebrated as descendants of Spanish black foot pigs could be registered as an American heritage breed in North and South Carolina (and, indeed, across the country)?

In the course of this book I directly examine such questions and show how complicated it is to make such deceptively complicated descriptions.[1] But I also note that it is possible to speak of "heritage," even in the absence of any real generational depth—and even when producers and consumers do not assume any such depth—because the word can also connote more general qualities of depth. Indeed, a central quality of the foods that are described as "heritage" is the way they are felt to embody deeper meanings or characteristics. Such depth may be attributes of their process of production or flavor. In this way, depth of meaning can be contrasted to other qualities—like being cheap, insipid, bland, or commercial—and thereby can represent foods described in this way as being opposed to, or distinct from, the generic products of an industrial food system. In this book I illustrate the ways that this oppositional possibility instantiates a critical contrast between the compromised values of our current food system and what is often thought of (simply, if quite confusingly!) as "real" food.[2] Heritage connotes generational, historical, grounded depth (and it is only one among many signifiers held to instantiate these qualities in the food world), which I argue is reliably embodied in something otherwise notoriously hard to know: the real thing.

This elusive but compelling truth, the real thing, is a powerful motivation for the complex and challenging efforts I have seen made by farmers, chefs, consultants, and ordinary eaters who are aiming to transform the industrial food system or some specific dimension of it. This is not only a question of finding the real stuff, not just a matter of seeking and spending and getting, but also of knowing what it is. Perhaps above all it is a commitment to the notion that the real is a veritable entity, something that can be brought into being, made concrete, and accessible in everyday life. While figuring out what people can possibly mean by "the real"—or even by "real food"—is undoubtedly a messy task and full of ambiguity, these commitments to the real, as well as the capacity to discern it and the wherewithal to acquire it, are not only abstract, metaphysical matters. The guiding problem I discuss in this book is, in fact, trying to understand and demonstrate how real pigs come to embody these material and symbolic characteristics. Finding and making such pigs, lively animals that incarnate quality, is a project with sociocultural as well as political economic dimensions. The book before you is my attempt to flesh out the endeavors of those working to bring us real pigs.

ACKNOWLEDGMENTS

This book was made possible by the generous support of many friends and colleagues. Much of the writing was done over the course of research leaves provided by the College of William and Mary, and I thank the college for its support. I have also benefited from invitations to present parts of this work at the Universities of Chicago, Michigan, and Western Michigan; the Massachusetts Institute of Technology; the Radcliffe Exploratory Seminar; the School of Oriental and African Studies at the University of London; and the Weltkulturen Museum, in Frankfurt am Main. I am grateful for these invitations and for the generous comments I received from these diverse audiences.

A number of scholars have offered their critical support. I presented various essays that would become parts of this book at the 2008 and 2009 Symposia on Contemporary Perspectives in Anthropology. I would like to thank, in particular, Misty Bastian, Tim Burke, Grey Gundaker, Dorothy Hodgson, Janet MacIntosh, Adeline Masquelier, and Rachel Reynolds for their insights at those events. At various conferences I have benefited from the company and comments of Judith Farquhar, Robert Foster, Cristina Grasseni, Donna Haraway, Deborah Heath, Karen Ho, Hannah Landecker, Laura Lewis, Paul Manning, Anne Meneley, Diane Nelson, Harris Solomon, Amy Trubek, and Harry West. Kriszti Fehérváry, in addition to always being an enthusiastic supporter of my work as well as a font of stories about the Hungarian devotion to pork products, did me the tremendous service of using the manuscript for this work in her graduate seminar in Ann Arbor. The comments I received from her and her wonderful students made an enormous difference in the final work. I had a spectacular time organizing a conference with Marisol de la Cadena in 2010, and the best part of it was beginning a conversation with her about animal life, the political possibilities of ontological matters, and a sincere questioning of the value of anthropology. I have enjoyed disagreeing with her at least as much as I enjoyed agreeing with her, and I look forward to seeing what she makes of Colombian cows. Gillian Feeley-Harnik and John Hartigan offered invaluable comments on chapter 4. Gillian, in particular, provided such a detailed, thoughtful, and inspiring critique that it provided one of the central themes of the book as a whole. I cannot thank her enough for her beyond-generous collegiality. Paige West offered a generous and clear critique of the book that was essential to my final drafting of the work. Ken Wissoker and Elizabeth Ault at Duke University Press have also been great supporters of this book, and their accessibility and enthusiasm have made working with the press a pleasure. Tim Stallmann created the maps. Heather Paxson has been a constant and remarkable interlocutor throughout my research and writing. It was her work on artisanal cheese that first alerted me to the work being done on alternative food systems in the United States, which helped make it possible for me to imagine this research and give it some direction. Her invitations to speak at a Sawyer Seminar and later at Radcliffe were genuinely appreciated, and her insights and questions about my research and chapters have been tremendously helpful in crafting my arguments. I have also been exceptionally lucky to be carrying out this work on "my" pigs at the same time that Alex Blanchette was engaged in his phenomenal work on "his" pigs. Alex's remarkable grasp of the interface between labor, care, and animal life (of all sorts) in the contemporary American political economy of hog production has been a source of real inspiration. I was delighted to serve on his dissertation committee, but the truth is that I learned a hell of a lot more about my own work from him than he benefited from my suggestions. Both Heather and Alex read far more of this manuscript than any colleague can be expected to, and I am sincerely thankful for their unflagging support. Above all, I want to thank Margaret Wiener and Chris Nelson, members of my writing group, for their detailed comments on almost every page in this book. I learned a great deal from their wonderful work, as well. It will be impossible for me ever to think about this book without thinking of Chris and Margaret (and Atsuko, Siobhan, Fifi, and Sophie) as the friends who shared not just writing but also living in Carrboro and Chapel Hill, where so much of this research was carried out. Wherever we are, they will forever be a part of my life, not only my work, and that is something to be very, very grateful for.

On a purely personal note, I must thank Kj and John F. for helping to keep me sane by encouraging me to do something ridiculous. I am forever in their debt. Or perhaps I just owe them a Triscuit.

Fieldwork is always a privilege, as strangers become the best of friends and share aspects of experience that cultivate profound forms of intimacy and empathy. Carrying out this research almost literally in my own backyard, in central North Carolina where I so loved living for twelve years, only amplified this privilege. The nine individuals featured in the profiles I present here were very generous with their time and offered me support that exceeds anything I could give them in return. There are too many farmers, vendors, and market customers for me to thank them by name, but I have learned something from every one of them. I really appreciate Mike Jones's support for my work and his constant willingness to talk to me about anything and everything—and pigs, too. Charles Sydnor—known to everyone as Doc—is a master rancher at Braeburn Farms, and I have not only learned a great deal from him about grass and cattle, but I have been sincerely humbled by his respect and enthusiasm for my work. I learned a great deal while having a very good time working alongside Marshay Privott. I can hardly thank him enough for the few months that we were able to do chores together. A number of unimaginably talented chefs offered their support for my work, and many of them took the time to talk with me extensively about their work and their interest in pastured pork. In particular, Adam Rosen, Aaron Vandermark, and Jeff Barney made very helpful contributions to my work. Andrea Reusing not only talked with me, but she also gave me the opportunity to work in her award-winning kitchen at Lantern alongside her phenomenal staff. Fernando Lara put up with me during the summer of 2009 while carrying out his herculean tasks in prepping a thousand delicious and exhausting concoctions every day in a way-too-small kitchen. I learned a great deal from him and from Miguel Torres and Monica Segovia-Welch, as well. I thank all of these hard-working cooks. Andrea Weigel, who writes about food for the *Raleigh News and Observer*, also offered some valuable insights, for which I am grateful. Steve Moize and Jeannette Beranger of the Livestock

Breed Conservancy had a number of conversations with me about their work and this added a great deal to my understanding of this project.

I do not know what to say about the Carrboro Farmers' Market except that it has been my home for part of every week for the past seven years. Working side by side with the farmers, bakers, cheese makers, and cultivators of all good things has almost always been pure joy. First Sarah Blacklin (whom I profile here) and then Erin Jobe, the managers of the market, welcomed my work, shared extremely helpful information with me, and engaged in thoughtful and fulfilling discussions about farming, food, and community. I am grateful to them both. I first got to know John O'Sullivan (also profiled in this book) at the market, and I want to offer him my great thanks here. John is a bottomless source of insight and understanding about local food, agrarian history, and community politics in North Carolina. Whenever he expressed his approval for the work I was doing, it was tremendously reassuring for me to know I might be on the right track. John has done the entire state of North Carolina an important service in his career, and I am the beneficiary of that as his former fellow citizen and as his colleague and friend.

Eliza MacLean is the best. Nothing you will read in this book could have even been imagined were it not for Eliza. She is the busiest person you could ever meet, but she took the time to teach me pretty much everything I know about anything I have written about here. From my first days mucking about on Cane Creek Farm to my final days in Carrboro manning the high-tech mobile trailer of the Left Bank Butchery, Eliza has been my guru, guide, and dear friend. She has also always let me know how thankful she is for my help to her, which is embarrassing considering how much I have benefited from our nonstop jabbering relationship. On top of all this, Eliza made it possible for my getting to know all the brilliant and beautiful members of her family—Quinn; Enid; and my sweetheart, Elizabeth Basnight—who have greatly enriched this book, my kitchen, and my life. I cannot wait to get back to Saxapahaw, as often as possible, to see how Cane Creek Farm grows over the years and to spend time with just about my favorite people on the planet.

Just about my favorite—but I will reserve that esteemed status for Ezra Weiss and Julie Corsaro. If it weren't for Ezra, the three of us would never have lived for so long in North Carolina, and this work would never have happened. So I am thrilled that he was happy to stay in Carrboro way back when. But I am especially proud of the way he has grown into a fine and compassionate young man. His enthusiasm for animals and farming kept me enthusiastic, and I am delighted that he is going to keep his toe in farming—and in North Carolina—for a little while longer. Of course, I love him dearly. And he took many of the great photos in the book. Julie is my alpha and omega, and her tolerance for my filthy boots, my ungodly early Saturday mornings, and a ridiculous amount of pork leave me humbled. Her simple tolerance for me is rather inexplicable, but I could not live without it.

—

An earlier version of chapter 3 appeared as "Making Pigs Local: Discerning the Sensory Character of Place" (*Cultural Anthropology* 26, no. 3: 440–63), and a version of chapter 7 was published as "Configuring the Authentic Value of Real Food: Farm-to-Fork, Snout-to-Tail, and Local Food Movements" (*American Ethnologist* 39, no. 3: 615–27).

INTRODUCTION

One of the first pigs I encountered in my ethnographic research was an enormous boar with a thick mottled coat. With coloring that vaguely resembled that of a calico cat, he was the sire of a great many hogs that would be "grown out" (or raised) and taken to market by Eliza MacLean of Cane Creek Farm, then located in Snow Camp, Alamance County, North Carolina. He went by the name of Bill Clinton (but known on the farm as just Clinton).

Clinton is no longer with us, though his legacy lives on in one of his equally prodigious offspring, Junior. Pigs like Clinton and Junior have become iconic today of efforts to re-create industrial food systems, to revitalize—or perhaps reinvent—commitments to slow and local foods. This commitment speaks not only to the conditions of these animals' production and the regional practices associated with their husbandry, but also to their eventual consumption as pork. Chefs and food enthusiasts of all kinds across the United States are engaged in a bit of a pig romance (see, for example, Dickerman 2006), since the many and varied ways in which pork can be prepared or used to enrich a host of other dishes—from lardy confit of root vegetables to maple bacon doughnuts—is now a well-established dimension of contemporary American cuisine. When I asked a well-regarded chef and a regular customer of Cane Creek what attracted him to pigs like those sired by Clinton, he was less concerned with their ancestry than with their flavor. He told me he was "looking for a pig

Fig I.1 Clinton, a large Farmer's Hybrid boar (foreground).

with some fat on it."[1] Of course, fat is not just a question of the flavor of the pork, it is also a vital physiological component of the pig's life—so production and consumption join together in their common concern for excellent fat.

If we take a moment to consider Clinton, we can see that he possessed a number of qualities that were critical to his own life and to the community of farmers, chefs, and consumers that were interested in him. How did Clinton get to be a pig with fat? At his heaviest, indeed, he weighed close to a thousand pounds. But are pigs not always fat? And if not, why not? If a chef is looking for a fat pig, perhaps that suggests that only certain types of pigs—pigs of a certain stock or lineage—can be counted on to yield sufficiently fat pork. Or perhaps it simply means that any pig can become a suitably fat pig if it is raised in the proper fashion. What might it mean for pigs to come in recognizable types—in Clinton's case, the Farmer's Hybrid variety? How does this question of pig classification relate to the desirability of the pork the animals yield? Problems like these are often understood in terms of yet other qualities, like being "natural" or "heritage." Moreover, these esteemed qualities of heritage and breed are very much a part of the material dimensions of Clinton's life, as well as of the conditions in which he was produced and reproduced. The fact, for example, that Clinton had a thickly bristled coat made it possible for him and his descendants to be raised outdoors. Even in inclement weather, in places like northern Iowa and Sweden, hairy pigs such as these can endure bitter cold with only straw for bedding. Just as important, hairy pigs can survive the often scorching summers of places like North Carolina. It turns out that pigs will get terribly sunburned without this hairy protection, though they also need adequate wallows in their pasture to keep cool since pigs cannot sweat. Furthermore, pigs raised outdoors get a good amount of exercise, which often means they "grow out" a little more slowly than other pigs, which also require substantially different conditions of production.

A fat pig like Clinton, then, possesses a host of related qualities. And all of these characteristics speak to the relationship between place and time, as well as that between history and community. Such qualities are markedly valued by the categories of slow and local food, which explicitly connect value and region to heritage and taste as well. What is generally less noted, however, is how relevant such qualities are to the ways in which communities are put together and often drawn apart. The relationships that shape communities—in the contemporary United States overall and perhaps especially in North Carolina, which has undergone a tremendously rapid transformation in recent decades—are often brought to the fore when matters of locality, history, and even aesthetic judgments about things like taste are the focus of social movements like those centered on pasture-raised pork and local food. I argue that these projects and practices raise critical questions of class—in particular, questions that anthropologists have been asking about food (specifically, its meanings, value, and availability) for a very long time.

The contemporary practices centered on pasture-raised pigs in the Piedmont of North Carolina are the focus of my account in this book. The pigs in the Piedmont raise problems relating to the transformation of place and the ways we inhabit it. They exemplify people's interests in praising the virtues of heritage, as well as capitalizing on its cachet. Promoting forms of value like heritage also depends on developing and circulating ways of knowing this value, so I pay attention to the various modes of discernment embodied by artisanal producers as well as selective consumers that contribute to the qualities that make for good pigs and good pork. Above all, farmers in the Piedmont as well as customers shopping for pork from healthy and happy pasture-raised pigs are in search of "the real thing," a phenomenon and an experience with unique characteristics that are in some ways irreducible and that make them worth seeking out. In this way, a concern for authenticity is a prominent feature of this work. I explore authenticity—the commitment to producing, preserving, distributing, and consuming "real" pigs—throughout this book. Authenticity is plainly an ethnographically observable motivation,[2] but it is also a complex symbolic form that I argue needs to be better theorized, rather than dissolved as epiphenomenal in a constructivist framework of invented traditions and fetishized commodities. This book winds through multiple sites and practices—a host of elaborate locales—across the North Carolina Piedmont to detail these themes of place, discernment, heritage, and artisanship, all of them held to be authentic. My aim is to describe and analyze the ways that many people's commitments to the reinvention of food are realized and contested through what they consider to be (as my title reveals) *Real Pigs*—that is, lively pigs that yield delicious pork, all possessed of an authentic character. In the remainder of the introduction, I spell out the theoretical orientations and methodological practices that have guided my research on these matters.

An Anthropology of Food

Anthropology has had no shortage of works dedicated to the study of food. As Judith Farquhar notes, "for anthropology from its inception, food has been good to think with" (2006, 146). The past fifteen years or so have seen a true explosion in the literature that relates food to sociocultural questions (for numerous examples, see Holtzman 2006; Mintz and Dubois 2002; Sutton 2010). My approach to the study of food is part of an effort to bring political economic and phenomenological concerns into a common framework. A number of works have looked at the way that food has played a central role in the reordering of social relations and, in particular, in the production and consolidation of relations of social hierarchy. Preeminent among these is Sidney Mintz's pathbreaking *Sweetness and Power* (1985). In his historically grounded text, Mintz describes the ways that sugar production generated very specific conditions of enslaved labor in the Caribbean; shows how this mode of production provided a template for industrialized labor in the British metropole; and shows how the sugar produced by the industrialized plantation transformed the British diet in ways that both facilitated the creation of a resource-limited and time-disciplined working class and made that class dependent on a cheap, abundant, stimulating, and drug-like food.

Mintz's work—like the many works drawing directly or indirectly on it (Gewertz and Errington 2010; Nestle 2013; Patel 2007; Schlosser 2001)—provides a model for thinking about how the production, circulation, and consumption of foods can come to embody transforming regimes of hierarchy and labor, inculcating innovative and compelling tastes while also consolidating the power of those who stand to profit from these regimes. While this analysis is more directly relevant to the industrial confinement pork I discuss in chapter 1, it does form an important backdrop to the pastured-pork practices I address here. At the same time, I am reluctant to portray American consumers of industrial foods as the benighted dupes that Mintz's work and the literature following it often make them out to be. Even some of the most erudite and committed farmers I work with eat foods from a variety of sources and cannot scrupulously restrict themselves to only local food. One farmer likes to joke about taking long trips across the state to processors or customers and tells me how she stops at Bojangles for a sausage biscuit—or, as she puts it, "some of their confinement pork." Moreover, the reflexive implications of ideological critiques like those inspired by Mintz's work not only suggest a misrepresentation of consumers' motives and values, but they also preserve a place of exception for the critics, who are somehow sophisticated, enlightened, or self-disciplined enough to withstand the inescapable grip of industrial foods on our diets. As Julie Guthman asks in her trenchant critique of these perspectives, "if junk food is everywhere and people are naturally drawn to it, those who resist it must have heightened powers. When Pollan waxes poetic about his own rarefied, distinctive eating practices, the messianic, self-satisfied tone is not accidental. In describing his ability to overcome King Corn, to conceive, procure, prepare, and serve his version of the perfect meal, Pollan affirms himself as a supersubject while relegating others to objects of education, intervention, or just plain scorn" (2007, 78).

From a broader perspective, what is missing from these now myriad popular press critiques of so-called industrial foods is a recognition of both the way that all foods—industrial, "real," and otherwise—are enmeshed in a field of political economic forces[3] and the fact that all food-related activities are modes of cultural practice. The choice to pursue alternatives to industrial foods, or to look for niche-market meats, is not merely a mode of liberation from corporate structures of authority informed by rational insight. Quite aside from the facts that it is impossible to eat in only this way in the contemporary United States and that all consumers eat foods from a variety of sources, the interest in alternatives is itself a meaningful activity, motivated by a range of values that are themselves encoded in symbolically charged qualities materialized in food. Pasture-raised pork chops are not exempt from these processes of class struggle, nor are they simply the enlightened choices of conscientious consumers.

Mintz's work offers a useful—indeed, pathbreaking—paradigm that shows how to offer a historical perspective on a commodity supply chain. But his approach to the relationship between power structures and subjects' consciousness of consumption[4] reduces meaning to the reflex of a power-laden, but somehow symbolically transparent, process of production that is wholly separated from, yet still powerfully constrains, consumers who struggle to construct the inside meanings they attribute to commodity forms. A more promising, if still problematic, approach to the ways that food-related practices can articulate an order of political economic—and specifically class—relationships in a world of lived experiences (and not, as Mintz says, the mapping of working-class cultural meanings on economic goods) is offered by Pierre Bourdieu. His discussion of "The Habitus and the Space of Life-Styles" (1984, 169–225) illuminates the way in which class dispositions are embodied[5] and do not simply reflect dominant structures of political economy, but rather constitute the often unconscious—or taken-for-granted—values of a hierarchical order by means of the practical activity of subjects. His discussion of the "taste of necessity" that is the centerpiece of his entire chapter demonstrates that necessity is not sufficient to account for a cheap, heavy, rich, fatty working-class cuisine (and especially the diet of working-class men), nor is this a taste (after the fashion of bourgeois lifestyle choices) that is merely a demonstration of the unsophisticated palate of proletarian rubes. Taste is neither a utilitarian calculation (according to which poor people economize and eat poor food) nor an absolute measure of sophistication (in this view, the more cosmopolitan one's experience, the more cultured one's preferences). Instead, it is a set of dispositions that does not simply conform to but actively constitutes (and so may transform, or reproduce—lest we forget that social orders do have a remarkable capacity to reproduce themselves) a habitus.

Bourdieu's discussion of fish in the working-class diet is a little gem of analysis of how this works, offering insights into the symbolic mediation of class and gender relations in the material characteristics of the food itself and—especially—in the embodied character of tastes, preferences, and the actual eating of a meal:

> In the working classes, fish tends to be regarded as an unsuitable food for men, not only because it is a light food, insufficiently "filling," which would only be cooked for health reasons . . . but also because, like fruit (except bananas) it is one of the "fiddly" things which a man's

hands cannot cope with and which make him childlike . . . but above all, it is because fish has to be eaten in a way which totally contradicts the masculine way of eating, that is, with restraint, in small mouthfuls, chewed gently, with the front of the mouth, on the tips of the teeth (because of the bones). The whole masculine identity—which is called virility—is involved in these two ways of eating, nibbling and picking, as befits a woman, or with whole-hearted male gulps and mouthfuls. (1984, 190–91)

What I find especially compelling in this brief discussion is the way that Bourdieu pays special attention to the material properties of the food itself. Here, it is not simply the mode of sociality (collective, convivial versus atomistic, efficient), or the effects of the food (nourishing, satiating versus slimming, lightening) that are privileged dimensions of the working-class habitus,[6] but the material dimensions of this process of engagement (Weiss 1996) that allows the "fiddly" qualities of fish eating—embedded in the form of the fish as well as in the inept fingers of laboring men—to express and constitute the class-informed and gendered bodies of a hierarchically ordered habitus. Here, materiality and embodiment are each reflexive dimensions of one another, and their open-ended potentialities are fully realized only in their encounter (Heidegger 1962; Merleau-Ponty 1962).

In recent years a number of works in anthropology and related fields have taken up the wider challenge of joining political economic and phenomenological approaches to ethnographically based analyses in ways that build on the concerns with embodiment and materiality begun by Bourdieu, among others. In my view, the central dimension of the most compelling of these studies is a concern with quality as a feature of both material forms and the capacity for perception (Chumley and Harkness 2013; Fehérváry 2013; Keane 2003). Much of this work takes its impetus from Nancy Munn's now-classic *The Fame of Gawa* (1986), which uses Charles Sanders Peirce's understanding of "qualisigns" (1932) to describe the ways in which a system of values has been produced and ramified in a wider regional world on Gawa, an island in the Massim of Papua New Guinea. For Munn, qualities such as heaviness, quickness, and darkness are embedded in the sensuous character of a wide array of things and actions in the world. These shared qualities permit such phenomena to be joined together in practice to generate forms of value—that is, icons (or qualisigns) that share qualities of the productive processes (crafting, and fabricating, but also transacting and consuming) through which they are created (Munn 1986, 17; see also Manning 2012, 12–13). In this way, we can grasp the social (or, as Munn refers to it, the "intersubjective" [1986, 9]) creation of value as embedded in the characteristics of the material world, performed in the course of social interaction, and embodied in the perceptions of active subject.[7]

Beyond the relevance of quality as a mode of evaluation, how to go about tracing concrete qualities (especially in a complex process like raising pigs; processing, distributing, and marketing their pork; and then preparing and consuming this food as part of a meal or other dining practice) poses vexing theoretical and methodological questions. How, for example, might the quality of "natural" be registered as a sensuous quality in the course of feeding and watering a pig; then in the processing of its pork as a value-added product (for example, using sausage spices, smoking techniques, and cooking or curing methods); and finally in a chef's preparation of, say, a grilled bratwurst? What allows participants in this nexus of activities to recognize the niche-market product in question as "natural" at every moment in this chain? And how might the meanings of "nature" be modified, reinterpreted, or translated from field to slaughter facility to menu? Robert Foster (2008) has offered an exceptional account of a commodity chain that is almost the perfect ideological opposite of that used with pasture-raised pork, the commodity chain of Coca-Cola. Foster also deploys a framework that is inspired by Munn's (1977) interest in the perception and fabrication of qualities in the production of valued goods, conjoined with Michel Callon, Cécile Méadel, and Vololona Rabeharisoa's (2002) understanding of the way in which diverse actors, often with very different, even contradictory interests, work to qualify and requalify products as they circulate across networks of dispersed actors participating in an "economy of qualities" (Foster 2008, 7). Furthermore, the qualities revealed in this expanding, iterative process of requalification does not entail just the sensuous appreciation of the material product—or the animals—conjoined in this economy; it also includes the perspective that different actors have on one another as they participate in this economy. For example,[8] a farmer may select for pigs that have a certain size or body type, and produce these animals because he or she imagines that local chefs will be looking for certain attributes in the pork they purchase from farmers. In turn, a chef may trim or season that pork in anticipation of what he or she assumes diners will expect of a pork chop in a restaurant, thereby requalifying that pork product in the process Foster (following

Hannerz 1999) describes as defining a "network of perspectives" that includes "perspectives that people in one place might have on people in another place as a result of their being aware of each other's inclusion in the same translocal commodity network" (Foster 2008, xvi). To flesh this model out further, consider the following commonplace operation of this "network of perspectives." Consumers at farmers' markets, usually in a not-quite-translocal network, routinely demonstrate their assumptions concerning farmers' activities by asking about the production techniques they use for raising their livestock (for example, "Are your pigs raised outdoors?" "Do you feed your chickens organic grains?" and "Do you use antibiotics?"). The presence of the farmer at the market serves to ratify (or not) these consumers' qualifications (that is, the way in which they attribute significance to a pork product), and the host of ways in which they may present themselves to these customers (for example, wearing rustic garb, having family members help run their stands, or presenting photographs or brief descriptions of the farm and its livestock) offers up concrete qualities that are available to the customer. The sensuous qualities of these face-to-face encounters become evidence of an array of wider values—of, for example, a "natural" process, a "trustworthy" interaction, or an "authentic" sociocultural practice—and no doubt a host of other meanings that can be attributed to this experience within a niche-market economy of qualities.

In this book, then, I find that paying attention to such qualities and how they circulate provides a useful way to combine political economic concerns with a phenomenological perspective on lived experience. Insofar as qualities are always modes of evaluation, they are always subject to a politics. Discernment, judgment, appreciation, and the like are all forms of perceiving in the thing itself a set of sedimented values that include certain preferred qualities as legible and relevant, while discounting or excluding other claims as irrelevant or wrong. "Knowing," for example, that "fatty pork" is "really" a good thing is a sensuous claim that can be made by looking at, handling, cooking, and eating a pork chop (as well as by raising the pig from which the chop is taken in the intended way); it plainly entails overcoming or rejecting other—often quite powerful (for example, medical, actuarial, and nutritional)—claims to the contrary. For this "knowledge" to hold, it has to appeal to some kind of authority (for example, connoisseurship, depth of experience, or sophistication) that ranks different kinds of knowledge (educated as opposed to rustic or cosmopolitan as opposed to plebian), and so quality demonstrates a political dimension. Moreover, attention to the network of perspectives through which the process of requalification proceeds makes it clear that certain perspectives carry more weight than others. One way to see this is to see how certain attributes are readily incorporated into the network, while others fit only uncomfortably. The well-being of the pigs that are protected by animal welfare certification, for example, is a quality that carries weight at markets and among chefs, aggregators, and consumers, but there are very few, if any, similar qualifications that can certify and materialize the health care protection of the laborers who feed and water the pigs or process the pork cuts that are part of this same network. Furthermore, once we place this network in the dynamic demographic context of the contemporary North Carolina Piedmont, we can see how such perspectives are transformed over time, as certain actors in a network come to the fore while others are bypassed or marginalized. This focus can also allow us to see how certain innovations such as "local foods," "artisanal products," or "sustainable practices" (Paxson 2012) come to be sought out as evidence of particular qualities. In short, tracking requalifications in an economy of qualities gives us some insight into pressing political economic matters.

Finally, I should note that there is a reflexive dimension to this concern with this network of perspectives that forms a chain of qualifications. Certainly my own perspective as an anthropologist and ethnographer— as well as an occasional activist, advocate, cook, and consumer—can be taken into consideration. But, more importantly, the qualities of a network themselves are integral to the perspectives that constitute and qualify the network itself. What I mean by this is that actors in the world of pasture-raised pork routinely refer to making "connections" through their work and lives as a meaningful activity that motivates them to participate in these networks. This is not so much a premise of any network, per se, but is itself a privileged quality that actors attempt to realize through their practice. Connection, then, is a dimension of a network, but it is also a feature of multiple perspectives and a quality that (most people in the network hope) can be perceived in the practices and products that bind the network together.[9]

Knowing Pork

The network of perspectives I have just described also served as a methodological guide for this project. This research was formulated in a farmers' market, but that single site quickly proved to have put me firmly in an entangled, multisited "place." There were three primary "sites" in which I carried out this work—farming, marketing, and cooking—but each of them is widely dispersed across a range of locations. They also entailed a few auxiliary sites that I will address here. Moreover, the locations I describe here are almost entirely contained in the Piedmont and even more specifically in the regions known as the Triad and the Triangle (see chapter 1 for more detail on these locales).

The first field I worked in, sequentially, was quite literally the field—that is, the paddocks in which these pastured pigs are raised. I began by working with some regularity, a few days a week at first and later for most of one summer, at Cane Creek Farm, owned and operated by Eliza MacLean. I learned the daily routines of chores, how to feed and water pigs as well as the range of other livestock found on the farm,[10] and the temporal organization of a pig's life on pasture. Breeding and feeding are the central activities of the farmer-pig interface, as pigs are moved across the landscape, from one pasture to the next, and fed increasing or decreasing rations of grain to supplement their wooded and pastured resources (pigs enjoy woody mast, grubs, and a variety of plant roots) in an effort to facilitate the reproduction of livestock (when it helps to reduce their weight a bit) and to "grow them out" for market (when you want them to gain weight quickly). This work in the field also included a consideration of the energy, soil fertility, and mechanical (for example, fences, vehicles, equipment) inputs that are needed to maintain a sustainable agricultural operation; an appreciation of the way in which labor is recruited and trained in farm activities; an understanding of complex infrastructure (including housing, bedding, wallows, and water resources) required for raising livestock that rotate across pastures; and a consideration of a host of economic questions relevant to investment, growth, and diversification of farms as businesses. Most of my insights into agricultural practice are derived from my extensive fieldwork at Cane Creek, but I have worked in some capacity on over a dozen farms across the Piedmont since 2009.

My work at Cane Creek and with MacLean is the central node in my work, and it led to the other activities that constitute the niche-market network I traced out from the farm. I have talked to a number of farmers, activists, chefs, and others about processing, but I have had the opportunity to visit only a few processors. My perspective on meat processors is based primarily on my grasp of how farmers talk about and negotiate their relationship to processing and the problems many of them continue to have with it. However, I have spent almost every Saturday morning since January 2009 working at the Carrboro Farmers' Market selling Cane Creek pork. Direct marketing, as I discuss further in chapter 1, is crucial to the rise of pastured pork in North Carolina. It is one of the primary reasons that this niche has continued to develop, and it makes North Carolina one of the most successful states for niche-market meat sales in the country.[11] I have also visited and talked with pork vendors at fifteen farmers' markets in the Piedmont and have had discussions with countless more farmers and customers about their experiences working and shopping at these venues. Farmers' markets are incredibly rich and complex locations where the network is densely concentrated. Chefs and consumers come together, and farmers' activities are calibrated to the requirements of filling orders for restaurants, reserving products for chefs (hoping they will show up at their appointed hour so that the farmers can avoid costly delivery expenses), and working with customers to satisfy their desire for pastured pork while also trying to cultivate their interests in new products so that more unusual cuts of pork can be sold—and in the hope that customers will more regularly return to the vendor for more purchases. Farmers also calibrate their prices, share an enormous amount of information about farming activities—including discussing the cost of feed, techniques for adapting to unexpected weather, the ups and downs of restaurant orders, the challenges of animal processing, and the changing financial and regulatory environments for farming—and swap stories and socialize with friends. It is at the market that it becomes most apparent that this economy of qualities is, indeed, a network of perspectives, as diverse actors—consumers, chefs, vendors, and farmers—reflexively present themselves and incorporate others' expectations into their own activities. It is also one of the principal locations for observing the way that the competing values of this niche as a capitalist enterprise generates friction (Tsing 2005) with the values of artisanship and collectivism in the face-to-face sociality of market interactions.[12]

The third field in this network that I participated in extensively is cooking. In addition to cooking up more pork than I could ever have imagined and talking to innumerable market customers about pork cookery, I had the opportunity to work in the kitchens of restaurants in the Piedmont. Most important, I worked in the kitchen of Lantern, thanks to the extraordinary generosity of Andrea Reusing, the restaurant's chef-owner (and the 2011 winner of the James Beard Award for Best Chef: Southeast), who permitted me to work with her wonderful staff doing prep work before service for most of the summer in 2009. Working at Lantern gave me a further opportunity to understand the perspectives at work in this niche market, as restaurants calibrate their activities in consideration of the imagined tastes of their clients and the anticipated qualities of the products they receive from the farmers that provision them. At the same time, restaurants are critical sites for grasping the way in which such perspectives can change, as chefs, cooks, and other staff aim to educate customers about innovative menu items and food trends[13] and to offer feedback to farmers about the quality of the meat (and other foods) that they are looking for. The insights I gained at Lantern were indispensable to the work that I was able to do with other chefs and restaurants and with a range of "prepared food" and "value-added" sellers at markets and retail outlets in the Piedmont.

Each of these "sites" incorporates a consideration of the other two, and my understanding of each is shaped by my participation in this network as a whole. How people in this region participate in such a network is not just a methodological question, it is one of the core topics I explore in this work. Questions of race are deeply woven into the social history of the American South, North Carolina, and in rural and agricultural communities, and certainly in the making of place as I describe it. Yet I will suggest that problems of racial conflict are both a strongly felt presence as well as a glaring absence in the discourses and practices of this complex local food totality. On the one hand, there are many actors, as I describe below, who see the project of remaking food production and provisioning as a mode of social justice, one that seeks to rectify centuries of overt racial discrimination in agriculture, landholding, employment, and food resources across North Carolina.[14] These intentions are often explicit in the missions and practices of many activists. On the other hand, the limited presence of African American consumers at farmers' markets across the Piedmont, from Raleigh to Durham to Greensboro (cities whose populations are approximately 30 percent, 40 percent, and 40 percent African American, respectively) is certainly vastly disproportional to the population of these communities.[15] Furthermore, only a handful of African American farmers sell their produce at farmers' markets in the area, and the number of livestock farmers is smaller still. This certainly does not mean that there are very few African American farmers in the Piedmont, but their participation in the networks I am describing—especially those networks constituted by pigs and pork—is certainly not robust. At the same time, because there is such an interest in making local food into a more inclusive world, there is a good deal of discussion about race and histories of racism in the state. Often, the industrial agricultural sector (which I discuss in some detail in chapter 1) is seen as an institution that exemplifies this racialized legacy in everything from its employment practices to its environmental impacts and the food deserts it institutionalizes through its distribution models. In this way, this sector provides a kind of alibi that may deflect attention from the racial composition of markets, restaurants, and small-scale farming activities in the region. Race, then, is both a vital concern and easily overlooked in the Piedmont. In this way, it resembles the structural racialization in much of American life.

In the course of doing my research I had only very limited opportunities to work with African American farmers. The only African American livestock producer I knew of in the Piedmont was not raising pigs during the period of my research, but I was able to talk to him a bit about the history of his family's farming practices. I also worked with a few farmers who were not located in the Piedmont but were able to market their pork there.[16] In fact, a number of African American farmers who raise pigs either do so strictly for their own families' subsistence[17] or, more commonly (especially in the Coastal Plain), do so only on a part-time basis.[18] So, while I was able to work with a few African Americans who worked with livestock producers as extension agents, employees of institutions like North Carolina Agricultural and Technical State University (North Carolina A&T, whose history I discuss below), occasional farmhands, or people who had grown up farming, African American farmers are certainly not well represented in the sample of farmers I was able to work with. This is clearly an important omission, but I think it accurately reflects the demographic realities of pasture-raised pork production in the Piedmont, and the absence of African Americans speaks not simply to a weakness of my fieldwork but to the very racialized character of the world I am considering in this book.

Before I move on to a summary of the topics and questions addressed in the following chapters, I should add that there are some auxiliary sites, generally overlooked in popular discussions of food systems, in which I worked that added tremendously informative perspectives to the network. These sites include the work of advocates for this niche market, and these advocates—activists, educators, entrepreneurs, and farm extension specialists—are dispersed across the Piedmont. I have benefited enormously from my conversations (many of them cited in the following chapters) with advocates from the Carolina Farm Stewardship Association, the

Rural Advancement Foundation International, the Livestock Conservancy, staff at North Carolina A&T and the Center for Environmental Farming Systems (CEFS), and the owners and employees at Firsthand Foods. These actors participated in and sponsored such diverse events as the Carolina Meat Conference, cooperative extension activities at North Carolina A&T, the Farm to Fork Picnic, and Field Days at CEFS, each of which gave me an opportunity to meet with a range of people interested in meat. Moreover, Jennifer Curtis graciously let me work alongside her and her partners at Firsthand Foods, visiting farms in Nash County, farmers' markets and retail facilities in the environs of Raleigh and Durham, sorting meat orders, and going over business planning in the Firsthand offices in Durham. All of these interactions inform my understanding of the complexity of the activities that are needed to make this niche market—which is both extensive and tenuous—work across the counties of central North Carolina. I have attempted to capture the irregular character of the interactions of knowledge production, entrepreneurship, service, and public policy in these networks by including several profiles in this book that feature individuals who have long been dedicated to working in these areas. The profiles (as I discuss in detail in my introduction to them) are wide-ranging, messy, and even at times tangential to the core ethnographic concerns of this book as a whole, but I feel that this reflects the nature of the diverse and experimental activities of these individuals.

One final point about a set of perspectives that is not thoroughly incorporated into this book: the views of the pigs. This book is not as fully informed by the animal turn (Weil 2010) in the academy as it might be. This is primarily because, as I freely admit, the pigs with whom I carried out this research led lives that were, with very few exceptions,[19] directed toward their transition into meat. This is, therefore, primarily a book about pork. It would be absurd, of course, to suggest that this telos defines the complex lives and characters of the pigs.[20] My focus in this work does them this injustice—although, of course, any analytic framework is always partial and interested. I would add, however, that the perspectives of pigs often do shape this network, and not simply insofar as they are potential pork. Farmers are routinely drawn to raising pigs because they have compassion for the lives of these beings or feel compelled to find an alternative to what they see as—or know to be[21]—the degrading conditions of industrial farming. They also must adjust their farming activities to accommodate the particularities of individual hogs. When a particular pig is known to have a proclivity to work its way through fencing in a wooded area, cause destruction to a field through excessive wallowing, or be especially ornery in protection of other pigs, farmers have to accommodate the behavior and imagined intentions of the pigs they are raising. Moreover, customers and chefs are also drawn to the pig's perspective and often take a specific interest in the ways that these animals are raised and treated as they grow. These interests are not typically limited only to a concern with the quality of the pork these animals yield, although healthy meat and environmental stewardship are ways of registering this concern for pigs' lives. Chefs and customers routinely come out to farms to see and work with pigs and even talk about the relationships they may have formed on a farm, asking about "their pig" by name. I found the account of Will Cramer (profiled below), a farmer who gave up raising pigs after four years because of the affective implications of the process, quite compelling and moving, and I am grateful to him for allowing me to share it here.

One further note on these networks: I have generally used the names of the people I worked with in the course of conducting this research. Most of them have been enthusiastic in their support of my project (though none of them bears any responsibility for how it has turned out) and asked me to use their names. In a few instances, I have used pseudonyms or otherwise protected peoples' identities. This is not because there is anything especially sensitive or unflattering (I sincerely hope) that I have had to write, but simply because I was not able to get express permission from these people to use their names. In addition, I worked in a number of public settings (markets, restaurants, and conferences) where it would have been quite difficult if not impossible to get consent (for example, it would greatly disrupt sales at a farmers' market to ask customers for permission to describe their joyous appreciation of Cane Creek bacon), and I have done my best to render such public encounters anonymous.

A Précis

The chapters in this book are organized around the locations that I have just described. Chapter 1 is an exception in some ways, however. There I offer a brief history of contemporary pig production in North Carolina. It covers the industrialization of confinement hogs and describes the processes and conditions that made it possible for pasture-raised pork operations to develop in the ways that they have in recent years. The chapter is generally intended to provide a background to the ethnographic work that follows, and it relies on a good deal of secondary literature—some of it quite well known—for evidence. It also introduces a range of actors who figure prominently in the current world of pastured pork. Chapter 2 takes up the question of terroir as a way to explore questions of the relationship between food and place. I ask, in particular, about how places are made and how their specific qualities are discernible, registered, and evaluated. Here I am interested in the perspectives of the farmers, consumers, and others who live in the Piedmont—as well as residents of other regions who also recognize the Piedmont as a distinctive place. Chapter 3 considers issues relating to food and heritage. It explores in some detail the history and development of a particular kind of pig, the Ossabaw Island Hog, and considers the relationship between breeds (and, crucially, hybrids) as natural or cultural categories; examines heritage as a "value-added" dimension of animals and their products; and considers branding as a way of knowing animals, food, and their producers. Chapter 4 examines butchery. Butchering has become something of a performance art, a demonstrable craft that recruits cooks and customers to the niche market of pastured pork and provides a tactile means of embodying the qualities that constitute its sociocultural processes. The life of the pig, ironically, is poignantly rendered, abundantly valued, and laden with experiences of affect at the moment of its transition into edible cuts of pork. Next, chapter 5 discusses the quality of taste and, in particular, the flavor of pork fat as a way of exploring the important sensuous experience of eating. I consider alternative ways of conceiving of taste, from meat science to Proustian recollection, to draw out the historical and regional character of taste as a mode of innovation and tradition. The final ethnographic chapter foregrounds issues related to authenticity and connection as central motivations in the world of pasture-raised pigs. There I discuss both the relationships that are developed through conceiving of the network as a totality and those that are developed through grasping the pig itself as a unified, whole animal— from snout to tail, as the expression goes—as an icon of both connection and realness, values that are central to the world as whole. In the conclusion I take the concepts of authenticity and connection developed in chapter 6 and demonstrate how they are woven through a much wider array of concerns in this porcine network and beyond. These categories, I argue, carry a heavy ideological load. At times, they work to challenge corporate models of production and consumption, but they can also be used to reproduce many of the features of the social order that are burdened with a longer legacy of inequality and exclusion. In this way, I argue that the commodity form itself can be seen to exercise a hegemonic force in contemporary

American food politics. At the same time, I remain reluctant to dismiss the projects and efforts of the many people who are dedicated to reformulating this politics; indeed, in the course of this research, I frequently worked as an unabashed advocate for many of these reforms. My position, then, is less that of a critic who would denounce these efforts as old wine in new skins than that of a critically engaged actor trying to maintain a semblance of optimism, and I suggest that these reforms might offer the possibility of hope and the prospect of a more just and equitable food system.

Interspersed between the chapters are profiles, modified transcriptions from extensive conversations I had with people who have played a major role in promoting "real" pigs in the Piedmont. I offer a fuller introduction to these profiles and their purposes at the end of the introduction. Overall, this book proceeds from a discussion of place, heritage, and history through a consideration of artisanal craft and consumption to trace processes of requalification that are objectified and embodied in the lives of those who are working to imagine and construct an alternative system of meat production, distribution, and consumption in North Carolina's Piedmont.

Profiles

I have included nine profiles in this book. They are interspersed between the ethnographic and analytical chapters of the work and are intended to complement (and, I would suggest, complicate) the chapters in a number of respects. Each profile is meant to illustrate relevant themes of a given chapter or of the book as a whole, but from the distinctive perspective of the individual featured in the account. In this sense the profiles add a very particular kind of ethnographic evidence; they are not case studies per se, but they offer firsthand stories by individuals that address their understanding of, and relationship to, changes in agriculture, food systems, and—above all—pastured pork production and consumption in North Carolina. Some of the points these individuals raise are elaborated on in one or more of the chapters; some of them speak to common issues raised in other profiles; and some of them are perspectives, reports of expertise, and advocacy that—I hope—will speak to wider audiences.

There are a few salient methodological purposes for including these somewhat unconventional (at least in anthropological genres) profiles. To begin with, I wanted to demonstrate some of the diversity of actors who have contributed not just to this ethnographic project but also to the re-making of a "local" food system, and—more specifically—the creation of a niche market in pasture-raised pork. This project has made use of a specific type of multisited ethnographic practice. While almost all of the work has been carried out in the Piedmont of North Carolina, within that region I have worked across different domains of practice: farmers' markets, pig paddocks, restaurant kitchens, butcher shops, and classrooms. The book as a whole, then, is not focused exclusively on pork production, marketing, or consumption but tries to tie together these diverse processes (each of which is itself a complex and historically dynamic field of activities) by following both the pig and the people who move pigs and pork across the region. I have worked, therefore, not only with the chefs and farmers who are usually included in studies like this one, but also with advocates and entrepreneurs from the world of academia and public policy who play immensely important roles in these overarching processes. Including their perspectives in these profiles allows me to cover more ground than the scope of a book like this one might otherwise permit.

The profiles are the products of conversations that I had with the individuals featured. In every case, I have known and worked (in most cases, very closely) with these people over a number of years. The conversations therefore build on a wide appreciation of the kinds of activities these people have been engaged in and reflect a good deal of background knowledge that we share. I have tried to clarify this background in the endnotes or in chapters of the book where certain issues, practices, and institutions are discussed in more depth than is the case in the profiles. The conversations presented here have certainly been edited, but I have tried to capture the voices of the people being profiled, so I left them in a somewhat raw state for a number of reasons. I am not simply trying to add local color. Rather, I am hoping to demonstrate that the way people talk about their experiences and activities is as interesting and revealing about wider social and cultural processes as what they have to say about these things. In trying to capture a Hymesian "way of speaking" (Hymes 1974) that takes communicative practice as sociocultural evidence, I consider vernacular styles as evidence of a shared world. It is important to note the way that common expressions, turns of phrase, or lexical items recur in these profiles, and especially the way these forms are used by different people engaged in very different kinds of projects. Using these transcribed conversations "as is" allows those shared resonances to emerge in a way that could be obscured if the conversations were "cleaned up," or if I had asked each of these people to write about themselves and their work. While the texts appear to be somewhat disjointed or loosely structured,

I trust that they are nonetheless coherent and compelling accounts offered by people working in the field. Furthermore, there is a wider purpose to the conversational character of these profiles, insofar as they suggest the open-ended quality of discourse. These are ideas about potential, ways of imagining possible futures of a food system that is understood to be very much in the making. This quality is well conveyed, I feel, in the style of the conversations themselves. Moreover, the "messiness" of these profiles encourages the reader to make his or her own sense of these ideas and will—I sincerely hope—invite readers to draw their own conclusions and raise their own questions. In all of these ways, the profiles are meant to draw explicit and implicit connections between the form and content of these conversations in a productive fashion.

1

PIGS ON THE GROUND

From Pigs in a Parlor to Ten Million Confinement Hogs

The geographical focus of this book is the North Carolina Piedmont, a region that lies in between the Coastal Plain and the mountains of Western North Carolina. More specifically, my research has been centered on two primary regions: the Triad and the Triangle. The Triad is formed by the three cities of Greensboro, High Point, and Winston-Salem. It lies roughly seventy-five miles to the west of the Triangle, which is formed by the cities of Durham; Chapel Hill; and the state capitol, Raleigh (map 1.1). There are important demographic differences between these two regions, which include urban centers as well as many rural and agricultural towns. As I indicated above, my work here included discussions with pastured-pork producers throughout the Piedmont as well as with restaurant chefs and staff members; vendors and customers at a number of farmers' markets; and academics, advocates, and activists working on behalf of this niche market in "real pigs." In this chapter I want to briefly discuss some historical features of hog production and consumption in North Carolina; describe the radical changes in pig production in the state in the late twentieth century; and give a somewhat more detailed account of the origins of the efforts to revitalize and, in some instances, invent outdoor hog production in the state, which has really taken off only in the past twenty years. This overview is intended as background for the practices that are discussed in

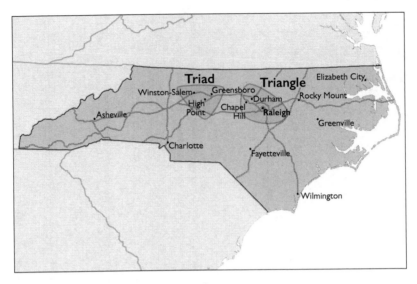

Map 1.1 North Carolina's Triad and Triangle.

more detail, and are accompanied by more ethnographic evidence, in the chapters that follow.

Raising hogs has a long and diverse history in North Carolina. While pig farming today is concentrated primarily in the eastern Coastal Plain, as described above, the enthusiasm for raising pigs across the state has been well documented. In 1982, John Raymond Shute, a politician and author, was interviewed for "Documenting the American South"[1] and talked about his experiences growing up in Monroe, just to the southeast of Charlotte (at the very western end of the Piedmont). Born in 1904, Shute described farms in Cabarrus and Stanly Counties when he was young:

> [Everyone] raised their swine and their chickens for their meat. As soon as the first frost came, that was the time to slaughter pigs and hogs. They would render their own lard; they'd make their own soap; they'd make their own sausage; they'd cure their own hams. Every house had a smokehouse. They'd burn hickory logs to cure the ham, and that ham was salted down along with the other [pork]. The sausage was put up in corn shucks. And you talk about something good to eat. Now you take sausage out of a corn shuck six months later with fresh eggs, and you've really got a breakfast. But as towns developed, they usually enacted ordinances prohibiting the raising of hogs or swine within

the city limits. . . . Consequently, you can see how it would develop as a separate industry located out where it was not offensive to anyone. You had what later became known, oddly enough, as "pig parlors." That's where they raised them and would slaughter them and cure them and everything. So that developed the swine business as really a separate industry from ordinary farming. But even so, every farm still had swine.

This account of a set of subsistence practices might seem romanticized, but it provides an image—though not an actual *practice*—that endured across North Carolina for most of the twentieth century (figures 1.1 and 1.2).

In 2009 an African American man in his twenties who had grown up on a farm in the far northeastern corner of the state—near Elizabeth City, in Pasquotank County—told me that he had only recently returned to his job near Burlington after "taking down the pigs back home":

There were five pigs from three families, and they got the whole thing done in four to five hours. The whole thing [killing and processing the hogs[2]] takes two full days. You season the meat for a day and then you grind sausage. You take the joints [rear and front legs of the pig, or "hams" and "shoulders" in pork parlance], then there are middlings— fat back bacon and bellies—and you salt them and put them up in the smokehouse. After the joints are cut out, then the girls come. They season the meat and grind up the trim for sausage.

I heard similar reports from farmers in the Piedmont who had in very recent memory participated in such collective hog-killing practices. Some of them were still raising pigs in family "parlors" and using their pork for subsistence or, as the expression goes, as "money in the bank"—pigs typically raised to be ground up into sausage for quick and easy sales to neighbors and friends.

On the whole, however, this kind of practice has been almost completely displaced by industrial hog farming in the state—indeed, by confinement operations in the three counties of Duplin, Bladen, and Sampson (see map 1.2), where more than five million of the state's roughly ten million hogs are raised (Factory Farm Map n.d.). How North Carolina went from pig parlors and neighborhood slaughtering and packing facilities to Smithfield Packing's processing 28.5 million hogs in fiscal 2013[3] is a story that has been told in more detail and with more rigor than I can offer here. My purpose is not to offer a thorough critique of this historical process[4] but

Fig. 1.1 and 1.2 Top: An undated image ("Hogs on Permanent Pasture") from the digital archives of North Carolina State University shows a famer on pasture in Kinston. Courtesy Special Collections Research Center, NCSU Libraries, Raleigh, North Carolina. Bottom: This image, from East Carolina University in Greenville, the urban center of the Coastal Plain, shows men at a pig parlor in 1957. Courtesy the Daily Reflector Image Collection, J. Y. Joyner Library, East Carolina University, https://digital.lib.ecu.edu/reflector/3057.

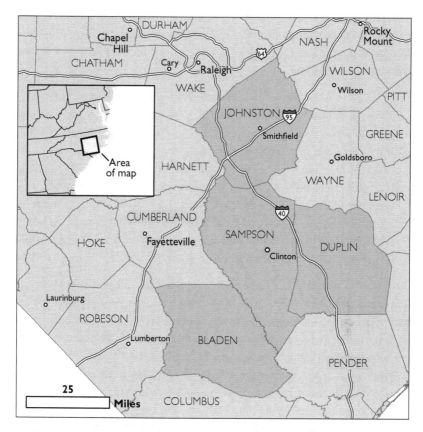

Map 1.2 Eastern North Carolina.

to emphasize some of the ways in which this process of animal confinement, the financialization of livestock farming, and the megaconsolidation of the industry contributed to and helped shape the development of the pastured-pork niche market at the very end of the twentieth century.

While I would not suggest that the image that I sketched above of subsistence pig producers on small-scale homesteads was an unchanging model that operated throughout North Carolina for over a century, I would argue that there were a series of momentous changes in the final decades of the twentieth century that substantially changed the pork industry throughout the world. These also had profound ramifications for the pig farmers and pork consumers with whom I worked in the Piedmont.

Here is what a former attorney general of North Carolina, Robert Morgan, wrote about the radical transformation in the state's hog industry. I quote at length since Morgan offers a concise summary of the extent of these transformations:

> In 1984, there were more than twenty thousand hog farms in North Carolina populated by 2 million hogs. More than a fourth of these farms, mostly in the east, had fewer than five hundred hogs, and only a small fraction of these more than two thousand. A decade later, the number of hogs catapulted to over 7 million, but the number of hog farms fell below five thousand. In little more than a decade, the number of hogs produced nearly quadrupled, while the number of farms dropped by three-fourths. Hog farming suddenly became big business as only 2.5 percent of these farms had fewer than five hundred hogs, while 84 percent had over two thousand each. (1998, 138)

How can we possibly account for this unprecedented expansion and consolidation of hog production in an extremely short period of time?[5] A series of policy and legislative shifts were put in place in the state in the early 1980s, in the period just before the decade that Morgan describes, which were designed to produce this consolidation and expand pork production to previously unimaginable levels. The story unfolds on a level that is both local and national (if not global) in its scope. As a student and analyst of social activity, I would normally be reluctant to suggest that a transformation of this massive scale could be attributed to the actions of a handful of people, but that seems to describe exactly what happened in North Carolina in the 1980s.[6] Members of the state's legislature, led by Wendell H. Murphy, an assemblyman from Duplin County, sponsored and passed a series of laws that made this sort of expansion immensely profitable and appear—as some agricultural economists at the time suggested—inevitable. Murphy was an executive in Murphy Family Farms, a hog production company founded by his family in 1962. In the course of his ten years in the General Assembly, his family business became the biggest hog producer in the United States. Murphy and his allies, both Democrats and Republicans,[7] passed a series of laws and amendments that paved the way for industrialization and contracting. They effectively eliminated state sales taxes on farm building materials and, later, on all farm equipment. Furthermore, they exempted farming enterprises from zoning regulations so that municipalities had very little ability to curtail the construction of facilities that housed thousands of animals. Finally, they gutted the environmental regulations that would have fined hog production facilities that illegally discharged wastes into surrounding streams and waterways. In effect, spills (whose existence the industry denied for years[8]) could be dealt with only by reporting them to authorities at the U.S. Environmental Protection Agency, who then had sixty days to take action. The combined effects of this legislation made consolidation of the hog industry much more viable and led to the development of the confinement systems known as confined animal feeding operations.

What made the industrialization of hog production not just viable but also enormously profitable for those who would come to dominate this process of consolidation were the drastically reduced costs of infrastructure that this legislation produced and the system of contract production that controlled the ways in which hogs were grown and marketed in the state. This system of contracts gives hog production its national, even global, character. The system was first developed and implemented in the poultry industry. As William Boyd and Michael Watts demonstrate (1997, see especially 154–57) the poultry industry became vertically integrated—that is, it consolidated the process of housing, feeding, transporting, processing (or slaughtering), and marketing the animal under a single company, or integrator—in the United States in the period right after World War II. They further show how this process was greatly facilitated by the political geography of poultry production—to wit, the fact that the American South was dominated by a series of small, near-subsistence farmers, whose marginal economic existence and skill set as farmers made them especially vulnerable to the generally onerous terms of the production contracts offered to them by the integrators to grow their chickens. Add to this the way that growers working under contract became, in effect, wage laborers for the integrators and the fact that ironically named "right to work" legislation was passed throughout the South in this era, and the conditions became ideal for poultry production to flourish in two states, Virginia and Arkansas, respectively dominated by the integrators Perdue Farms Inc. and Tysons Foods Inc.

This contracting system introduced tremendous efficiencies that allowed for scale to be ratcheted up enormously in the poultry industry. Hog production followed suit in North Carolina in the 1980s. The real profitability of the industry lies not in the volume and cost of the cheap meat that can be produced (indeed, the evidence suggests that pork is only profitable, when it is, because of the federal subsidies and tax breaks that the industry receives; see Blanchette 2013; "CME" 2014), but in the terms of the contracts that transfer most of the risks to the growers. These contracts require growers to raise their animals under conditions determined by the integrator, which generally require substantial investments in infrastructure to ensure that growers employ all of the infrastructure required by economies of scale and standardization in animal production: providing proper housing conditions, the use of temperature controls, administration of medications, meeting feed requirements, and so on. All of these costs are borne by the growers, who take out sizable mortgages to qualify for integrators' contracts. Farmers who are able to make payments on these mortgages—generally by selling off family-held land, usually to the integrator looking to find more land on which to construct confinement facilities—can be quite successful. The vast majority of growers, though, have to service their debt with the income they receive for their hogs, leaving farmers little or nothing on which to live. This story is far from unique: "John Cooper, a Newton Grove farmer who has worked under contract for three different companies, said he was lured into the business with promises of up to $100,000 a year. But after making $56,000 in annual payments on a $750,000 loan, he ended up taking a loss of $8,000 in his first year" (Warrick and Stith 1995a). The model created by this corporate success (that is, enormous profitability)—combined with the legislation passed by representatives who were direct beneficiaries of the laws they sponsored[9]—certainly made the consolidation of pork production and the exponential expansion of the industry seem like an inevitable result of industrialization.[10] Indeed, this expansion has proceeded apace, as the number of hogs marketed in the state reached 18,359,000 in 2013. Smithfield Foods, headquartered in Virginia, built the largest pork-processing facility in the world in Bladen County, North Carolina, in 1992 (in 2013 this facility processed 28.5 million hogs). In 2000 Smithfield took over the company that led the way in grower contracts in North Carolina, Murphy Family Farms (now Murphy Family Ventures), and Smithfield itself was taken over by Shuanghui International Holdings in 2013 for the price of $4.7 billion—the largest Chinese takeover of a U.S. company to date.

Even before the recent activities of Smithfield, the rate of growth in the industry in North Carolina attracted a great deal of attention and concern. The *Raleigh News and Observer* series (Stith, Warrick, and Sill 1995) that described much of the history I have just outlined was published in February 1995, just as this decade of legislative change and extraordinary expansion concluded. The stories in the series proved to be enormously influential for a number of food and environmental activists throughout

North Carolina (see the profiles throughout this book for examples). But what really alerted this community of scholars, farmers, chefs, and other advocates to the hazards of confinement hog production were a string of environmental catastrophes across the Coastal Plain in the 1990s. In June 1995, a few months after the newspaper series ran, a lagoon holding waste from a confined animal feeding operation growing over 10,000 hogs collapsed at Oceanview Farms, in Onslow County. More than twenty-five million gallons of hog waste spilled across tobacco and soybean fields and into the New River ("Huge Spill of Hog Waste Fuels an Old Debate in North Carolina" 1995). This led the state to reconsider some of the limits on environmental regulation that hog farms enjoyed. But the most destructive events for the industry were Hurricanes Fran and Floyd. Fran hit the North Carolina coast in early September 1996, making landfall near Wilmington. It caused $7.2 billion in damage and killed 16,000 pigs. Far worse, though, was the catastrophe brought about by Hurricane Floyd in September 1999. The storm hit North Carolina at Cape Fear and came straight through the heart of the Coastal Plain. Countless lagoons were breached, thoroughly contaminating surrounding rivers. This drew the attention of environmentalists across the nation, who descended on the plain at the turn of the century to develop programs for cleaning up the region and reforming the legislative framework that had generated these toxic conditions (Niman 2009). National nightly news programs broadcast footage of enormous herds of pigs standing on the roofs of their confinement facilities as the floodwaters rose around them. A hundred thousand pigs drowned in the weeks that followed (Randall 1999). Many contract farmers went bankrupt as the state endured losses estimated between six and eight billion dollars ("Hurricane Floyd" n.d.).

Of course, these disasters and the range of responses they generated did not impede the growth of the hog industry or diminish its profitability, as my summary above of the success of Smithfield Foods indicates. But they did create a widespread awareness of the costs and the wider impact of this industry that is critical to understanding the renaissance in pastured pork that is the focus of this book. Activists, academics, farmers, and consumers were aware of this devastation, and many wanted to take action to counter the effects of industrialized confinement systems. At the same time, some of the same forces of financialization and its consequent restructuring of class relations that transformed the hog industry have had a lasting effect on the demography and social organization of North Carolina as a whole. These abiding changes ushered in many of the conditions that also allowed the niche market in "natural" pork to develop and expand in the last two decades in the Piedmont. I will now turn, with a little more depth of focus, to the processes and agencies that promoted this niche market and that, although they were intended to reject the intensive confinement of animals, instead put pigs "on the ground."

Pigs on the Ground

It should be clear that the regional social and natural transformations I have described took place in such a rapid fashion that they could not help but generate a profound sense of displacement and rupture for many residents of North Carolina. In much less than a generation, farmers became critically aware of the imposition of a new system of pig and pork production to which they would have to react by getting big; getting out; or trying to figure out an alternative to the system of contracts and confinement, which was not yet imaginable in the 1980s and 1990s. The need to change was in no way simply a matter of a preference for modernization, as opposed to adherence to a traditional way of life. For example, one of the central features of the system of vertical integration is the way that it consolidates every aspect of production and marketing into a uniform combination of diverse elements. These elements are thoroughly standardized (for example, the quality and amount of feed and medicine per pig, the slaughter weight of animals, climate control in confinement facility, and the immobility of animals within confinement), which facilitates scaling production up to ever higher levels. The shift to integration not only imposes a major debt burden on the growers who opt to get big; it also prohibitively restrains those farmers who would prefer not to raise animals in this fashion. This is primarily because the standardization and scale of integration made it all but impossible for small farmers to process and market their pigs. While it used to be the case, as many farmers told me, that meat processors could be found in almost every town in every county of the Coastal Plain, most of these processors were put out of business by the integrators or, later, by the enormous facility built by Smithfield. These industrial facilities serve only those growers who have contracted with integrators, but the smaller processing plants could not maintain their customer base once contract growers were obligated to have their animals slaughtered and butchered in the integrators' plants. As I frequently note below, animal processing remains a major source of frustration for small farmers who are trying to produce pasture-raised pork.

Processing is a craft that, in many ways, is dying out as processing plants become fewer and fewer, and experienced, skilled labor becomes harder to find. Moreover, plants for processing large animals (that is, not poultry) are extremely capital intensive and subject to exactly the same expensive regulatory authorities as the enormous integrated facilities. While a few small, skilled processing plants serve the growing group of pasture-raised pig producers in the Piedmont, every farmer I worked with had difficulties with the costs—in terms of transportation, scheduling, or the quality of butchery[11]—of processing.

The other obstacle to raising pigs outside of the contract system is marketing. In the past, most pig farmers sold their whole animals to a processing plant, which also served as a meat packer. These plants then branded and sold the meat they aggregated from "their" pig producers. Under the contract system this kind of independent marketing becomes almost (but not quite) impossible. Since the integrator controls the entire production process, farmers who work outside of the contract system can no longer depend on packinghouses to market their meat for them. If independent pig farmers were able to find a processor that they could work with, most of them still needed to find a way to get their pork to consumers.

For individual farmers, wholesale distribution (that is, through a grocery chain, country store, or other retail facility) was not viable. Maintaining a reliable supply of pork that could keep a retail operation stocked year round was all but impossible on the scale that most smaller pig farmers operated, and the time and energy that it would take for a store to keep up its relationship with individual farmers made this kind of marketing prohibitive.[12] The only viable option, under these conditions, is what the industry calls direct marketing, a strategy in which each farmer packages and brands his or her own meat[13] and then sells that meat directly to consumers, usually at a farmers' market but sometimes at a shop on the farm itself or (in recent years) on the Internet. It should be clear, then, an independent small farmer must disaggregate all of the elements of the integrated system—growing, transporting, processing, packing, labeling, marketing (and, many hope, branding)—and that makes the farmer responsible for (or responsible for a way to engage in) each element of the whole process. Marketing, in particular, demands a set of skills that very few small farmers can readily acquire, as well as time and opportunity. It was only in the early 2000s, for example, that the first farmers acquired meat handler's licenses, which allowed them to transport their meat from a processing plant and take the product to market. Moreover, many farmers in the Coastal Plain lacked access to farmers' markets if they did want to market their product directly. The Piedmont is much more urban and more densely populated than the Coastal Plain and also has a more affluent population, better able to pay the premium price required for raising pigs on pasture. It is no surprise, then, that farmers' markets have been much more successful in the vicinity of Raleigh and Chapel Hill than they have been in Sampson County, and transportation costs, as well as market regulations that limit the geographical range of producers,[14] make it impossible for many small farmers to get their meat to customers.

Given the range of obstacles that small independent producers confront, it is not hard to see the appeal of a contract that guarantees farmers a certain price for each pig and relieves farmers of all of the complicated procedures required to take a 250-pound pig from the producer to the consumer. Of course, the contract system itself has imposed many of these obstacles. In any event, the debt burden it entails may be a risk worth taking for some farmers. At the same time, as I have already indicated, the potential catastrophes of vertical integration—not just for the debt-strapped producers, but for the ecosystem, to say nothing of the health and well-being of workers and consumers—generated an interest in North Carolina in creating alternatives to the contract system, and that interest exploded in the 1980s and 1990s. In what follows I present the story of how a specific group of actors—individuals, institutions, and a consortium of related agencies—worked to make it possible for farmers to raise pigs and market their pork outside of the confinement and contract system—that is, to put "pigs on the ground," in the vernacular of farmers and many local food advocates. Of course, this is only one story, and it focuses on a limited range of actors. But I am quite certain that pasture-raised pigs would not be found in the North Carolina Piedmont were it not for the activities I outline here.

North Carolina Agricultural and Technical State University (A&T) is a historically black land-grant research university in Greensboro, North Carolina. In the late 1980s, A&T hired Charles Talbott as a professor of animal science.[15] Talbott had gotten his PhD from North Carolina State, in Raleigh, working on dairy cattle, but when he was hired at A&T he developed an interest in swine science. As he told me, "I had seen what the confinement system did Down East [in eastern North Carolina], and I didn't like it." Talbott's chief concern was "food security. What will happen when diesel goes to $10 a gallon? How are we gonna move all of that pork thousands of miles to the consumers? How will we feed ourselves?" Talbott's concerns about food security led him to promote what he thought would be more-sustainable, lower-input, small-scale outdoor production practices as a counter to the industrial system.

At about the same time, Talbott told me, he became aware of the potential consumer interest in pasture-raised pork when he read an article in the journal *Art of Eating* (Behr 1999) that profiled Paul Willis, a farmer in northern Iowa who had rejected factory farming and developed innovative techniques for raising his pigs on pasture. I discuss this article and its wide-reaching implications in chapter 5. Here I want to note that what most impressed Talbott about Willis's operation was the quality of the pork he was producing, something that Talbott had not really been interested in until that point. "Chuck became more of a meat scientist after that," Talbott's swine specialist assistant, Mike Jones, told me. Talbott traveled to southern Europe, where he saw the way that pigs could be raised in extremely different farming systems and how their pork was processed, cured, and consumed at a much different scale. As Talbott put it, "these pigs were really at the center of community life. There were festivals around the slaughter process, and pork from those pigs served at these events. It was much more of a ritual than you see here."[16]

Talbott's interest in meat quality would have profound, if somewhat indirect, implications for the way that pork is marketed and for creating communities of discerning customers for different kinds of pork from different kinds of pigs raised in a distinctive fashion across the Piedmont. I detail the sociocultural dimensions of these transformations in the chapters that follow. What I want to focus on here are some immediate political economic consequences of Talbott's quest for quality meat.

After reading about Willis's innovative operation, Talbott contacted him to find out more about his work. By this time, Willis, while continuing to farm, had taken on a new position. His pork had come to the attention of *Art of Eating* through Alice Waters, the celebrated chef at Chez Panisse in Berkeley, California. Willis, persuaded that he was raising the best-tasting pork imaginable, arranged to send loins of his pork to her to sample. Waters, in turn, became so taken with the flavor of Willis's pork that she contacted Bill Niman, who owned Niman Ranch in Bolinas, California. Niman subsequently hired Willis to manage a line of pork for Niman Ranch, which so far had marketed only beef and lamb. Willis, then, was trying to organize a network of producers who would contract with Niman Ranch to market their pork under the Niman label.

When Talbott contacted Willis to inquire about his operations, Willis saw this as an opportunity to expand Niman's production capacity beyond the group of farmers in northern Iowa that he had recruited to the brand. Together, Willis and Talbott proposed in 2002 to develop a pilot project for Niman that would encourage pig farmers in North Carolina to raise their pigs according to the animal welfare, environmental, and meat quality standards that the Niman brand maintained. In return, Niman would contract with those farmers who could meet the standards, make a contribution to their farming infrastructure to allow them to work toward meeting the standards, and give them a guaranteed price. In this way, while not acting as a traditional vertical integrator, and—crucially—requiring that pigs be raised on the ground in pasture, not in confinement operations, Niman could help simplify the established obstacles of processing[17] and, above all, marketing that severely limited the viability of small-scale, sustainable pig production in North Carolina.

Innovation and Structural Constraint

It is not my intention to write a mystery, so let me say say right here that this pilot project did not last very long. But piecing together how this happened is entirely relevant to understanding the contemporary networks of pork production, distribution, and consumption that are the central concern of this book. An array of forces joined together to initiate this project, and it is a challenge to simply tell what happened apart from the diverse perspectives of the various participants in this process, many of whom remain active in—and, indeed, critical to—the world of niche-market pork production in the Piedmont and beyond today. Here, my story becomes less a narrative than an account of the various forces and perspectives that contributed to the failure of the Niman project but also gave rise to the contemporary order of relationships and practices that constitute that niche-market world, and especially its characteristic features, tensions, and aspirations.

We can start with the money. Niman Ranch did invest significant resources in this program, but there were other funds and significant institutions involved in this process of introducing, or updating, pasture-raised pig facilities and practices to small farmers across the Piedmont Coastal Plain who could sell pork to Niman. As Talbott was a research scientist at A&T, a good part of the funding for this project came from grants.[18] The Niman project made use of funding from the Sustainable Agriculture

Research and Education (SARE) program of the U.S. Department of Agriculture (USDA). In addition, important funding came from the Golden LEAF Foundation and Heifer International. Golden LEAF is especially important. It is a foundation established in 1999 with funds from the tobacco buyout—that is, money that the tobacco industry paid as part of their settlement with the federal government that precluded further lawsuits against that industry. Part of this buyout was paid directly to tobacco farmers, but other funds were provided to foundations like Golden LEAF in Rocky Mount (at the eastern edge of the Piedmont), which issued grants designed to help economically stressed tobacco farmers transition to other forms of agricultural production. In this way, pastured-pork production received a sizable impetus from these tobacco buyout funds, both in the form of grants and as direct payments that most farmers used to pay off debts and, in some instances, fund new pig production infrastructure.

At the same time that Talbott and his team were using these grant resources and helping set up Niman's entrepreneurial enterprise, Talbott was also working for A&T. North Carolina State University (State) was also participating as required by two of the funders, the SARE program and Golden LEAF. It is worth pointing out, then, that there were certain potential tensions built into this arrangement that bound state universities, granting agencies administered by the federal or state government,[19] and a private enterprise together. Suspicions of conflict of interest followed many of the members of the initiative, as some potential farmers wondered whether public resources and infrastructure were being used to develop the operations of farmers who were administering the grants. These kinds of reservations are entirely predictable—and I have no evidence to suggest that they were accurate—in such public-private and university-corporate projects. But it is also worth noting that the mission and history of State and A&T were not entirely compatible with the objectives of Talbott or Niman. State and A&T have recently cooperated in the development of sustainable agricultural practices, notably through the development of the Center for Environmental Farming Systems (CEFS) and NC Choices, its program dedicated to niche-meat supply chains. At the same time, State is deeply involved in the promotion of industrial agriculture across the state and the nation. Many of the people I know who worked on this Niman pilot project suggested that people at State were skeptical about promoting agriculture on such a small scale and were uncomfortable seeking funding for such operations when many of their efforts were dedicated to securing mortgages and promoting policies (like those of Wendell

Murphy, who is one of the biggest donors to State's athletics programs) that enhanced the profitability of industrial producers.

But it is also important to describe the ways that A&T viewed this project and related projects dedicated to small-scale agriculture. My understanding of these tensions derives from discussions over the past seven years with a number of A&T employees, as well as from long-term ethnographic work with recent graduates of A&T. As a historically black university, A&T is dedicated to a project of modernization. That is, it recruits students from the sizable African American community across the state of North Carolina, whose painful history of disenfranchisement and oppression includes not only slavery but also the consequences of land dispossession; debilitating poverty; discriminatory lending policies by the USDA; and unequal access to social services, education paramount among them, that follow from this legacy of slavery and Jim Crow. But A&T's central intention today, especially with respect to farming, is to move its students out of poverty and beyond the marginalized resources that have been available to them by giving them the skills and opportunities that will allow them to advance in the contemporary world of financialized industrial agriculture. One recent graduate of A&T I worked closely with told me: "They didn't want me to do this kind of [pastured livestock] farming. They wanted me to go work for Cargill."

Both State and A&T, then, were less than fully supportive of Talbott's initiative with Niman. Moreover, the structural tensions I just identified with respect to A&T, and the way they are related to a long legacy of racism, revealed a broader tension in the Niman initiative, as well. That is, race also figured as a dimension of the project as it unfolded. As I have indicated, the notion that pig farming should be an outdoor operation in open pasture appealed to some African American farmers as consistent with what they had learned from previous generations of farmers in their families. But others worried that this kind of pig production might interfere with productive land for other agricultural activities on their farm. The inputs that Niman offered often involved innovative techniques that made use of woods and untended land but that required setting up fencing, water supplies, or small structures in wooded areas. Many black farmers were reluctant to do this. My information about this reluctance is merely anecdotal, but it may speak to somewhat different understandings of what constitutes productive farmland, fields, and yards as opposed to dangerous, unproductive, wild woods[20] (Gundaker and McWillie 2005). When farmers participated in the project and provided pigs that they had raised to the processors that Niman contracted with, I heard concerns that these farmers were bringing in not pigs that they had raised themselves according to Niman's protocols for animal welfare and pastured production, but pigs that had been raised on neighboring farms, often by family members. These cases raise a valid question: What makes a pig "my pig" in a place where pig raising, slaughter, and provisioning had often been carried out by collective efforts in a context of limited access to land and widespread dispossession? Some participants saw this use of "other" pigs as jeopardizing the Niman market, while others saw objections to extending this market to a wider set of related farmers as racist.

Similar tensions emerged with respect to quality control in the pork these animals produced. Niman would sample meat from North Carolina pigs for a range of qualities, including size, tenderness, and fat content (marbling). When Niman's market specialists felt that some pigs did not meet their requirements, the result was often allegations of favoritism—and occasionally of racial preference. But not only were there complaints of racial bias; there were also concerns that the processors that Niman contracted with were not competent and did not butcher some farmers' pigs in ways that complied with the expectations of the program. As I have suggested above, and as I will discuss in many places below, many farmers, food advocates, and other actors feel that processing is an ongoing concern, so its intersection with possible racial tensions made for conflict that many recall even today.

There were, then, specific tensions that relate to the concrete history of North Carolina—its educational institutions; the long history of tobacco farming that was central to the state's economy for centuries; and the legacy of pronounced racial hierarchies, particularly in the Coastal Plain— that were clearly illuminated as the Niman project unfolded. But the collapse of the project was precipitated by conditions that were not specific to North Carolina, and it is conceivable that the project would have continued to develop, or perhaps limp along, had it not been for external forces. To begin with, Niman faced the problem of transportation costs. A company headquartered in Point Reyes, California, with its pork operations centered in northern Iowa was poorly prepared to deal with production questions that emerged in eastern North Carolina. More to the point, the costs of shipping pork from North Carolina across the country proved problematic, especially for a company whose brand was, to some extent, built on claims about sustainability. As a research scientist, Talbott often turned his attention to new projects—like the redomestication of the Ossabaw

Island Hog, which I discuss in great detail below—which limited his value to the entrepreneurial pursuits of Niman. Furthermore, Niman was facing significant financial pressures. Bill Niman, who had founded the company, was committed to innovative pasturing methods and animal welfare, but in thirty years of operation, the company was never profitable (Finz 2009). In 2006, Niman announced that it was pulling out of North Carolina. At the time, as MacLean notes, Niman offered "72 lines of sausage and other cuts," a figure that suggests that the company not only lacked marketing focus but also would face problems with sourcing enough animals to produce sufficient volume for each of these cuts to remain viable. Just after the project ended in North Carolina in 2007, Bill Niman left Niman Ranch over a conflict with its management team and was prohibited from using his name to market any of the meat he produced on his own land (Severson 2008). By 2009 the bankrupt company had been taken over by Chicago's Natural Food Holdings, its largest investor.

In spite of the fact that the Niman project "imploded," as MacLean puts it, it would be a mistake to call it a failure. In all sorts of ways, Talbott's efforts transformed the landscape of pasture-pig production in North Carolina, and a host of regional actors developed their commitments to niche-market meats because of these efforts and their aftermath. I think it is fair to say that the farmers, chefs, food activists, entrepreneurs, and artisans I describe below would not be participating in an order of relationships and practices surrounding niche-market pasture-raised pork as pervasive and complex as it is today without the foundation—problematic as it was and continues to be—established by Niman Ranch.

Where We Are Now

Once Niman pulled out, a group of farmers who had been given infrastructure and guidance in how to raise pigs on pasture found themselves without a market. In 2007, eighteen of the former Niman producers joined together to form the NC Natural Hog Growers Association, a growers' cooperative whose members planned to work together to find ways to market the pigs they had begun to raise. The Co-op, as many know it, has worked with chefs and entrepreneurs to find ways to keep its members' operations afloat. Their pork is featured in Whole Foods markets around the Triangle in the Piedmont, although their ability to supply a full range of cuts for these outlets is occasionally limited.

Marketing in niche markets remains a pressing question for most producers, for the reasons I have already discussed. The Co-op looks for outlets like markets, butcher shops, aggregators (businesses that can consolidate meat from multiple producers and sell it under a single label), and restaurants to sell its pork. But most farmers outside of the Co-op are heavily dependent on direct marketing, and for most, that means farmers' markets. The Piedmont has a substantial number of farmers' markets—over twenty-five in the Triangle and the Triad together, some of which are open twice a week for much of the year—so there is certainly an opportunity for most pig farmers to market their pork directly (if they can process their animals at costs that are not prohibitive). Indeed, if anything, the number of markets has exploded in recent years, which runs the risk of dissipating the customer base of many of the long-established markets. Margins in direct marketing are, as one might imagine, extremely low, and the costs of marketing itself—the labor spent packing, driving, and selling, let alone keeping track of inventory (which very few farmers do successfully)—are significant. Grants from the SARE program and Golden LEAF and the Rural Advancement Foundation International (headquartered in Pittsboro, North Carolina) continue to subsidize a number of farmers who take on innovative sustainable projects.

Beyond the production of pigs, pork marketing also takes advantage of the substantial interest in food among the area's restaurants and specialty shops. In 2009, *Bon Appétit* named the Triangle (focusing on Durham and Chapel Hill) "America's Foodiest Small Town" (Knowlton 2008). The James Beard Foundation routinely names a handful of chefs in the Piedmont among its finalists—and winners—in its "Best Chef: Southeast" category. Throughout this book, I describe the work of a number of restaurants in cultivating a taste for local pork and in generating enthusiastic and discerning diners for this product. Finally, it should also be clear that the media in all forms, from Instagram photos to *New York Times* restaurant reviews and university press books, have contributed to an expanding interest in pastured pork in the Piedmont.

This chapter has provided a broad background to the world of niche-market, pasture-raised pork in the Piedmont. There is a vast and growing literature on the degradations of industrial meat (Estabrook 2015; Foer 2010; Pachirat 2011; Schlosser 2001; but also see Blanchette 2013 for a brilliant ethnographic exploration of the factory farm as a utopian enterprise full of surprising relationships and complex biosocial interactions). Here

I have tried to describe only the conditions that were created in North Carolina (especially their precipitous expansion), conditions that many today cite as central to their commitment to finding an alternative to the confinement system. In what follows, I describe the range of values that motivate this commitment. I also consider the sociopolitical implications of this alternative system and try to demonstrate how they are situated in a much broader nexus of political, economic, and social forces. But first I turn to the profiles of some of the individuals who have figured prominently in the world of pastured pork in the Piedmont.

PROFILE: Eliza MacLean

—

Eliza MacLean is a farmer and the owner of Cane Creek Farm in Saxapahaw, North Carolina. MacLean was one of the first farmers in the state to get a meat handler's license, which allowed her to sell meat from her livestock through direct marketing—that is, at farmers' markets in Carrboro and Greensboro. A pioneer in the niche market of pasture-raised pigs, MacLean grew up outside of Philadelphia and lived in New England and California before coming to the Triangle (and she would want me to tell you that she has also lived in Clayton, New York, on the St. Lawrence River). I first met Eliza in 2008 at my local farmers' market, where she has been selling meat and produce since 2006. I worked on her farm in 2008 and 2009 when she was partnered with Braeburn Farm in Snow Camp, North Carolina, owned by Charles "Doc" Sydnor, and I have been selling with her at the Carrboro Farmers' Market almost every Saturday since January 2009. We had this conversation in the fall of 2014.

BW: I know you first developed your interest in animals working with Amish farmers when you were in high school in Philly. But tell me what you were doing in the Bay Area before you came to North Carolina, and how did you decide to leave?

EM: I was playing a little too hard. I had moved out there to prepare for vet[erinarian] school. And I was very interested in [the University of California at] Davis because they had a really good wildlife and large animal [program] at the time, and the only other one was Penn [the University of Pennsylvania]. And I really wanted to explore and do all the fun things that you do in S[an] F[rancisco], but really start gearing myself toward good scores on GREs [the Graduate Record Examination]

Fig. 1.3 Eliza MacLean with the author.

and Davis vet school. And I really felt a bit afraid with four or five years under my belt that that was never going to happen because I was having way too much fun. I took on a lot of responsibility with a couple of veterinary clinics. I invested in one and became the owner manager of one. It just seemed like I was bypassing vet school to work with animals, have my own business, and follow the Grateful Dead and play. And I got really into long-distance running.[21]

Where vet school would have never fit into all that, I thought the only way to actually live that dream would be to come home—and I was homesick for my family. I was kind of adrift. I applied to [the University of California at] Berkeley and Duke [University] for a two-year environmental toxicology program and got in, and everybody said, "You're coming right?" And I did. And that was 1994.

I did an awesome master's program on the Saint Mary's River at White Oak Plantation, at the border of Georgia and Florida, where I got to do captive breeding work, as well as work on my master's thesis which had to do with the secession of a 150-year abandoned rice paddy. [We looked at] what came back after all of those canals were gone and the hydrology had been changed. That was fascinating. I did the wildlife, and two other students did the hydrology and the vegetation. I got to work with *fantastic* animals late at night. Birthing bongos and catching black rhinos, working with the school vet staff.

I decided I really should be in vet medicine. But I couldn't get in to NC State's vet program, for a number of reasons. I had a biological clock [ticking] and a lot of veterinary experience, and I just decided to take a job at Duke. I managed the ecotoxicology lab and tried to figure out why I had been unsuccessful at getting pregnant. And I ended up in the infertility clinic as a Duke employee and got to carry through to conception and have these two beautiful kids. And then with two kids, vet school was out of the question.

So I became a farmer when the kids were born in 2000. I had a little petting zoo with my goat herd. I did child care for other moms, pet care to make it work. By 2002 it was time for me to get some real work. I did tons of little jobs. I worked as an editor for environmental presses. But I started looking around seriously to think about farming from a toxicological standpoint. Because we had had extremely little training at Duke in that. I feel it's still the same issue twenty years later! And livestock farming is still one of the worst actors. Why are ponds and streams all eutrophic? [Hurricanes] Floyd and Fran had happened. Now in Pennsylvania, where my parents live, they have some amazing farm link programs where the old farmers teach new farmers and sustainable practices come in, and the state helps out. But nobody was doing that around here. And I thought, "Aha! There we are."

I kept meeting people and ended up working with the American Livestock Breed Conservancy and did some work with them. I set up their farm tour on the CFSA [Carolina Farm Stewardship Association] Farm Tour program. I ended up with a lot of numbers of people who were raising animals. So I could call and see who could bring their cute little Dexter cattle and fancy Guinea hogs [and] to see who could bring their animals to the campus at Central Carolina Community College [in Pittsboro].

Setting this all up, I met a guy named Chuck Talbott because he had Tamworth hogs at A&T. Now they couldn't bring them to the farm tour, this was 2002. But he said, "Come see what I'm doing! I've got these crazy wild Eurasian hogs on my farm." And the guy was such a crack-up, but he said, "Whenever you want, I've got a job for you at A&T." I approached Chuck with an offer of a part-time position—I had two little children I need to take care of—and he literally hired me the next day. I got to the A&T job never having had a single idea that it was a land-grant historically black university, and here I roll up to campus, this hippie chick in a purple school bus. The whole thing was a riot.

BW: I tell everybody there would be no pastured pork in North Carolina if it weren't for Chuck. When you got there, what was he up to?

EM: He had just happened upon an article in the *Art of Eating* which was talking about the taste and the quality. Health benefits to flavor, to animal husbandry—it [pork] met every expectations of consumers as good food and a good livestock product. He had just got the first Golden LEAF grant. And he was trying to put together relationships between the Animal Welfare Institute; Niman, who Chuck had started working with through Paul Willis from the *Art of Eating*; Heifer [International]—so that there could be a pass-on program that made sense. A&T and NC State had grants from the SARE program that required them to work together. The idea is to get these tobacco farmers that are accepting the buyout [funds] to diversify in some way. It all of a sudden became a little darling in many different ways. But it was not supported by either university.

BW: Why not?

EM: First, I think A&T truly felt we were trying to put black farmers back in the Dark Ages.[22] They really were almost insulted. And then we'd run to State and they said, no, nobody's doing that, we're only interested in building big barns and getting big financing, and the bank won't go for these small operations. But we went for it anyway because we had a market in Niman Ranch. We did have people committed to buying these hogs, there weren't too many things we had to put together. Processors [were a problem], but there were processors down in Duplin and Johnston and Sampson Counties where these farmers were. They had these growers' schools going, run by John O'Sullivan and Mike Jones, and they had just hired me.

I could manage the herd at A&T, and then A&T finally put the kibosh on it when Chuck wanted to put Ossabaws on their land—they said no, they couldn't support it, they didn't have the land for it. And that was the end of Chuck at A&T, and then Niman offered to take me on as their field agent in 2003 and 2004.

It became much easier for me to develop my own farm, without the scrutiny of A&T, once I was working for Niman, because that was seen as a huge conflict of interest. All of the farmers that were working under the Golden LEAF grant were part of the A&T breeding program. So all of these small farmers were producing pigs to pass on [to] the next generation of incoming farmers, and these were coming home to the swine herd at A&T. And I was getting them ready to go, making sure they were artificially inseminated, and getting them back out to the farmers. And then Niman offered me a job, and A&T let the door hit me hard going out it.

I worked for Niman until 2006, and that's when Niman pulled out. AWI [the Animal Welfare Institute] picked me up, and I audited processors for them. That's when Whole Foods came in to pick up the farmers that Niman left, and they developed [an animal] welfare program of their own.

BW: What can you tell me about the fallout of Niman, both for you and for the area?

EM: I think that it was systemic. They had a huge number of pigs in the Midwest, their headquarters was in Oakland, and they had this pilot program in North Carolina. I was charged with getting more East Coast farmers, and I got some. And then all the processing came to a screaming halt. They didn't want to play with Niman and Whole Foods, because they would accept pigs, process them for Whole Foods, and Whole Foods would send them *back* to Niman. And then the processor was getting screwed. And I was down at the processors when I worked for Niman. The processors were doing everything right, but some farmers were bringing in horrible pigs. So we had to go back to the drawing board, and we really worked on consistency. And after a while the race card got thrown in, and black farmers felt like the white guys got their pigs to Niman, but not the black people, who got marginalized.

Along came NC Choices, but the black farmers didn't want to have anything to do with that. They didn't want to be a part of what they thought was a little "club." They were happy to get the stuff from Niman to set up the outdoor pigs, and then go on their own way. But the Co-op really did get going when NC Choices and A&T [and] some folks in [cooperative] extension really pushed for them to incorporate. But it's run by one of three white farmers—a great guy—of the more than fifty black farmers we got going over three years. That was part of the mission of Golden LEAF, to target resource-limited farmers. And it ended up being geared to black farmers.

Very quickly when I worked with Niman I realized that I couldn't survive on what they were paying, I needed to direct market my pork. And thankfully Lantern was opening its doors, Magnolia Grill, some other restaurants in town. The folks we set up Down East, the last thing any of them wanted to do was direct market. They didn't have a market. I was lucky to be in a place where there was demand for that higher-end product when Niman stopped buying pigs. And a market [in Carrboro]. And accessibility. Chefs brought their whole staff out [to the farm]. I insisted that every single one of them come out so that the wait staff and everybody else could tell the story. And that was really fun. And that made me keep my farm in good nick, too.

Anyway, lots and lots growing pains. When Niman imploded, they got rid of seventy-two lines of sausage and other cuts and just focused on pork products in Iowa, and beef and lamb in California, and next thing you know, Bill Niman himself is bought out of his own company!

BW: This is all 2006, and you're out on your own, and then you partner up with Braeburn?

EM: Yeah, 2006 and 2007. 2005 and 2006 we [Braeburn Beef and Cane Creek] provided a lot of the product for the CFSA banquet. We met through our product. We were finally getting up our numbers enough where we could actually supply something like a banquet. And our names were on the table. I really enjoyed Charles [Sydnor], and he wanted tremendous things to happen on his farm. It felt like the stars were aligning. I was nervous, but I felt like it was what I should do. I also thought it would put me [geographically] closer to my partner, but it didn't.

I got my parents involved, and we really, really carefully—I thought—went through it all. And it really looked like it was a great opportunity. I just think the number one thing was scale. Charles wanted to scale up, and that entailed a lot of issues that I wasn't really equipped to deal with. So we couldn't make it work. We thought this was a place where it could work. I could do the direct marketing, but to manage the place and find staff that stuck around year after year was just hard. So we dissolved our partnership in 2011.

BW: So what's been the upside of this for you in the whole grand scheme of things?

EM: It's annoyingly personal, but it has everything to do with Enid and Quinn [her twins], and shifting every single priority around them. My life can be a monster that swallows us all, but it gives them something to identify with and be really proud of, and that's very community based. I love the sense of community. I love the sense of purpose. I appreciate what I've learned, and the challenge—that can be splendid. But also that when it's not fun, it's just mine. I don't have to make it so hard on a whole staff, or a company. There are little triumphs every single day, there are beautiful ways of commingling with these animals, of learning about oneself, about teaching other people. It gives me a lot of pleasure to give people the best product for their event or their wedding. Or to just hear that they got creative and just made their own bacon and they loved it. Ninety percent of the time we get great feedback.

And I've always wanted to make a difference. Whatever I do, I try to be in the top of it. I liked being a pioneer here. But it's never "I'm going to do this because no one else is." It's that there's a need, and I feel that I have enough drive that I might be good at it.

I feel like I still get to choose a lot of who my customers are. And I've been so busy that I haven't really noticed who else has jumped into this game. I thank God that Firsthand came along, because I couldn't handle all of the bigger orders I was getting. We thought with Braeburn that we might end up being an aggregator for other peoples' animals, like Hickory Nut Gap.[23] But what quickly ends up happening is you end up raising other people's animals to control your quality. They all take serious time! You can't keep your eye on all the other balls.

What we learned in the early years is that nobody knew the cost of anything they were producing. So we've definitely fine-tuned the pricing of all these markets. But there's just a lot of them. And there's a lot of people that are excited by the food—but they can be fickle. They can go somewhere else, and if we're dependent on them to show up and spend that $100 every week—and they don't show up—then we're in trouble. I screamed with the pedal-to-the-metal for as long as I could to find that sweet spot, to get big, to deal with the demand; to get small to deal with the authenticity and the quality. In some ways I'm right back where I started, but that's where we are now.

—

John O'Sullivan is an emeritus professor of sustainable agriculture and local and community food systems at North Carolina Agricultural and Technical State University. He recently retired as codirector of the Center for Environmental Farming Systems (CEFS). He has played a vital role in working with small farmers across the state to develop their business skills to get them, as he says, "to do a better job as a business." I first met John in 2008 through my work at the Carrboro Farmers' Market, where he is not only a regular customer but also a local celebrity: he is known by all the producers at the market, most of whom he has worked with at some point over the past thirty years. John and I also share a wider intellectual legacy, as he has a PhD in African history from the University of California at Los Angeles and has done a good deal of fieldwork in West Africa on regional economies. We had the following long conversation in October 2014.

BW: How do you describe your work?

JO: It's hard to convince anybody who is trying to make an informed decision about farming. There are trade-offs if you want to be this type of [sustainable] farmer. It's very hard to convince people that the costs and benefits will work for the person, or that over time there won't be changes. Farming and fishing are different from running a coffee shop. Probably the skill set that you need to have to do this [run the coffee shop] will be the same in six months. But each year in farming—learning your land, learning the animals, whether it's their food needs, or how they can be handled, how aggressive they are—all of those things are a dynamic. The weather, feed costs, energy costs, public policies—here we are, we have this beautiful little system and there's a disease outbreak and the government comes in with this heavy-handed decision and huh? You are caught out!

I was talking with a farmer the other day, and it turns out there's a farmer who is having a baby, and another farmer who has young kids. They are giving up the farming. It's a full-time commitment you make to farming. And then there are trade-offs. When you're twenty, twenty-five, just trying to do it, and make it happen, and prove to yourself that law school isn't what I want to do, I want to be a farmer. And then you can *do* it—for two or three years, and you feel, "Wow, this is so awesome!" But then [you think] "this isn't as fulfilling as I thought it was

Fig. 1.4 John O'Sullivan. Photograph by Lisa Forehand.

going to be. And I met this great guy, or girl, and now we're thinking of this." The dynamics of this are very difficult.

BW: Yeah, farming is different. But lots of skilled positions are like that, aren't they?

JO: But now let's flip the story—go from today back twenty-five years ago. The story of pigs is very, very different. On the one hand, the market stuff has gotten into place. I do think that, in my opinion, Obamacare has really changed the equation, just in terms of what it is that I'm trying to do and the risks that I'm taking. If I can get medical care, I can run pigs on a little bit of land. And I can do it part time, because one of the nice things about animals, if I set it up well—one can raise pigs on a little bit of land, because now there are infrastructures [like markets] for getting yourself set up. And you can go in the direction of raising pigs that *can* be fulfilling.

But, again, it's very hard, people don't think in these terms. They think they can do it all, and they want to do everything themselves. But even very accomplished farmers with a lot of animals, it's just too much to get on top of. But if I were Mike Jones's kids, and I knew pigs, and I knew the outdoors, and I wanted to live in NC [North Carolina], I could get something going, I could be a teacher or a FedEx driver and have pigs and know the heck out of it. And here's my asset base of land and labor and love that I'm putting into it. Now the question to me is, what is my return on *that?* What do I need? It's obvious—the number one enterprise in small farmers is cow-calf operations.[24] Now, why is that? I can afford the risk, and there is this *ethos*, at least for white folks. There's nothing greater in my observation than to be from Auburn University, and to have a pickup truck with wheels about as tall as I am, and to have a belt buckle and boots, and just be standing there and talking about your cows! And it's so funny too, because, talking to those kinds of producers, there's very little of the economics that we can talk about. There's talk about the minerals and their soils, and the different breeds—that's what gets them excited! They do know where they're making money and where they're not. They're maintaining their asset base, and you make enough that you're not losing money. But now if you add that your health care costs are covered, it does become more viable, and you can do that raising pigs part time, too. Anything you can do to reduce your costs helps out.

BW: So you always taught me: to make money in farming, you need two things—either own your land or make your money from some other source, from what lots of farmers in NC call a "public job."[25]

JO: It's cash flow—a lot of the financial stuff is really complicated. If you've got to have the cash flow to pay for your operating inputs *and* put bread on the table, then you've got some serious problems.

BW: What do we do about scale? It's great that these niches can be profitable for those farmers that can figure it out, or have some other income, or can balance farming with something else—but can you really feed people that way? Because when you start to talk about people doing it on a part-time basis, now you're talking about people raising not hundreds of pigs, but maybe not even dozens of pigs, just a handful of pigs. How can we feed everyone that way?

JO: I don't know the answer. What we have created, with the way our economy is structured and our society is structured—we're more of an urban people now, and that doesn't even begin to explain the complexity of the questions. The food demands of our society, I don't see how it's even going to get done going forward. If I were Cisco I would be sweating bullets in terms of projected demand, convenience, food safety for the global system.

But given that—it's just like where we started with the question, is it possible to be a niche farmer in NC—and the answer that I'm giving is not for Nebraska or Montana—here there's no way that this will work as the *base* for what we want. If farmers had realistic *demand* for their product, how would they live as opposed to how would they *want* to live? What are *their demands*? If I want to have WiFi, and I want a big screen TV and an NFL package, you can have all of that, but it costs money! If you have to factor all that in on the cash demand side and then try to respond on the cash *supply* side, that really gets complicated. Versus, let's say, living in Franklin County on family land, [in a] basic, single wide [trailer], maybe a bathroom, electricity, that's gonna hold for a while. Can we configure our supply to our demand as well as our demand to our supply?

Now let's go back up to the question you asked. Most Americans' idea of a meal is a function of the five to eight minutes they can take to cook—we've configured things so it's not possible [to satisfy all demands]. However, there are repeated entrance points into our lifestyles in which more simple foods, more true foods, are available. There are more spaces for small part-time farmers to make some income. Let's try to figure out a system in which this *can* work. There are now markets in Carrboro and Durham and South Durham, etc. If the system were to really grind off—suppose it really shuts down. In the short term, it's going to be really difficult. Like the Europeans did in 1945–46, eating leaves and wild plants. The deer will be *gone*, we *will* learn how to eat the squirrels! But then, we'll have a base that allows us to have the butternut squash, the potatoes, the sweet potatoes, the corn, as we reconfigure given the new constraints. That, to me, is where things are.

BW: Does that make you an optimist or a pessimist? If you really think there's an apocalypse coming?

JO: It's so easy to see that. There are a lot of indications around the edges that things are not working great. But people *are* positive in places around the world. Even in Port-au-Prince [Haiti],[26] the kids are learning to play soccer, they're thrilled with a new T-shirt.

I was born before the bomb, the technology of mayhem that we have produced that are out [there]. That may lead to [a global] shutdown. I don't think the question of feeding the nine billion [people in the world] is the issue, it's feeding the three billion that [would] survive!

BW: Getting back to your points about demand side and supply side. In the Piedmont, some farmers have pretty high demands. They want to ask, how can I have a summer vacation and send my kids to great schools? It's kind of a paradox. There are high consumer demands that farmers have, yet living here is where there is demand for their production.

JO: North Carolina is a very special place in that it values small farmers—because of its heritage, land ownership, and traditions of farming. There's a mix that is possible here that everyone accepts. There are people who have done it; there are farmers that are leaders. Now let's look right at that [question of farmers' demands]. Let's go down to the North Carolina Natural Pork Co-Op [the North Carolina Natural Hog Growers Association]. Is it possible to set yourself modest goals and have the asset base down in that part of the world where it's not terribly expensive? They like to raise pigs. And the market has come to them, repeatedly in different ways. The pieces are in place, they're still tenuous, and they're always going to be.

As I see it, they had Niman, but that didn't work out; they had Whole Foods; they have Firsthand, but even there you need consistency and you need the volume. And is this still possible? I think it is. I don't know what the answers are. There's a farmer that I know from Franklin County, and I asked [him] would it be possible to franchise—that would allow you to get better control over those tenuous pieces, and you control for consistency, and you're raising those animals in the right way, and it has to be scheduled so that it's coming when the market wants.

BW: Isn't that what Niman tried to do?

JO: I'd agree with that. Big guys and little guys—and then the big guys get bought out—that's what happened to Niman. Feed prices went through the roof, and there was no market for pigs, and he got forced out. Now, we had a model for the viability of small farms in North Carolina with the tobacco program.

BW: Tell me about that program.

JO: It starts with the New Deal and the Agricultural Adjustment Act, but it's specific in terms of a commodity like tobacco. And it was set up on a county basis, with land that was producing tobacco, and the supply of that land was controlled by the government through the FHA [Farmers Home Administration]. And the question was not production of tobacco but being able to *market* the tobacco. And quantity and quality were controlled by the government's Crop Specialization Act. That was set up based on what the tobacco companies told the government they needed for tobacco for the coming year. So there was a stabilization. That's the way the thing worked—there were a lot of issues with it, but it lasted for fifty years.

BW: Well, what happens when suddenly nobody wants tobacco? Or says that the government shouldn't be subsidizing tobacco?

JO: Well, the big difference was that the companies found they could get the same quality from Malawi, and they weren't gonna pay for NC tobacco! So what I'm saying is, if you're trying to build a local food system, is there a way to set it up so we have supply management within the constraints of what we know of a market, and that it's economically viable and meets the needs of a local market that wants local products? Now, we don't have to worry about industrial pork because that's going to be at Walmart. We're producing a local product that is set up and is clean, and there is demand for it.

BW: Is that beyond those already going to the farmers' markets? Can you reach a wider world?

JO: There are markets that want to have local farms in North Carolina. At Fort Bragg, NCGT[27] is supporting this kind of program. The Fort says, "We serve 100,000 meals a day." They want to have agricultural land on the seven counties that make up the Fort because it's a lot easier to be a paratrooper on agricultural land than [in] subdivisions. Okay, we say to the Fort, if you want to have agricultural land, then you have to pay for it to be viable agriculture. I think the same kind of thing could be part of a land-use plan for a state, like North Carolina. Couldn't you have policies that build a framing of what is "local" and then manage supply and demand so that the farming could be viable with distribution and processing? I'm saying it is possible because we did that with tobacco!

BW: So tell me your story, and about you and pigs.

JO: There was an opportunity to come to A&T in 1983 to work in international agriculture. A&T had two projects in French West Africa, and they needed someone to work with communities over there as the home campus coordinator. One of the projects was in Guinea, and it was to set up an agricultural research station in [a] network, a research station that had an extension component in Conakry [the capital of Guinea]. The other one was in Niger, and it was livestock. It was trying to move cattle out of Niger into Nigerian markets. I hadn't been there before, but I worked in the Mali–Ivory Coast [cattle] system. And it's a grass-fed system, and it is really well fit to its ecosystem. Well, this was 1982–83, and [President Ronald] Reagan defunded all of these kinds of aid efforts to put more [money] into security and military response. So we lost all of our funding. But it happened that A&T had a position in cooperative extension. The dean of international programs helped me get connected with that.

I started with a thing called the Farm Opportunity Program. This started as a way to get small farmers just do a better job as a business, as a modern farm. And we had people out there called technicians that were farmers helping other farmers. So I spent the first two years just traveling around listening to farmers, way up in the mountains, where we had a Tennessee Valley Authority–type program called the MAP—Mountain Agriculture Project. This was the first time I bumped into things like high tunnel production. I found a couple of mentors across the state. These were tobacco guys, and they were really *thinking*. So with that base, I had that awareness, and the parallel to the African cases—the same issues of production quality, connecting with customers, thinking about markets, producing for markets, and on and on. We had people Down East, but that was a lot harder because of the social constraints

BW: What were they?

JO: Well, in Columbus County—as you're going towards Wilmington . . .

BW: Wasn't there a big [Ku Klux] Klan presence there?

JO: Yeah, there was. I didn't realize there was still so much segregation. I asked one agent to take me to a farm. And he said, "Well, I never been out there!" And we got out there to the farm, and he's pushing me in front to ring the bell. Lo and behold it's a black family, very thought-ful and interested. Now usually these agents would take the lead and say, "Ah, these are my farms! This is the county, and you guys are from the state!" But here he was pushing *me* to the front!

I was working as a farm management and marketing specialist at an A&T cooperative extension program. We were always seen as part of the government because we worked for "the state," and they [farmers] didn't want to tell us any numbers or let us see anything written down. And the experience of African American farmers was not good in terms of government support and government agencies. But over time, coming from A&T, I do have some access, if I'm willing to start the conversation on *other* things and then listen carefully to what their interests are.

Now I was always just looking for the enterprises that were of inter-est to producers and consumers. And as we saw people trying to do a better job on cost management in tobacco, I saw that there was a *cul-ture* around it. And you could have different communities—blacks and whites talking, saying the same thing, listening to each other and in agreement about "this guy put too much soda on his field, this one got too much rain." Everyone can talk together about tobacco. Everybody understands what's going on with tobacco. The social network of deci-sion making, it's all there! What they call in business school a "com-munity of practice."

But you can see that the days of this are numbered. The USDA is get-ting pressured—"What are you doing funding tobacco!" Things needed to change, and people knew that. And that's when I started looking around at farmers' markets and direct marketing. We got some money from Kellogg[28] in the early 1990s.

At A&T in those years I had no production specialist working with me. I was totally there as a farm management marketing person. I was working with people at NC State on this, but not at A&T. Then came Chuck Talbott who was hired to be a professor in animal science. So Chuck came to A&T in the late 1980s, with this fascination in specialty hog production, such as one could find in Spain and Italy. He wrote [an application for] a grant from SARE early on—he had his doctorate from State—and he's interested in this stuff, and he's getting connected with Niman and Paul Willis. And he got his interest in SARE, and he kept moving the goalposts, and he kept seeing new possibilities.

So it was a challenge for him. Now, you want to get black and white producers together, all you gotta do is *talk* about small-scale pig production, call a meeting, and it's amazing what will happen. People in North Carolina have roots growing up on their farms. So in that process Chuck got connected with Ed Mitchell[29] in Wilson County. The connections were making themselves. And there was this interest from people like Niman and Willis up in Iowa, and what they were doing as businesses was available to North Carolina through Niman and Iowa State. So Chuck puts together his team of Eliza and Mike. And others get connected through them. Whole Foods is interested. So it was obvious. This was in a bunch of counties Down East. They were trying to put together a Niman network. They got commitments. That's how infrastructure like hoop structures and high tunnels got down to Duplin County.

As it turned out, of course, Niman was a house of cards, in the sense that anybody at that size is. If they got it right at that size, man, they were a smaller fish, and they were going to get gobbled up, and that's what happened!

We had consultants hired to work in extension in the east. After Chuck's project ended, we hired Mike Jones over into extension as an area swine production agent. Eliza had by this time left to go out on her own. Mike started the process in Duplin, and then the work was carried further by Michelle Eley [a community development specialist] and Niki Whitley [a livestock specialist]—both A&T cooperative extension program specialists. And they helped us set up the producer schools, because they had expertise in production and knowledge of animals. We set one up down in Duplin County. And the Co-op comes along out of the growers' schools.

Niman was a part of this story. In the mid-1990s, Niman was looking for an eastern supply chain, so they didn't have to bring pork all the way from Iowa. But Niman falls apart. One of the problems for Niman was the processor link. We didn't have the slaughter facilities that understood what Niman was looking for, that could be a good fit. It took a while for Acre Station and Bailey's[30] to come on board. They couldn't get a bigger processor to work with them. There was this floundering period, and then the wheels came off the Niman model.

BW: Is this when you started working with CEFS?

JO: CEFS began in 1994, just after Niman started up out here. And I was part of the team there that was planning the creation of a sustainable agriculture systems model, which is what CEFS emerged as out of all that discussion. Parts of CEFS were the grass-fed dairy [cattle] and the beef [cattle] unit. Along with the Systems Research Unit. We created a systems research model to look for the best management policies. We had an organic unit, the small farm—in those days it was called the student farm, and it was designed to connect to universities. And I connected myself with it because I saw that the small farm unit *should* be able to provide extension and offer information about alternative production practice on a small farm. I didn't know what the mix ought to be, but I knew that was what producers were interested in. But it wasn't until 2004 that I was able to change over to the small farm unit, which had begun as the student farm.

CEFS was there from 1994. We did have a swine unit. CEFS was located on a facility known as the Cherry Farm, run by the NCDA [North Carolina Department of Agriculture]. Just a production farm around the hospital there in Goldsboro. There was an old confinement swine operation there that was very outdated and had developed serious waste-management issues left over from archaic production systems. It had leaking lagoons, with documented pollution coming down to the Neuse River through underground water movement. What the [state] Department of Agriculture said, and the university said, is we need an alternative to this—let's do a swine unit. We had the hurricanes in 1996 and 1998.[31] We were a mess! We couldn't feed animals, etc. It put us back, we were really slammed. The legislature had money allocated for us, but they pulled it back. We've never recovered from the floods, really—CEFS and this new direction in extension.

NC Choices came along in 2004. It was funded from a Kellogg grant. At this point Nancy Creamer[32] got [the] Sierra Club and Environmental Defense [Fund] to put their money where their mouth was and be willing to let NC Choices connect with a customer base for producers with sustainably produced pork on the ground and to defuse the tension between environmentalists and swine producers. A very important part of what goes on in North Carolina is the willingness of parties to let a middle exist, that doesn't blame one side or the other for whatever, but can work together. And these are the systemic questions that we need to be working on: how can we manage the environment *and* recognize the producers, even in confinement, who have stakes in the system?

What I love about NC Choices is they make connections between producers and consumers together [they have educational programs]. Let's get a chef in there to say, "What is this? I can't use this if it looks like this." That's the only way to make markets work!

BW: And that's what you were trying to do with the producer schools.

JO: Exactly!

BW: And how did that go?

JO: Oh, terrible! [Both laugh.] It's just a challenge. To try to get people to think of their farms as a business is just a challenge!

2

PIGS IN A LOCAL PLACE

Central North Carolina might seem an odd region in which to examine the complex relationships between taste and place invoked by the culinary concept of "terroir." While the region might have its time-established foodways; a variety of much-debated recipes; and distinctive agricultural products and practices, each with its loyalists, we have seen above that the demographic and political economic transformation of the state has been striking. These transformations, as I indicated, are especially apparent in the pork industry—no small irony, given the centrality of pigs to the Carolinian cultural and agricultural imaginary. To recap: North Carolina has seen an astronomical increase in industrial pork production, from 2.6 million hogs grown in 1988 to over 8 million in 1997, and to well over 18 million pigs in 2013. As recently as 1993 North Carolina was the fifth leading state for pork production in the United States; it now competes with Iowa for the status of leading pork-producing state (see Duke University Center on Globalization, Governance and Competitiveness n.d.; Iowa State University 2004). The devastating effects of industrialization on watersheds, soil nutrients, energy costs, labor, and the pigs themselves have been thoroughly documented (see Kaminsky 2005; Morgan 1998; Niman 2009). This radical transformation has generated a landscape of displacement, as small farms are increasingly consolidated under the contractual obligations of vertical integration, and long-standing methods of raising livestock give way to confined animal feeding operations (Page 1997).

Such industrialization characteristically undermines the kinds of depth and connoisseurship required for an appreciation of terroir, the "taste of place (Trubek 2008) valued among advocates of slow and local foods. This commitment to taste as a qualitative feature of place would seem to face a significant challenge in a landscape as disrupted as central North Carolina's. Yet this commitment and the connection between taste and place are quite relevant to understanding the widespread interest in what is expressly described as "local food" across the Piedmont. To recognize and appreciate the commitment to something like terroir, we need to critically examine this changing social, ecological, and gastronomic landscape and look at the ways that the connection between taste and place is being forged in the practices of a host of actors across the region.

In no small part owing to the growing awareness of the perils of the industrial food complex (Kenner 2009; Kingsolver 2008; Pollan 2006; Schlosser 2001), as well as a dynamic group of environmental activists (see, for example, Jennifer Curtis's profile below), this region has seen a significant growth in interest in alternatives to this production system. As I outlined in chapter 1, the growth of pig farms whose owners subscribe to sustainable practices has been a central outcome of these many efforts.[1] Moreover, the market for pork from these farms is central to the rapidly increasing interest in local foods in the Piedmont. As one animal scientist at North Carolina State University (NC State) noted, "over the past five years, meat sales have been surging. Consumers want to buy pork from farmers" (Morrow 2005). There are, as I suggested, a host of labels that are applied to the products of these alternative pig farms. "Niche-market," "natural," "pasture-raised," and "outdoor" are all terms used, with varying degrees of precision (or strategic ambiguity), to describe the pigs in this alternative food sector. However, given the preeminence of direct marketing as a strategy for farmers to sell their pork to consumers, such pork is most often marketed by producers—and sought out by consumers—as a specifically local food. The Carrboro and Durham farmers' markets, two of the main sources for directly marketed niche-market pork in the Triangle, both have locality inscribed in their bylaws. All products offered there must be sold by their producer (and not, for example, by a third party hired by the farmer to market his or her goods), and all must be produced within a fifty-mile or seventy-mile radius, respectively, of the market. Indeed, when I told one farmer that Smithfield, the largest pork processor in the United States, with production facilities in North Carolina, was bringing out a line of pastured pork, her response was: "That won't affect us; 'local' will always trump any other label." So, in the heart of a state thoroughly transformed by the dislocations wrought by industrial pork production, pasture-raised pork has become a central feature of the local food scene. Furthermore, farmers who produce and sell this pork deploy a sense of locality as one of the distinctive qualities of the meat.

The political economic motivations of the pastured-pork market are unmistakable. Piedmont farmers and foodies alike are critically aware of the devastation, in particular the environmental degradations, wrought by the industrialization of pigs. In contrast, many historical issues of hog farming in the region relating to labor, class, and race are less fully incorporated into the politics of local food. According to my research, especially among consumers at farmers' markets, the largely cosmopolitan producers and consumers of this niche-market pork describe themselves as committed to supporting local farming systems and opposing the perils, especially ecological, of the corporate, industrial food system. However, they rarely refer to the problems of racial disparities that are rife in North Carolina's agricultural production or express concern for the condition of workers on local farms as often as they ask, for example, about animal welfare. To be sure, these cosmopolitans in the Piedmont are progressive in their politics and often work assiduously to make local food more affordable and provide outreach to underresourced consumers in the region, including a growing Latino community. This is true of a number of institutions and programs such as the Rural Advancement Foundation's Agricultural Justice Project, which seeks to certify farms and label foods that are produced according to standards that support "farmworkers, living wages, safe working conditions and collective bargaining rights" (Rural Advancement Foundation n.d.), and Operation Spring Plant, which works with African American and limited-resource farmers-in-training, as well as offering legal services for farmers seeking to redress the long-standing devastating loss of black-owned farms promoted through discriminatory lending policies of the U.S. Department of Agriculture (USDA) (see Operation Spring Plant n.d.; Land Loss Prevention Project n.d.). Nonetheless, many participants in this largely white, middle-class movement do overlook problems of inclusiveness, a point to which I return throughout this book.

My approach here is informed by the concerns of "locavores" for sustainability and environmental justice, and I understand these concerns as part of a broader process through which social actors grapple with the places they construct and inhabit. I consider one specific feature of the relationship between pigs, an agricultural icon of the Piedmont, and the movement to promote local foods—namely, the connection between taste and place as cultivated and embodied in the production, circulation, and consumption of pasture-raised pork. These connections are constituted as a network of perspectives and incorporate a series of requalifications in a process spelled out in the introduction to this book. My ethnographic evidence, drawn from my work with farmers, chefs, restaurant workers, and consumers at farmers' markets, demonstrates how these diverse sites are fields in which place is constructed in action and experience and imbued with concrete meanings and orientations. Pasture-raised pigs provide an excellent entity to use in outlining loose networks among diverse actors—human and otherwise—whose activities constitute the places held to underlie "local food" processes, including tastes. Their porcine paths take us from the intimate gustatory pleasures of pork fat to efforts to combat the dire social inequities of environmental, human, and animal degradation at the hands of industrialization.

Places in Perspective

Eliza MacLean, whose profile appears above, has been raising pastured pigs at Cane Creek Farm since 2003. At her farm I worked in all aspects of pig production and reproduction, from the daily care and feeding of over 250 pigs (among many other species) to tracking the development of a registered line of a specific heritage breed—the Ossabaw Island Hog—being revitalized on the farm.[2] My experience at Cane Creek also involved marketing. Cane Creek pork is sold directly to restaurants, to a few local grocery stores, and at three farmers' markets in the Piedmont. We can begin at Cane Creek to examine some of the ways that place is created through the paths forged by pigs in the Piedmont, and, in turn, how places made by these relations shapes the pigs (and their pork) in qualities ranging from their parental skills to their genetic viability, environmental impact, and succulence.

North Carolina is also renowned for its exquisite pork barbecue. Eastern and Piedmont barbecue, which overlap in the Triangle, have their recognized styles of preparation and legions of aficionados. But even this cursory evidence suggests that, in North Carolina, the production and consumption of pigs is indicative of a concern with the specificities of places and tastes and their implicit interconnections.

Rather than assume these interconnections as a given feature of locality and foodways, I problematize such links between place and taste (as well as the very category "local food") by asking how places are constituted and how taste becomes one of place's constituent qualities. Local food is widely celebrated in the Piedmont, and pastured pork may be a critical index of locality, but these assertions beg the questions of how place is established and what are the concrete, experiential qualities through which it is grasped in social practice. More than attempting to specify the qualities of "the local" and their relationship with distinctive foodways or agricultural niches, I am concerned with what Henri Lefebvre calls "the production of space"[3] (Lefebvre 1991). What is valuable about Lefebvre's model is the way it combines attention to the political economic restructuring of everyday life under neocapitalism (39) with considerations of the felt qualities of lived, bodily experience. I focus on these correlated concerns and propose to follow the pig through its many places to show how pork production and consumption might reveal how a place's tastes are cultivated within what I am calling a shared, if also contested, sensory field. A taste for quality pork, at once an ancient tradition and an entirely new cuisine in the Piedmont, is being carefully crafted through a range of venues in a process attuned to the materiality of ecosystems, landscapes, animals, and meat; built through social relationships among farmers, artisans, and activists; cultivated in the educational mission of menus and market tastings; and thus suffused in place. Exploring this sensory field within the production of space allows us to grasp how characteristic dimensions of place—above all taste—invoked by local-food advocates in the Piedmont have been remade by remaking pigs and pork.

The relationship between place and food, especially qualities of taste, has generated a great deal of interest in recent decades. Part of this interest derives from the work of environmental activists dedicated to sustainability—a highly contested term (Kloppenburg et al. 2000)—who understand food as an expression of the cultural, agricultural, and ecological resources on which it draws (Berry 1990, 145–53; Dover and Talbot 1987). "Eating is an agricultural act," as Berry famously puts it—or it would be, were it not for the fact that industrialization has devastated the connections between farmers and eaters, stultifying the tastes of consumers: "The industrial eater is one who no longer knows that eating is an agricultural act, who no longer knows or imagines the connections between eating and the land, and who is therefore necessarily passive and uncritical—in short, a victim" (Berry 1990, 153). It is certainly the case that many local-food activists in the Piedmont are motivated by these ecological, anti-industrial arguments. Such critiques form a cornerstone of efforts of farmers, chefs, and others to regenerate robust connections between farms and eaters. Desirable as these objectives are, Berry's essentialized "connections between eating and the land" are problematic terms with which to approach linkages between taste and place in any kind of comparative (that is, anthropological) framework. "Industrial eaters" inhabit a world that is not empty and abstract but, in fact, full of places.[4] Such ecological perspectives presume that places have specific, intrinsic qualities (subtended by natural and cultural activities) that are expressed by eating and so realized as taste: "Eating ends the annual drama of the food economy that begins with planting and birth" (Berry 1990, 145). But this is more a normative assertion than a claim with much anthropological relevance. People eat and taste the world over. Understanding how the taste of food reveals what place is requires a broader perspective.

Recent anthropological and sociological work on the relationship between taste and place engages the cultural category terroir from a variety of perspectives (Barham 2003; Trubek 2008; Trubek and Bowen 2008). Amy Trubek points out that terroir is less a quality in the material substrate of the land itself than it is, as she says, "a category for knowing and discerning" (2008, 2). She also notes that the formal French definition of "terroir" as "the earth considered from the point of view of agriculture" (xv). This definition suggests that terroir is always perspectival; it is a dimension of the material insofar as it is registered in human practice. It is, therefore, an aspect of the way in which place is inhabited, and not simply an inert property of the location itself. Indeed, even in France terroir is most routinely referred as *le gout du terroir* (the taste of place), or place considered from the point of view of a very specific mode of perception.

In her excellent recent review of the concept, Heather Paxson (2010) details the controversies and challenges that surround the use of the term "terroir" in comparative regional contexts. Since it is a term that derives from a specific French historical context that putatively has long-standing traditions of appreciating the regional character of distinctive agricultural products, can we apply the word cross-culturally? For some people, terroir is principally a regulatory mechanism intended to support communities of practice in highly competitive global markets through a process of denomination or domain-specific standards (such as Appellation d'Origine Contrôlée in France or Denominazione di Origine Controllata in Italy). For others, terroir is not simply the taste of the territory or the soils in which the product is grown; it is the outcome of long-standing practices and techniques used to make the product. The fact that le gout du terroir is generally understood to have emerged as a category with respect to the appreciation of wine, an agricultural product that is plainly an amalgam of nature and culture, indicates that this appreciation of the interconnection of place and taste entails a complex understanding of place as itself a mode of inhabiting the world.

Moreover, Paxson describes the ways that North American experiments with terroir in the world of artisanal cheese represent a critical response to the deterritorializing effects of industrial farming, just as ecological concerns motivate much food activism. But Paxson's perspective situates these environmental concerns within a wider project: "*terroir* provides American producers with an opportunity for *reterritorialization*, for drawing meaningful lines of connection among people, culture, and place to invest place anew with affective significance and material relevance" (2010, 446). She argues that connections between place (conceived of in ecological, material, agricultural, and cultural registers) and taste invoked by the term "terroir" are under construction ("reverse-engineered," as Paxson puts it, with the French model as a goal) as the food system is reterritorialized. Taste's grounding in place, then, emerges within the construction of place.

This process of remaking place is the wider framework within which to situate the current interests and actions of the locavore movement. Places are suffused with experiential qualities (like taste) and provide a grounding for sociopolitical projects (Casey 1998). This is not a normative framework that assumes that only richly integrated social and natural regions constitute expressive places. Rather, I see place as a constitutive feature of human habitation (Casey 1998; Merleau-Ponty 1962). Defining the contours of the production of space and modes of dwelling allows us to specify how a politics of food is spatialized. Why, for example, does opposition to industrialization or commodity agriculture invoke place as a remedy to these forms of production? Why is "local food," among all legitimate rubrics for collective action, such an effective category? How are problems of industrialization, animal welfare, environmental degradation, and the exploitation of labor spatial matters to which "locality" offers an alternative? Specifying how places are constituted, and the qualities with which they are imbued, helps us grasp the force of the politics of space entailed in appeals to locality.

Lefebvre's work on the spatial character of everyday life is complex and open to a wide range of interpretive uses. He describes space as a social

Fig. 2.1 The anthropologist in the field.

product, not merely a conceptual schema to be read or decoded, or a physical container for social action. What he calls "three moments of social space" (1991, 33) provide my heuristic point of departure. These moments are: (1) spatial practice, activities through which subjects interact in and with spatial relations, assuring their production and reproduction (the know-how of a farmer carrying out his or her chores on a working landscape might be an example of spatial practice); (2) representations of space, ways of conceiving space and codifying it in objectified models, plans, or schema (an architect's blueprints are a case in point); and (3) representational spaces, "embodying complex symbolism, sometimes coded, sometimes not, linked to the underground side of social life" (33), such as a food activist's efforts to imagine an alternative system of consumption or distribution. This conceptual triad, which Lefebvre condenses as space as "perceived-conceived-lived" (40) is foundational to his discussion of the structure of everyday life. In this chapter I explore space as "perceived-conceived-lived" to characterize the conditions that permit tastes to evoke places for Piedmont advocates of local food.

Making Place

To suggest the complex character of place as a "perceived-conceived-lived" phenomenon and demonstrate some of the ways that pigs and pork figure in this complexity, let me illustrate how local pork finds its way onto menus in the Piedmont. My wife and I once enjoyed a very fine meal in one of the newer establishments that has arisen on the locavore food scene in the Piedmont. On each dining table was a small placard listing the produce that had been procured at market that week, and the farms from which each crop had been harvested. The menu, service, culinary techniques, and accompanying details all emphasized locality and seasonality and provided a sense of grounding in the moment in the broadest sense. At the end of the meal, we asked our hostess why the chef or owner had chosen to prominently feature a large portrait of Mark Twain on the otherwise spare walls of the interior. "He wants to remind diners of the southern roots" of the restaurant, she readily told me. This might seem a remarkable response, given the fact that the menu featured robust and flavorful Italian dishes (to say nothing of the clearly Italian name of the place), a cuisine it further celebrated in regular, seasonal "community table" dinners that featured *carta musica*, spicy Sicilian rusks, *farinata*, *torta di zucca e riso*, *foccacine al griglia* (grilled focaccia), and *mataroccu* (crushed tomato and almond pesto), with gelato and zabaglione for dessert, accompanied by grappa. In what sense might Mark Twain, a chronicler of the Mississippi by way of Connecticut, evoke the southerness of this place in central North Carolina? Indeed, what is the place in which this restaurant—Italian in its cuisine and southern in its roots—is grounded? What kind of terroir was our dining experience meant to express?

In 2009, I worked in the prep kitchen of Lantern, whose menu and signage highlight its affiliation with all things local, including its prominent place in the founding of the regional chapter of the Slow Food movement. It features a pan-Asian cuisine, with ingredients acquired as much as possible (which is to say, about 80 percent) from North Carolina sources. When Lantern participated in the James Beard Foundation fund-raisers in Manhattan, it offered a picnic plate featuring deviled eggs, strawberry snow cones with candied fruit and marshmallow fluff, and barbecue sandwiches. While not indicative of the fare served up on a daily basis at Lantern, the chefs told me that these foods were meant to highlight the regional offerings of the Piedmont—what could be more North Carolina than barbecue and early season strawberries?—and to emphasize, yet again, the importance of local food in their operating ethos.

These two modest examples pose a question: What do we mean by place when we talk about its taste? Any unified notion of place as a territory, geographical zone, or material ecology is incompatible with these examples of how local foods operate in practice. Restaurants emphasize attachments to a specific local network, a community of laboring farmers, artisanal meat processors, sustainable fisheries, and an array of things edible. But each expresses these attachments in diverse cuisines, presentations, and applications (that is, dishes) that articulate place and locality in ways that vary with the performance, the context, and the diners. In each iteration, the distinctiveness of place shifts with respect to the social relations of interlocution: Italian and pan-Asian cuisine can also be the Piedmont's local foods; strawberries bespeak North Carolina in May when served in Manhattan; savory *porchetta* over polenta might evoke grits and smothered pork chops.

I do not mean to disparage or even make light of these efforts; they plainly work. Nor would I dismiss the notion that taste is a constitutive feature of place. Rather, these examples suggest the complexities of articulating locality and characterizing its qualities with respect to taste, food, and culinary practice. Local food operates as a representation of space (in Lefebvre's terms) in these performances—that is, it provides a conceptual model meant to promote or direct the production of social space. It orients diners, consumers, and producers to the spatial character of their practice as local (as opposed to cosmopolitan, international, or traditional, among other spatiotemporal possibilities). These complexities suggest we need to be careful in specifying what a taste of the land or territory might amount to, given how highly contingent these places are, as well how a taste of such a place might be framed (for example, as a material feature of regional ecologies, a respect for culinary traditions, or trust in a community of purveyors to provide good meats and produce). How do such relationships constitute place, and what is it about places that becomes characteristic of the foods procured and purveyed in them?

Heritage Pigs: A Sensory Perspective

The Carrboro Farmers' Market, as I noted above, requires that all its vendors produce everything they sell. This stipulation contributes to the social dimensions of place, helping sustain a sense of what is often described

Fig. 2.2 Farmer's Hybrids

as a "connection"[5] between farmers and consumers—and food—very much along the lines promoted by Berry. The social activity of the market, including conversations that range from the health benefits of products to agricultural techniques and recipes, is itself discussed by vendors. And these discussions include criticisms of the very ethos of creating connections between farmers and customers. As one food activist put it to me, for some people the Carrboro Farmers' Market is a place where customers "put two little tomatoes in a basket next to an egg, and then socialize a lot"—a well-established critique of the elitism that embeds the sociality of such connections in the food itself. Nonetheless, such venues, as well as recurring events in the region such as the Annual Piedmont Farm Tour and the Farm to Fork Picnic,[6] help articulate a sense of place through food among those committed to local food. These venues work to develop what I am calling a sensory field, in which perceptual qualities like health, well-being, social responsibility, and connoisseurship are elaborated. What other qualities of the place constituted by these sociomaterial, or natural or cultural, connections might be situated in this place-based sensory field?

Pigs make important contributions to this sensory field. When I asked MacLean what makes the Ossabaw a distinctive breed, she said the standards to which breeds are held might be defined in terms not just of size, appearance, and behavior, but also of taste. Pigs, she notes, are monogastrics ("like us," she says), not ruminants (like cattle, or sheep), and therefore "they are what they eat." The taste of the animal will therefore directly reflect the seasonality and locality of what it consumes. "If you feed pigs pumpkins in the fall, they'll taste like pumpkin," MacLean says. Such claims about taste, while by no means typical of pastured-pig farmers in the Piedmont,[7] are supported by a range of regional institutions. Many restaurants support local pork for the tastes it offers. Interest groups and academic agencies, like the Livestock Breed Conservancy in Pittsboro, and the Center for Environmental Farming Systems in Goldsboro, promote outdoor-raised pigs and specialty breeds for the qualities, like taste, that these practices support. Furthermore, there is a growing literature in meat science that presents intriguing findings about local pork and taste (discussed further in chapter 6). Comparing the taste of Ossabaws raised on a diet of hardwood forest mast (for example, acorns, hickory nuts, and the seeds and fruits produced by woody plants) with the taste of those raised on corn and soy, Charles Talbott and coauthors report that forest-finished Ossabaws were judged (by a "three-member, highly trained sensor panel" (2006, 186) to have a "deeper, more complex flavor" (188). At the same time, the judges of this "deeper" taste report to a high degree that such pigs have what is called (by pork industry standards) an "off-flavor," a category labeled "dark turkey meat" in meat science (189). To reconcile this apparent discrepancy (pork that tastes so good that it tastes bad, or "off"—the technical term for which in the food taste business is "funky"), Talbott and coauthors determine that "for niche-market applications, a new 'On Flavor' classification may be required to distinguish differences in conventional sensory models" (189–90). This conclusion is a fascinating commentary on the cultivation of animals and tastes together, as innovative sensory features of a local landscape. At issue here is understanding not just how taste reflects an ecological niche or how transformations in animal husbandry generate distinctive taste profiles. Rather, we see how the dynamic interrelationship of animals (distinctive breeds), husbandry (diets, pasturing, acreage, and processing), and testing protocols and qualities (including juiciness, tenderness, chewiness, and "pork flavor" [190]) is transforming the understanding of what taste is given by these local innovations. The taste of monogastric pigs may express the conditions (material, social, and otherwise) of their production in a local place, but we need to revise our understanding of what the taste of pork is to appreciate that "on flavor" pork taste. This process of remaking taste, discussed below, is central to the ongoing requalifications that constitute the complex meanings of pasture-raised pork in the Piedmont. An appreciation of this innovative taste—a capacity for discernment, both objectified and subjectified—is, therefore, a dimension of a reconfigured sensory field entailed in the reproduction of pigs in a local landscape.

If these findings in the husbandry and meat science of pigs are components of the elaboration of locality as a sensory field, so too are culinary practices particular to pork. The taste-testing protocols by which pigs are evaluated use chilled loin chops as a sample (Talbott et al. 2006, 187). This is the standard cut adopted by the niche-pork industry, first established by Niman Ranch: "the company takes a loin chop from every shipment from every farm and grills the chop to be sure it meets Niman standards" (Behr 1999, 14). MacLean, too, wants the Ossabaw to be recognized as a breed that will incorporate standards that include a "long, lean, loin" that is still "well marbled" with fat, as this is what her restaurant chef clients most desire.

Although the loin chop is highly profitable and marketable, Ossabaw pigs are known (in part) for a genealogy that links them to Ibérico pigs from Spain, pigs that are renowned for their superior hams (that is, pork legs). Currently, much of the ham produced by MacLean's pigs ends up ground into sausage, due to the costs in time and labor of processing hams and the versatility that grinding pork into a range of sausages affords. But occasionally Ossabaws—especially Ossabaws bred with other varieties of pig—are used to produce hams. In the spring of 2009, I attended a ham tasting held at a wine retailer's establishment, at which wines were paired with hams made from Cane Creek Ossabaw crossbred pigs (called Ossabaw Cross) that had been wet cured and smoked by a local chef. I want to examine this marketing event in some detail, as it demonstrates some ways that pigs (and the people who love them) help constitute local place as a sensory field.

A Curiosity for Cured Meat

This event charged customers a modest fee to sample food and wine. Not surprisingly, the thirty or so attendees were largely affluent, but included among these were a few people at lower echelons of the restaurant business (that is, not chefs), many of whom were friends of the wine and meat purveyors. Food production processes were framed in the remarks of the wine merchant and ham producer in a manner indicative of wider patterns of place-making activities characteristic of the "local food" community in the region.

The wine retailer introduced the event by noting that links between taste and place are relevant to the store itself. The walls of the shop are lined with large photos of vintners from Europe who "are working on a small scale to support sustainable agriculture. This is exactly what we want to do . . . with the wines that we carry, buy things from small farmers from around the world who are concerned about protecting their own wine traditions, in their own homelands." Here, the category of locality is invoked as an ideological commitment (supporting "sustainable agriculture," "small farmers" "protecting . . . wine traditions") as well as a transposable framework, in which the local is a quality that can be found in practices around the world, extracted from other "homelands," and deployed in any spatial context. In this way, the local becomes a discernible property of practices that can be enacted anywhere. "Local" European wines are available in the Piedmont.

Next, the chef who prepared the hams introduced the tasting and MacLean to the crowd. "Thanks so much for coming out," the chef began. "It's great to have the support and curiosity in cured meats that are done locally." She told the audience that the ham was made from an Ossabaw Cross, adding that MacLean "has been at the Carrboro Farmers' Market for—five years now? . . . She's actually moved her farm from Saxapahaw out to—is it Snow Camp? So, Eliza, thanks for raising the hog, and what *is* an Ossabaw Cross?"

Before I get to MacLean's response, I want to note that this off-the-cuff introduction incorporates the themes developed here: it links a series of places across the Piedmont (the market, the farm, Saxapahaw and Snow Camp) with the animals raised on the farm, and—crucially—includes the audience within this sensory field: "It's great to have the support and curiosity in cured meats that are done locally." Taste—referring here to a community interested in a specific taste, which is presumed to have a regional relevance—is expressed as a feature of locality.

Here is the response MacLean gave to the question "what *is* an Ossabaw Cross?":

MACLEAN: Our farm is now on huge acreage where we raise a lot of different animals, but the pigs are still sort of carrying the name and getting further and further known. A purebred Ossabaw Island Hog has become of interest to a lot of people across the country—it's a smaller, long-legged, prick-eared, furry, funny little black hog with white joints. But it's not very big. It's not a very easy animal to raise or market. It's a little wild, a little wily. They're very smart, very interesting, but kind of small, and they have a particular kind of fat that's actually really hard to make bacon and sausage and things like that with. So what I did was crossed it, developed a boar line and a sow line, and I actually have a breeding herd of a fifty-fifty cross between that, the Ossabaw Island Hog, and a five-way old-timey cross called the Farmer's Hybrid. And that ended up being a great part of our marketing strategy. I can do all the things that I want to do with fresh ground product and hams and loins and things for the restaurants in this area, and I have a fast-growing, larger-type, very colorful hog with all the fun attributes of the Ossabaw, like [the] sort of better-for-you fat profile and incredible flavor that you're tasting.

QUESTION FROM THE AUDIENCE: Has anyone else done this cross?

MACLEAN: Not that I know of, but people buy them from—or buy the purebred Ossabaw and try crossing them on other things like the Duroc or Berkshire—I don't think that would work very well, but a leaner type hog.

QUESTION FROM THE AUDIENCE: So you're the first one to do this cross?

MACLEAN: The first one to think of it as its own breed and really raise it year after year and keep a breeding herd, and play with it a little bit—so.

COMMENT FROM THE AUDIENCE: I think it makes a darn good ham. [Laughter.]

Telling Skills

There is much to say about this impromptu account of local pig production at Cane Creek. This is the kind of story that MacLean, her staff members, and I tell in numerous settings. The Ossabaw Island Hog, from which the Ossabaw cross derives, has its own complicated narrative history. The Ossabaws raised on MacLean's farm are said to be descendants of a group of Ibérico pigs that were brought to the New World in 1539 with Hernando de Soto's conquistadors. Abandoned, or perhaps shipwrecked, on the Atlantic coast, a feral colony of these Ibéricos survived in isolation on the island of Ossabaw, off the coast of Savannah, Georgia. The island remained largely undeveloped through the end of the twentieth century, and Ossabaws developed the characteristic qualities of an insular breed: they are small in stature yet possess a remarkable ability to store fat. This remarkable ability also produces a tendency to develop type 2 diabetes, which made the Ossabaws of interest to medical researchers. Moreover, the Georgia Department of Natural Resources wanted to exterminate these "wild" and "wily" pigs because they were destroying the nests of threatened loggerhead turtles. Thus, a group of twenty-three pigs were imported to the mainland for a National Institutes of Health research study in Columbia, Missouri. From there, Ossabaws made their way to the program in swine husbandry at North Carolina Agricultural and Technical State University (A&T) and so to MacLean's farm (Kaminsky 2005).

But note that what MacLean concentrates on in her comments to the people who have come to taste hams is what I would call her "farming skill," incorporating a number of distinct, but related activities. The notion of "skill" (Ingold 2000) is important, as skills are embodied dimensions of a sensory field: "The breeder's skilled vision is never detached from a certain amount of multisensoriality" (Grasseni 2004, 41). Such skills are ways of grasping and integrating knowledge, technical ability, and bodily activity into a locale.[8] Such a "field" is not merely a technique deployed in a given time and place, but a mode of activity through which time and place are reproduced. Beyond animal husbandry, MacLean's skills cover a range of sensory modes of knowing. For example, she offers an understanding of the personality of these pigs—they are wild, wily, smart, and funny—features of Ossabaws' temperament often discussed on the farm. Sometimes these qualities are seen to be an expression of their history described above: a wild, wily, smart, little pig that got that way in adapting to the limited resources of its island habitat. When I first started working at Cane Creek, I was told that you could see the evolutionary adaptations of the Ossabaws in their behavior. The sows build nests together when they farrow (that is, give birth to litters), and they tend to eat in a more sociable fashion than many pigs do. That is, they line up in front of their feed and make room for smaller pigs to get access to the food as well. All of these activities were seen as evidence of an adaptive legacy to enduring for centuries in an insular, resource-poor environment.

Fig. 2.3 Photo by Ezra Weiss.

Fig. 2.4 Photo by Ezra Weiss.

Fig. 2.5 Photo by Ezra Weiss.

Fig. 2.6 Photo by Ezra Weiss.

At other times, these qualities are thrown into relief with references to the challenges of breeding Ossabaws. An essay by another pig breeder on "The Unfortunate Demise of the Ossabaw" describes the pigs this way: "Ossabaws are a feral breed of hogs. They are small, difficult to manage and, for feral pigs, very lardy. All those traits work against any commercial exploitation: 'small' means slaughter will cost too much per pound of pork, 'difficult to manage' implies expensive and irritating and 'very lardy' means you've got unusually lardy carcasses" (Putnam 2009). My point here is not only that "wild" and "wily" with "a particular kind of fat" might also mean "difficult to manage" and "lardy" (a characterization MacLean forcefully rejected), but that the characteristics of the Ossabaw (whatever their origin, and however positively or negatively they are described) are never neutral, objective features of animal behavior or breed standards. Rather, these are dimensions of the skills needed to husband the animals. Indeed, "wily" and "difficult" might be the same qualities, but their presence in Ossabaws is an expression of MacLean's sensory skills in raising her animals. Behavior, then, is a potent admixture of colonial narrative, natural selection, and farming technique located in place—or, perhaps, in a trajectory of places, from Spain to Ossabaw, Saxapahaw, Snow Camp, and ham tasting. Indeed, it is an attribute of the Ossabaw that is defined within the economy of qualities through which this pig moves.

This narrative account of the breed also configures place as a representational space, in which the Piedmont becomes a locality by virtue of its narrative connection to similarly "tellable" places. To tell this story as an account of how Ossabaws become a local pig, MacLean's skills are required to successfully make the region into a place habitable by Ossabaws (and those who would consume them), and so recognizable as a place with this critical local-food environment. Such narratives are a striking way in which pigs and pork provide a novel representational space—a way of imagining new spatial possibilities for inhabiting the Piedmont as a place—and a place of distinctive and discernible qualities, now often inhabited by residents who are relatively recent arrivals to North Carolina[9] with little connection to past modes of living here.

Critical to these mixtures, and at the core of MacLean's technique and story, is the breeding process she describes. Her description of the distinguishing physical characteristics of the Ossabaw ("long-legged, prick-eared, furry . . . black hog with white joints") refers to those features of hogs that are not simply descriptive terms but attributes that serve to establish these animals as a breed. Ear shape, height, color, each are distinctive standards, features necessary to the recognition of a breed. MacLean goes on to describe the ways that this breed, now registered and standardized (Livestock Conservancy n.d.), has been crossed with the Farmer's Hybrid to produce not just an Ossabaw Cross, but "a breeding herd of a fifty-fifty cross." The specific standards of the Ossabaw Island Hog breed are germane insofar as they become expressed not just in an animal, but in a breeding herd—that is, as the expression of a specific farming skill, a practice that links knowledge of animals, their histories, and their possibilities with a method for perpetuating (literally reproducing) their desired qualities over time.

While the Ossabaw Cross is not the only line of animals being raised at Cane Creek Farm, and many kinds of pigs (for example, Tamworths and Gloucestershire Old Spots) might be raised there, there is a significant effort made by the Cane Creek staff to monitor the reproductive lives of pigs. Sows are moved according to how recently they have given birth to ensure that they are fattened up sufficiently for lactation after they have farrowed yet do not get so obese that they are unable to reproduce again once their litters are weaned. Pigs are removed from their mothers when they are weaned, and these "teenagers," as they are called, are selected for breeding stock or sent off for fattening. As one staff member put it, "we'll decide to keep these and make 'em sows instead of sausage." These daily practices of adjusting feed, moving animals, sorting offspring, and so on do not make this kind of farming an exact science of breeding: as one staff member said, "we'll pretty much sell any kind of pig we raise." But it does make breeding an expression of a skill, a multisensory set of capacities that allows the process as a whole to be reproduced in a distinctive locale in space and time.

Note, moreover, that the pig provides an anchor to these diverse skills. The animal itself is at once a model and objectification (or representation) for how place should be organized and a representational form that embodies an imagined mode of inhabiting place. The Piedmont becomes a place with a distinctive (if fabricated) heritage of farming, breeding, and marketing. These material practices that are used as historical claims (to a Spanish colonial era in the case of the Ossabaw, but also to the early twentieth century when pigs were raised in parlors and fed on acorns and mast in woodlots around farming homesteads—the activities recalled by John Raymond Shute in chapter 1) are also part of the way in which this recognizable place is given temporal qualities. That is, pork production in pasture-raised operations permits the Piedmont to generate a sense of place that has historical (if also emerging) depth and tradition. These are precisely the qualities that characterize terroir, so the taste of place entails a grasp of the historicity of the Piedmont as well. In all of these ways, the pig permits places to be reinhabited through imagined connections to that which is culturally distinctive by means of an alternative past, one not unraveled by dispossession and industrialization.

Pork Education: Developing Discernment

All of these skills point toward the effective consumption, and more specifically eating,[10] of these pigs. Careful attention is paid to behavior and breeding because a commitment to animal welfare, breed revitalization, and sustainable land management (enterprises central to the daily activities of Cane Creek Farm) depend on the specific orientation of these skilled practices toward the most productive and profitable ways to eat pork. In production, this means the creation of the Ossabaw Cross—a hybrid of a hybrid, a revitalized breed crossbred with a well-established hybrid (the Farmer's Hybrid, the line promoted by Niman Ranch and its pastured-pig farmers)—an animal that has a number of qualities that are fully realized when it is eaten. Fast growing and large, they produce portions that satisfy the desires of consumers—especially chefs—and have a fat profile (higher in omega-3 fatty acids than omega-6s, and hence cholesterol inhibiting) that is good for you and good (or is it "funky"?) tasting. These features of an Ossabaw Cross demonstrate most clearly that concrete farming skills entail the dynamic constitution of a multisensory field and how, therefore, they are central to the process of making pigs local. The Ossabaw Cross is an amalgam of animal husbandry, marketing strategies, and social networking (perhaps also cardiology)—abstract processes that are grounded in sensory skills. These skills include the breeding practices discussed, an appreciation of how restaurants portion their meat, and, of course, a recognition of incredible flavor, all at once immediately sensible attributes of the Ossabaw Cross and qualities whose appreciation requires careful discernment. Moreover, they are qualities that give evidence of the continuous process of requalification, as breeders consider markets for consumers, and markets reposition husbandry practices as local—as well as humane, healthy, and a range of other qualities. But it is especially by means of the edibility of this pig, the Ossabaw Cross, that the various attributes of the narrative, the techniques, the strategies, and the scientific know-how that go into producing local pigs achieve their integration.

Thus, it can be said (with apologies to Berry) that agriculture (or animal husbandry) is a culinary act. Pigs are reconfigured to match the gustatory preferences of a consuming public.[11] It is only by virtue of the exquisite taste of the Ossabaw Cross (bred to satisfy the demands of chefs and consumers for flavor, health, and apportionment) that the storied past of the Ossabaw; the skilled breeding and pastured lifespan of these animals; and the pleasures of a rich, satisfying meal are placed in a unified sensory field. Taste, then, becomes one means of confirming the character—those attributes that make the Piedmont distinctive and recognizable—that is built into this region as a place.[12]

The reciprocal sensory dimension of the production process, then, is not simply the market or consumption, but a discerning public[13] understood to be (but also made to be) knowledgeable about and desirous of good pork. It is these practices of discernment with respect to porcine qualities that render the Ossabaw Island Hog, with its Iberian origins, a recognizably local food. Discernment is critical to the relationship between consumers and producers, and furthermore it grounds qualities of taste in a material landscape, a network of perspectives, and specific places. When purveyors identify a "curiosity in cured meats . . . done locally" as part of their successful marketing practices, they are positing a capacity—at once subjective and material—to appreciate qualities in pigs in particular places. Lauding the "off flavor" of Ossabaw pork as a desirable quality makes an appreciation of innovative tastes part of a reconfigured sensory field that reproduces pigs in a local landscape. In both cases discernment is objectified (materially embodied in the pig) and subjectified (expressed in the experience of consumers). As in the classic Bourdieuvian case, customers exercising such discernment also come to qualify themselves as legitimated subjects who are authorized to make discerning judgments (Silverstein 2006, 492). This discernment might be presumed (to a degree), but it can also be cultivated; indeed, the two go together, as a given curiosity is critical to appreciating the taste innovations that local foods—like the Ossabaw Cross—generate. In this sense, such discernment entails a set of dispositions that are neither inert rules for how to render judgments nor preferences that are mere expressions of a class position. Instead, they are orientations to ways of knowing that make it possible to generate new forms of knowledge, judgments that seek out new modes of evaluation.

In this way, this carefully selected animal, raised to meet the requirements of a discerning (if somewhat diverse[14]) public, is a kind of a switch point (Munn 1996) between material conditions (of production and consumption, incorporating skills of species rotation, growth rates, portion size, and fat content) and symbolically qualified characteristics (including a colonial narrative constituting heritage, a "wily" and "funny" hog, and a deliciously "funky" fatty pork). The Ossabaw Cross reminds us that these are not distinctive levels of appreciation. They are copresent dimensions of a concrete reality—a living, breathing, meant-to-be delicious pig—embodied and experienced in the world. This embodiment entails a coordination of skills deriving from diverse sensory practices (such as observing, feeding, crossing, selecting, and sorting) fully realized in sensory qualities of taste specific to that range of skills. The locality of such pigs, and thus the development of taste as a dimension of place that they exhibit, is an expression of the ways this highly innovative and wholly contemporary hog is bound to the distinctive place constituted by this sensory field: a way of seeing, feeding, breeding, and finally tasting an animal.

Equally clear is that among the skills that are the foundation of this sensory field are many forms of consumers' discernment. The materiality of the natural or cultural processes that establish the sensory field is rendered as social value through the taste of this pork, a taste that is recognizable as a value only when it has been cultivated through processes of skilled appreciation. The culinary discernment that marked the ham tasting event is repeated in venues across the region. Indeed, selling pork at the Piedmont's farmers' markets, where the clientele is (largely) committed to local food and typically exhibits a curiosity for pastured pork, is routinely an exercise in cultivating discernment among already discerning consumers. At a typical market, vendors offer advice on how to prepare pork; propose alternative cuts for various dishes; retell the many narratives of the Ossabaw to culinary tourists; and extoll the virtues of small, well-marbled pork chops. Again, marketing becomes a skill of qualification, educating customers about everything from how animals are fed to how to feed your family with an unfamiliar pork shank, and thereby hoping to turn customers into subjects imbued with a sense of the place from which their food comes. Cultivating discernment, in short, helps generate the value held to inhere in such local pork.

Pork tasting (at least in the form of ongoing conversations about barbecue) is the birthright of all North Carolinians. The Farm to Fork Picnic, held in early summer, displays numerous ways of cultivating discernment in pork. This event couples chefs and farmers from the Piedmont and charges customers a significant fee ($60–$100 in the period 2009–12) to attend. The 700 tickets available routinely sell out weeks before the event, which bespeaks both the affluence and locavorous interests of the community. The chefs and restaurant staff members with whom I spoke in 2009 were all impressed with the range of pork dishes available at the picnic and the quality of the pork offered. When I asked why they thought there were so many pork dishes, many Lantern staff members said: "It's North Carolina; you have to serve pork." Fair enough—but it is worth noting that only one vendor offered whole-hog barbecue, and the other pork dishes included *cochinita pilbil* roasted in banana leaves, artisanally cured head cheese, and slow-braised and grilled pig tails. Such offerings depend on both having an interest in things pig—"It's North Carolina, you have to serve pork"—and on showing an interest in using that first interest as a foundation on which to develop new interests, expand tastes, and cultivate new forms of discernment. Many professional cooks see the revitalization of heritage pigs as an opportunity to promote just such new forms of discernment—or, as they often put it to me, "to educate the public" (see the profiles of chefs and butchers below for examples of how they describe this process). The role of niche-market pork as an icon of discernment produces some intriguing and complex culinary problems. At Lantern, for example, the pork shoulder one month was slowly braised and simmered in a coconut sauce. The item was never a big seller, a fact I discussed with the manager one day. "Yeah," she said, "customers don't even know what it is. We need to educate people about it."

This comment points to a specific paradox in cultivating discernment characteristic of heritage pork. All of the chefs I spoke with love this product. Every one of the line cooks and prep cooks at Lantern, for example, said that their favorite dish on the menu was pork shanks. However, many of the chefs I spoke to in restaurants across the region said that they could not make money on pork dishes. "People don't want a pork chop when they are going to spend a fair amount of money on dinner. . . . Even though we're in North Carolina, people don't think of pork when they think of fine dining," one hotel chef told me. Nonetheless, he offered local breakfast sausage as a free part of the breakfast served to hotel guests to attract them to dinner. Indeed, all of the pork he served was from Cane Creek Farm, and he cured his own bacon and blended his own sausage from MacLean's pork. The pork chops at Lantern were monstrous double-cut portions, carrying a hefty price tag. The sous chef told me in the summer of 2009 that they had been butchered and trimmed improperly in the past ("they left too much bone on the chops") but were now well-cut by the processor. Still, he said, Lantern couldn't make money on them—in that season, they would just break even. "It's important that we keep it on the menu," though, he said. "We want people to see that we support local pork." It may be the case that there are profit motives that shape this practice of losing money on pork or even giving it away; the symbolic value of a loss leader (pricy though it might be) could yield higher profits in the end. But according to restaurant staff and owners, they support local pork because they understand the cultivation of discernment to be central to their operation. "Educating diners," as a great many chefs put it, is part of what restaurants do. Their use of niche-market pork is driven by this interest in promoting an appreciation of good things.

How might we characterize this discernment? What are the conditions that make it possible? What kinds of tastes are promoted when educating diners? And how do pigs and pork facilitate these practices? These forms of education and discernment should be linked to the "curiosity in cured meats" discussed above, the always-already present interest in pork in Carolina, to see how these prior interests and new modes of education contribute to a sense of the local. Discernment depends on a given interest, an appreciation for certain qualities (think bacon and barbecue) into which degrees of discrimination and distinction (unctuousness, "depth," and "funk") can be introduced. That is, discernment requires both continuity and transformation. This point was illustrated for me in discussions about cured pork. In 2009, MacLean was considering working with a partner to develop a facility for curing meats. Some older businessmen who had a long history of curing and marketing country hams in the Piedmont were invited to Cane Creek Farm to speak with MacLean. When I spoke with them, they said they had raised pigs since they were young, but they realized "ham was the thing," and they got out of the pig business to concentrate on curing country ham from pigs raised by others. When I heard MacLean talk with the potential partner about these men's experiences, she was unhappy with their claims. For her, the disconnect between pigs and hams was problematic. "These guys are just supporting the lousy genetics of industrial pigs," she noted. While her objections were at the level of animal welfare and farming techniques, the potential partner—who was working closely with a local chef to develop curing recipes—was uncomfortable with "country ham." He preferred to develop a line of prosciutto, *culatello*, and Tuscan sausages. "We don't really want to produce country ham," he said. "We're trying to cure artisanal meats."

This discussion indicates the value that discernment plays in shaping a taste for pork—that is, in characterizing pigs as local. The shift from "country ham" to "artisanal meats"—not identical, but akin, to the shift from industrial to pastured pigs—requires already existing conditions of possibility that permit forms of innovation to emerge. It is only the compelling interest in pigs and pork (exemplified, for many, by industrial pork and commodity country hams) that allows the introduction of novel categories (pastured, artisanal, and local) to be understood and appreciated.[15] These modes of continuity and transformation are requisite features of any form of discernment. Note, too, that the shift from "country" to "artisanal" correlates with how the adoption of revitalized animals and techniques of breeding permit the reimagination of emplaced connections to an alternative past. Inhabiting place in a local fashion is a matter of innovation, never just continuity. In all cases, narratives of discernment provide a means of underwriting the value of the local.

I need to note one other crucial feature of this process, especially as it relates to the category of terroir. As capacities for discernment are being inculcated and the sensory field of the Piedmont is materialized in pastured pig production, narration, marketing, and tasting, the region takes on distinctive qualities that make it a recognizable place—a place known for being "foodie," for its progressive commitments, or for its working landscapes. As all of these qualities make the pork that is produced in the Piedmont into local pork, it is also the case that the local becomes a knowable category with distinctive qualities and attributes. To be local, then, is not just to be geographically marked, differentiated, or located; it is to possess the kinds of qualities that make locality a value that is esteemed in this economy of qualities. The value of local becomes concretized and enhanced even as discerning judgments about local products (like pastured pork) circulate in this economy. In the chapters that follow, I pay close attention to these qualities of the local—in particular, the way in which it is felt to embody connection and (to a degree) authenticity—to show how the values of pasture-raised pork are ramified across a series of domains and practices in the Piedmont.

Conclusion

Highlighting the role of discernment and the integration of sensory fields should alert us to social concerns that are a consequence of this way of thinking about taste and place. If place is made through the recognition of critical qualities (skills and tastes, both objectified and embodied), it is important to ask what—and, more important, who—is not recognized in such place making. As I suggested above, issues of race and class are uneasily incorporated into the politics of local food. The historical prominence of African Americans in hog production in North Carolina, for example, is well established. What is less clear is the role that African American farmers will play in producing local pastured pigs. As I have indicated, a number of African American farmers and African American institutions—such as historically black colleges and universities like A&T—in North Carolina have ambivalent relationships to these categories and processes. While there has been outreach to African American farmers, and by African American agricultural extension agents, to facilitate and promote pastured pig production, a good deal of skepticism, if not antagonism, remains. African American farmers often reject the categories of local and cooperative, even as their traditional practices include annual hog killing and processing among small groups of neighboring family farmers. In short, their practices are local and cooperative even if they do not embrace these categories (or enjoy recognition for their practices).

The uneven adoption of these categories demonstrates that local is not simply an existential condition of being in a place, it is a specific orientation to how space is produced. The category of "local food," then, is a way of evaluating sociospatial relations.[16] These values tell us why a commitment to local food is so often seen as a remedy to the degradations of the industrialized food system. It is precisely because the local is not simply a geographical designation, but a representation of a mode of producing places imbued with the concrete sensory qualities I have described for the world of pastured pork, that it can serve as a counter to those dominant processes—like industrialization, animal confinement, and deskilled labor—for which locavores seek alternatives. It is no surprise to find that the food produced through these dominant processes is so often described by discerning consumers of local food as tasteless, since tastefulness is one of the main qualities by which status as the local is confirmed. I would add, though, that the fact that so many citizens of the Piedmont are so uneasy about the terms in which the local is extolled—although they would seem to inhabit the same places as the extollers—should give us pause when we think about the kinds of connections that are and are not produced locally.

The ambivalence surrounding these categories, persons, and practices demonstrates that place is a way of making—an active process, open to innovation and contestation. Place is never a given. The local works as a way to make sociospatial relations and so to evaluate practice. This analysis implies that we can think of a taste of place as promoting transformation and not just preservation, as much of the language of the Slow Food movement (Petrini 2006), for example, implies. Indeed, the necessity of discernment for any appreciation of such tastes indicates that taste is tied to the promotion of emerging sensory fields, as new modes of discernment refine an appreciation of the given qualities of any place. Such tastes cannot be reduced to specific times and places. Rather, a concern with the connection between taste and place—grasped as a sensory field that produces space—helps us better understand how places are made. Greater attention to the possibilities and limitations of these wider activities and the array of elements (culinary, animal, commercial, and technical) that participate in making place may help us appreciate the specific qualities (both recognized and excluded) of the local.

PROFILE: Sarah Blacklin

—

Sarah Blacklin was the market manager of the Carrboro Farmers' Market from 2008 to 2013. She moved over to work with NC Choices, starting as a volunteer in 2011 and later becoming its program coordinator; she was appointed director at the end of 2014. We talked about her work in markets, agriculture, and livestock in September 2014.

BW: So tell me your story.

SB: I grew up in Carrboro. I've been in Carrboro since I was ten. There's definitely a local kind of contingent in this ag[riculture] scene. I started at UNC [the University of North Carolina] Asheville doing dance movement, to work a lot more with my hands—I'm a more auditory, tactile learner. When I moved to UNC Chapel Hill, I had to make up my own major. Technically I was a cultural studies major, but I had such a hodgepodge of experiences—with dance, and then I was also working as a farmhand [at Maple Springs Garden]. I was able to piece together kind of a curriculum based on my experience. I got a lot of credit studying coastal environments and tied some of that into my interest in folklore. Changing environment and changing culture. That was what interests me, but there wasn't any way to study that!

Fig. 2.7 Sarah Blacklin. Photo by Kirk Ross, courtesy of the *Carrboro Citizen*.

And one of my teachers when I was working Down East also owned a B&B in Ocracoke, and he ended up being my boss down there. I went to Ocracoke, and I was mostly interested in developing my understanding of fisheries. I spent a lot of afternoons learning from older folks in that community. And then I came back, did a lot of landscape work. And then Leah Cook knew me through Ken [Dawson, at Maple Springs Garden] and [she] said, "Hey, we need a new market manager, because Sheila [Neal] was going to open up Neal's Deli." This was December 2007. So I got that job, then [I] spent five years managing the market. And in the last year and a half, before that [2011–13] I started volunteering at NC Choices.

BW: How did you decide to work with NC Choices?

SB: It went back to working with my hands again. I was a vegetarian for a little bit, so I wasn't really a huge meat eater. But I got into it because Reggie Hatch[17] encouraged me to go to Terra Madre [the Slow Food conference held in Turin, Italy], and that was in 2010. So 2010, we raised the money, and I went to Terra Madre, and I met these gals that were running the Portland Meat Collective. It was just after they got it started. So I introduced myself. I was like, "What is this?" I was really curious about butchery, you know, working with your hands and actually having a payable skill and trade—that really interested me. I was like, "Oh, people actually *make money* doing this!"—and that's always a challenge.

BW: "Bootleg sausage"—do you know about that term?

SB: I do—Hank Wilson[18] used to do that. He always told me that he used it to like pay for their [children's] school clothes and sell it by the side of the road!

The whole concept of like NC Choices is like a laugh to these folks: "Why would [you] have to sit there and have to figure out how to sell different parts of the hog? We'd sell it in a day—we'd sell the whole animal in a day!"

That's when I got really into it. And then I volunteered with NC Choices at the [Carolina] Meat Conference. And that was when I met Casey [McKissick] and I was *thrown* into it. And they needed me to do stuff, and Drew [Brown, the chef for Firsthand Foods] showed me some really basic stuff so I could help out. That was just for the one day at the conference. Really enjoyed that, and then just after that I started volunteering and [did] a few small contract jobs with NC Choices for another year and a half.

At first, I did work on an early survey. The second survey I did was by phone. I called every farmer with a meat handler's license in NC—700 people! Now I am the director, as of recently. I came in as a coordinator.

Last year all of our projects were in [processing] plants. So that was another crash course. We were entirely funded by the Rural Center[19] to provide tech[nical] assistance to small processors. So that meant driving to processors. I did a lot of volunteering at that time, too, doing things like visiting plants to let processors know that they could apply for these grants. Many of them don't have a strong web presence or website, so I would go to these plants—we really had to recruit these participants. And that was really helpful for me. We spent a lot of time working with processors, figuring out what are their technical needs, what are their inventory needs?

BW: What do you know about the history of NC Choices?

SB: NC Choices was a CEFS [Center for Environmental Farming Systems] initiative. It started with [a] partnership with [the] Sierra Club and other environmental organizations to develop alternative markets for niche pork producers. It later grew to develop conservation practices for outdoor hog production. And then they started looking at pastured pork, and it was really production focused. But soon after, they were just listening to farmers complaining about processing, where there appeared to be a bottleneck, because there really wasn't any other institution doing anything about this. So they were like, "Okay, we gotta do something about this!" And then Jennifer Curtis, Casey McKissick, and the NC Choices team at that time realized that there's extension, there's all sorts of agencies that were working with production, the need is more *processing*, it's more *postproduction* packaging, marketing, how to sell your whole animal, who's making money, etc. So that's when they started looking at postproduction processes and supply chain work really took off.[20]

BW: So how much do you work with the production side of things?

SB: Not as much, and that's actually because that's been driven by our constituency. So we team now with production people. There's Amazing Grazing, who focuses on rotational grazing, and that's another group out of CEFS, so we don't duplicate that. We're not doing as much of that, but we still need to have a farmer production specialist on the NC Choices team. Now Amazing Grazing doesn't do as much for *pork*. And we're still not into poultry that much, though it's all a part of our umbrella of focusing [on] local pastured meats. But beef and pork tend to be our focus at this time.

BW: What do you do about meat quality?

SB: Some of our workshops we're running this year are on this. That's an avenue that we can explore a lot more. Casey has done a lot more on this—he's looked at final product, compared to how that animal is raised and what that animal is fed. And we're going to have a meeting to really focus on our mission, and this is one question on the table. There has been great research done on this out of Clemson [University]. But we need to know where is the focus now? What is going to have the greatest impact? What we've ended up doing is working on better inventory management to make sure you have a more *consistent* product primarily within the processing facilities and working with them to retool and increase capacity. We really don't have the *team* do [work on taste and quality].

NC Choices has been entirely grant funded for thirteen years, so that limits what we can be. But there is a tendency to have [a] little bit of mission drift when you have to chase the funding. But I think we've done a damn good job at that, though it is a constant challenge. It was good to spend time in the processors.

Our primary funding has been from [the] Golden LEAF [Foundation] this year, but we've also received funding from USDA's Southern Risk Management and Education Center to continue to do some work with women in the livestock meat industry. We were funded through the Rural Center from 2012 to 2014, and before that we were funded primarily through Kellogg [the W. K. Kellogg Foundation] and other grants. To my knowledge, there was pretty decent Kellogg funding in the past, which was nice. But now the funding environment is just much more competitive. As of last year, we didn't know if we would have *any* funding. So it was really tenuous.

Golden LEAF funding is for working with transitional ranchers and livestock farmers interested in branding and marketing their products. We're not targeting transitional farmers, but many traditional farmers were tobacco farmers. They are pretty well equipped to make that transition in direct marketing meat in terms of volume and a good baseline of farm knowledge.

BW: Is direct marketing one of your main objectives now?

SB: Well, our focus is really supply chains. It's direct marketing in the sense that *you* retain control over that animal throughout its life. Direct marketing is dependent on a healthy supply chain. We are a resource for those producers that want that direct marketing. It's more—if those producers are interested in direct marketing, we're a resource for them. The idea is to increase more pasture-based systems in NC, and in order to do that, . . . the businesses across the supply chain need to operate in a relatively healthy and profitable manner. Direct marketing is often an entry point for that.

BW: What is the main challenge you face?

SB: It was much easier to learn and enter into the world of farmers' markets. Meat is not as inviting, I find, in terms of information exchange.

It's been more of a challenge for me. It's just *so many different pieces*! I mean, that's also why I'm attracted to it. Animals, animal welfare, distribution, cooling, regulatory. There's a lot more of what I would consider the people-oriented side of things [at the market]. I've had to be a lot quieter, and just really observe. There's a lot of terminology. There's the 4-H side where kids are *grown* into this. And then there's the post-production side, and there's only eight high-volume processor[s] that provide the services for our farmers, and they don't really have the *time* to talk to this lady that wants to know more, ya know? And I don't need to be the person who has all the answers.

BW: What does NC Choices see as its main challenges as an institution?

SB: Defining its mission. That's hard. It's a harder question than it seems. We tend to like to bring everybody to the table. But it's important to figure out—are we just working with underresourced farmers? We typically work with small-scale pasture-based farmers who don't use antibiotics or added hormones, right? But within that, what do the words "local" and "niche" mean? That's where we've hung our hats. Both of those words are intentionally fluid. So it's given us some time to try to understand the market. Because people have associations with these words—we depend on that! But who do we work with, who do we not work with? We don't have a membership, we don't have a fee, nor do I think we will. So [we're] homing in on "what *is* NC Choices?" We haven't shut any doors, but it may be time to figure out who we work with and what we do.

We really are the niche-meat specialist for cooperative extension. We will do the programing. CEFS is a nonprofit, so we can use the nonprofit organization to cast a wide reach. Yes, we act like we're consultants, and we also act like a nonprofit. We provide networking opportunities, educational programming, and technical assistance for producers, meat processors, buyers, and food professionals

BW: What have you seen change? Is it fast changing?

SB: Scale is becoming more important. I don't think people are disillusioned with farmers' markets, but now a lot of livestock producers want to skip that step. Ten years ago it was so much more about the *story*, small-scale farm, this rotation of fifty different species. And while that should still be central, the conversation keeps switching to supply chains' scale. You know, how do I get someone like Bel Campo [an aggregator in California]? Are models like that applicable here? Can they really work for us? How do we keep our integrity but scale up?

Any time you lose that direct market, that *story* doesn't matter as much since the consumer hasn't formed the trust that comes with a direct relationship with the producer. Third-party certification will *kind of* tell the story, but [third parties] are really more of a resource to validate the product's quality and wholesomeness. You typically have to have a *huge scale* to have your *brand* tell the story.

BW: Tell me about the diversity of the clientele you work with.

SB: I don't find our clientele diverse from a racial perspective, though we're seeing that slowly changing, and more minority and women farmers are entering into the business. That said, there's a lot of room to grow in that department. The types of business models are varied—ranging from small farmers to traditional cattle producers and ranchers to rural livestock cooperatives. We certainly have people attribute an ethos to small-scale pastured production, and that attracts most of our clientele.

BW: Tell me about Women and Meat [Women Working in the Meat Business]. I know this conference, which has become an annual event, is coming up, and you've been active in promoting this aspect of the field.

SB: It's a fascinating topic. I like to do things that make me feel more empowered. And that typically revolves around culturally gendered activities that I wouldn't learn by being exposed to it. Like, I get excited by changing my oil. Everything from working Down East with fishermen to being a farmhand kind of ties back to screwing with the gender boundaries. Because all of those activities are gender-charged. So I don't even think of it as food per se. It's more the cultural identity and cultural associations with things that make you feel more empowered. Other words can be put in there—"tough," "masculine," sure—but I think at the end of the day, it's confidence. And when you do that, and you're crossing a gender line, it then invites this kind of community that says, "Huh, I can do that. I didn't know I could do that!" It's simple, but it's very real. You find it in music, you can find it in any field. And I've found that with livestock. But it's a little different because you have very traditional communities at the heart of the movement.

BW: One thing that's interesting is that the gendered practice is focused on butchery.

SB: Well, this year we are going to team with Amazing Grazing for our Women Working in the Meat Business event, since they hold workshops for women around pasture management and everything from vaccination to loading a trailer. We come in with focused programming on postproduction, as in the marketing, selling, pricing, packaging of the meat product. I think it's just crossing the cultural lines to make sure we provide resources to this growing constituency of women farmers. I think at the end of the day, I think that's what it is.

Even in recruiting for these sorts of events, you can see some cultural barriers. Many times in the older generation, but there are certainly exceptions. Sometimes the barriers are real or perceived by women, but there is a cultural foundation for why [fewer] women own and operate livestock businesses, although it's changing. I was at an event with cattle producers, and I asked [the husband in] a couple, "So, have you asked your wife if she wants to sign up for this women workshop?" And she's around sixty years old. The husband answered, "Oh, she doesn't want to do that." He also poked fun at her for not knowing how to let the cows back in once they'd been out of the pen. And I'm like, "Well, if she comes to these workshops and she learns . . ." You do certainly find the opposite, too. The livestock world is changing, and there are many men supportive to see more women in the industry. However, sometimes the biggest challenge is just that women don't have as much of an established network of other professionals to turn to and talk to since they are a relatively new addition to the community.

If you grow up with 4-H you can have your dairy cow, and you milk it, and you learn about showing her, and a ton of valuable life skills. However, most kids typically leave 4-H when they reach seventeen or even earlier, so there's an opportunity there to tie in the meat business side to the curriculum. I think part of it is, I want to pump up my gym shoes and say, "I can do this, too." And it has nothing to do with strength, or whatever. It's just cultural norms! And I think people are drawn to breaking them.

I never want to make anything gendered through my work, but the reality is I think I do anyway, because I have an interest in it. But I want this work to be inclusive, and what I love is the mix. I don't think I would do well in Portland [Oregon]! I love having [a] traditional cattle producer next to this person, next to this person. I don't want to just follow trendiness, since that can ostracize certain people. I want to follow hard-working people and bring them together, [both men and women of different backgrounds], without putting myself too much in a corner.

PROFILE: Jennifer Curtis

—

Jennifer Curtis is the founder and co-CEO of Firsthand Foods, an aggregator of pasture-raised livestock that markets meat to consumers, chefs, and retailers. The company, based in Durham, North Carolina, purchases whole animals that meet careful standards of pastured production and animal welfare from small farmers across the state and processes, packages, and brands this meat for sale to restaurants, schools, and other customers. Jennifer served as the director of NC Choices from 2006 to 2013, when she came on board full time at Firsthand. She has had a long career as an environmental activist across the country, from California to North Carolina and throughout the southeast (a career that we discuss below). Our conversation took place in October 2014.

BW: Tell me your story. How did you come to meat?

JC: I had an internship in college and worked for two really, really dynamic professors—one botanist and another more just a do-gooder environmentalist—and they got me deeply engrossed in the lack of regulation of pesticides. This was my real life education in civics and public policy. I did study a whole premed track, more biological sciences, so it's a combination of policy and science for me.

But what I ended up doing was getting an internship at NRDC for eight years—and that turned into the best job of my life, the only job of my life, because everything after that has been consulting—in 1988. That's the Natural Resource Defense Council. I was in San Francisco, and it was what I learned in college—how the government was failing us—that got me into policy analysis. I worked with lawyers who were suing the government and scientists coming up with evidence to support that. It was really a comprehensive approach to problems as they came along. It was a really neat team environment, really top-notch people, I learned *so* much.

But what I became passionate about over the course of doing that were the farming communities. I was sent out to work with them. And so I got to work with extension agents, and crop consultants, and farmers doing things differently. And I worked with NGOs and the certification organizations and came to realize that, wow, doing things differently

Fig. 2.8 Jennifer Curtis.

was much more complicated than just, "Let's get rid of the pesticides and the world will change." I mean, these guys need real alternatives to deal with coddling moth[21] and invasive diseases. This is very complex. So then I became interested in policies that would promote good practices rather than penalize them for bad things. The carrot versus the stick.

That started to define how I wanted to work in the world. At the end of eight years I became extremely frustrated by the rate of change—sometimes zero. Or you'd make progress, and then there'd be a political change, and you'd be set back to where you started. And changing food systems didn't seem to be happening in food policies, it's really more in the marketplace. So I became more and more interested in market-based change. When I left NRDC I moved out here [North Carolina], going back to grad[uate] school in environmental management and policy [at the University of North Carolina at Chapel Hill], and got a consultancy with Gerber baby food. That started out as a little project because they have extensive apple acreage in North Carolina, out in the western part of the state. There used to be a whole plant dedicated to Gerber, and the south is the first crop of apples because it's warmer, but it has the most pest pressure. It's the most challenging for pest control. It was the last holdout for any kind of research on alternatives.

I worked with them as a bridge builder—researchers, farmers, and private-sector interests to leverage public dollars to research alternatives. And that's what it took. Because researchers can't go out and get money, you have to show you're engaged in the community. Gerber had a very specific interest. At NRDC in 1989 I had worked with many other people on a report known as the Alar and apple report [Sewell and Whyatt 1989]. It was the first time that an environmental agency told the story about how the government was failing children when it comes to pesticides. There are twenty-six carcinogens in baby food. Of course, the only one the media focused on was Alar. Overnight, moms were throwing their apple juice down the drain, people wanted organic apples, the organic apple industry was freaking out! It catapulted a whole new interest in alternatives. Michael Pollan was one wave. Well, this Alar report was the very first wave of "Ah! They're not taking care of us! We need to do something! We need an alternative." And then organic grew, and that led to regulation and certification. This led to state regulation, which led to the national movement. Well, the apple growers sued the NRDC for infringement of a public good—food! And that led to twenty-seven laws across the country [saying] that you can't disparage food.

It was a fantastic education, but I really wanted to do more on the ground. NRDC wants to make incremental change. And I definitely adopted that—but you need the Greenpeace, the radicals, there to make you look reasonable, too!

Working with the NRDC made it possible for me to work with Gerber for five years of fabulous consulting. I was able to learn how to be a consultant, to think about how to bring people together, and how I bring value to the room. We developed research dollars, and the researchers finally worked on mating disruption, pheromone mating disruption in coddling moths—totally nontoxic, and they figured out how to do it in

North Carolina. And now that's the national standard! And they got rid of organic phosphates.

Next, I worked on a huge sweet potato project. Multidisciplinary, multistate. The amount of chemical use in the southeast for pest control—it's insane. But Gerber lost its institutional memory: they let go all of the team that worked on Alar and apples and coddling moth. But I realized that the private sector *could* do the research and make a change. And I saw farmers who said, "Yeah, if my buyers say don't do that, do this, I will *do* it!"

I leveraged work with Gerber into working with the WWF [World Wildlife Fund] on a project in Florida. They sent me down to do an ag[ricultural] issue audit in the southeast because they have a project on Everglades restoration, and they realized that their biggest enemy was agriculture. And they wanted to change the dynamic and make it more collaborative. And they weren't sure which ag commodity to work with because all of them use water, all pollute water. After a year of research and stakeholder interviews, we ended up working on cattle ranching. And that is what I'm probably the most proud of. Because we got all the science behind it to show that if farmers in Florida north of Lake Okeechobee, which is used like a toilet,[22] could *hold* water [instead of releasing it into the lake], it would reduce phosphorous loads to both coasts [of Florida]—and to the lake—thus saving many, many species of animals, and they could still farm. But they could get *paid* for environmental services. So it turned into a cost-share program for environmental services while still farming, instead of flooding [the lake] and turning it into one big lagoon. It was all documentable, and the state bought into it, and now it's a standing program—without an NGO—where the state funds farmers to be environmental stewards. I *love* that! It took ten years, and I was in on the first two years of it.

BW: Did this project get you into meat?

JC: Yes! Right around then Michael Pollan had a piece that was a prologue to *The Omnivore's Dilemma* [2004], where he bought a beef animal and traced it. I was like "Whoa!" And the way he brings an issue to life—he rounded it out for me. It started to be not just about this animal but the health implications and the ecology aspects, the whole thing. And then I had a kid, and she started to eat. And she didn't like carbohydrates, and she didn't eat fruit. I wasn't really a strict vegetarian at the time, but I didn't really know how to *cook* meat. I think the first time I bought some meat, I bought some ribs—and they are kind of hard to cook (but my kid loves ribs now). I had also gone to grad school here and knew enough about the hog system to get an interest in that.

That report came out in the *N and O* [*Raleigh News and Observer*] right after Hurricane Fran, a series called "Boss Hog" [Stith, Warrick, and Sill 1995]. And it completely opened my eyes. I thought, I gotta figure out how to work on that one day. But I still didn't have any work in North Carolina. I was in the southeast consulting on sweet potatoes and Florida on cattle. But then Gerber fired the people that were interested in pesticide risks, and the time I had put into this approach—I was out of work for a couple months, and I took myself down to the Swine Unit dedication ceremony at CEFS with my mom, and I thought, hmm, Center for Environmental Farming Systems—they're doing stuff on sustainable hog production, let me check this out. This was 2006, and NC Choices was just off the ground. I met Nancy Cramer [the director of CEFS], and the *next day* she called me and said, "I'm looking for someone to take over NC Choices." And then that led to seven years of doing all sorts of stuff for CEFS.

Well, I quickly realized that they were never gonna be able to employ me for long unless I helped raise them money. So the first grant we got was a conservation innovation grant for a million dollars to do on a farm—outdoor pasture-based hog production research—from [the] National Resource Conservation Service [part of the USDA]. And then we did a renewal grant for much more that included a lot of pilot projects.

Chuck Talbott pulled together this grant funded by the Golden LEAF Foundation partnering with Heifer International, Niman Ranch, A&T—this is before I got to NC Choices. I come on, and Niman announces it's leaving. Chuck is still trying to figure out how to complete his research and produce his results. I didn't ever work directly with Chuck, but I got to know Jim Green, the forage specialist at NC State. I hired his student to be my coordinator. I'm a project manager, but I'm *not* the person to go tell farmers what to do.

Pretty quickly I realized that the number one issue for the pig farmers that Chuck was working with wasn't an issue of demand, it was processing. So then I began my journey of understanding what is meat processing, why is it important. There was a lot of bitching. That was tiresome. This was all over North Carolina. Now I have to figure out how does NC Choices add value for a handful of farmers that are selling direct to consumers? There were some tricky politics among the stakeholders of CEFS. And I'm really only able to work with direct marketing as a strategy. So what I can ask is, why is *my* local co-op not able to sell *local meat*? I'm really not a marketing specialist, but I have to develop a marketing project for NC Choices, since that's what these farmers that I *can* work with need.

Most of the farmers weren't interested in doing anything different based on the *research* I could bring to the table on environmental systems. It's different with hogs. You can do cattle sustainably, but the impact of hogs, even outdoors, still needs work. It was frustrating to raise money and do research, but there wasn't enough support for that research to go anywhere. But now we're kind of known around the country as the state that has more direct market opportunities for hog farmers. That's really not true in Iowa or elsewhere.

BW: What makes processing such a problem here?

JC: It's only a problem for *us* [for niche-market producers]. The big boys have the capital. It's the politics of Smithfield. They have been so exclusionary—they don't just want to beat you, they want to crush you. And there hasn't been a solution to the problem of pastured-pork environmental impacts. Rotation does help, and there are things you can do. But our research shows you've got to keep pigs off fields for three years and grow produce to move nutrients off.

[Soon after I started working with NC Choices,] *The Omnivore's Dilemma* came out, and it really *did* change my life. What happened with NC Choices was, it was still looking to define its mission, but it had already been kind of branded! It had a logo, the opportunity to become a marketing project. But they weren't sure what they could *do*. Because they couldn't make sales for farmers—the university [NC State] had real problems with that. Some people were excited about NC Choices, but they really didn't know who CEFS was, so that was a hard way to move the project along. We helped to raise grant money to raise the profile of CEFS. This all culminated in me putting together the statewide action guide for developing a sustainable local food economy [Curtis et al. 2010].

At the same time we were figuring out the issues on the ground—and our grant from Kellogg [the W. K. Kellogg Foundation] said "scale it," so we have to figure out how to do that. And that led to us incubating Firsthand Foods without having any idea what that is going to be. And working with my local co-op, I realized that they were not going to have time to develop relationships with thirty hog farmers across the region to assure a constant supply. Somebody needs to be organizing this for them.

BW: So it was volume that you were concerned with?

JC: It was volume, consistency, freshness—scale. There's no one on their [the co-op's] staff that wants to do this. But in the meantime, Whole Foods was doing this, and you could see them making an effort. But a smaller grocery store, no. They were so disinclined to buy the whole animal.

NC Choices managed that supply for a year, and part of our job was to get the co-op going on this, and the relationship was direct, but aren't we a nonprofit? Working on behalf of a co-op? I didn't like it.

It was a pilot. And it gave us an indication that there was a business that was needed to do this. For me, there was a two-year period where I was just as involved in growing CEFS to work on a wide range of sustainability issues, and getting to be networked across the state, and realizing I had to make a choice: am I going to go deep into meat, or am I going to stay generalist and go where the opportunities are? Only being able to work on the direct marketing was a real limitation. But I decided, well, I'm not much of a risk taker, so Firsthand Foods had to be fairly well developed before I could get that going.

BW: So tell me about the actual origins of Firsthand—when do you realize that an enterprise of some sort is needed?

JC: Well, I'm doing this pilot at the co-op. Kellogg is saying how are you going to scale it? And this entrepreneur, Fred Callahan,[23] calls me who says he's trying to help this food product company to develop a purpose for its cattle traceability program,[24] which is developed for the whole Canadian government. Now, he had this technology, and he was a consummate entrepreneur. He had no mission—the mission was "figure out an application for this product." And Fred says "take me along with you" as I'm visiting farmers and markets. He's looking for business opportunities. And I'd never met anyone like that. I'd worked with academics and NGOs my whole life, and his attitude was so different! He went to a processor, saw a farm tour. He looked at all of the players and he just said to me—after I'd been working on this for two years—"you need a consumer products company in the middle making all of this happen." And I was like, "A what?" I'm just *not* a private-sector person. I just logged that away, kept talking to him. And he realized that these small farmers at the farmers' markets—there was huge growth here, but there was never going to be enough customers for *his* [Fred's] product. He had to go after bigger fish. But I wouldn't have started Firsthand if I hadn't met him.

We got this project with NC Choices, and Fred helped fund a study of a type of business that might be a broker. We went to the Center for Sustainable Enterprise at Keenan Flagler, the UNC business school, and got a summer intern to figure out this broker-type business. The advice we got was: figure out where you are going to make money before you start a business. And who was the biz student? Tina [Jennifer's co-CEO at Firsthand].

She got the mentoring, and we got a low-cost financial model on becoming a broker where we would resell *pieces*, and we realized we couldn't make any money doing that. There wasn't enough value we could add along the supply chain for us to add another layer. We had to take on more of the supply. We worked with the Business Alliance for Sustainable Entrepreneurship, an advisory group that the Kellogg Foundation pulled together, and got early business coaching—like think about your brand, think about your name, etc.

And then we went for "Launching the Venture," which is a competitive class at UNC. We got in the class, and we were able to show that there were sales at the co-op. They weren't *our* sales, but there were sales. So I was the community partner, Tina was the student. And we were one of eighty. First semester, down to twenty-five. Then on to [the] financial module, one of eight that graduated, and we were voted most likely to launch. At that time, 2009, we still thought, we need to see if there's some money to launch this as a pilot. We're still part of NC Choices, and I'm looking for grants. We went to the Tobacco Trust Fund, they turned us down; again, turned us down; third time, we got it.

BW: Who is the Tobacco Trust Fund?

JC: They are a state program voted on by the legislature, and it's all about transitioning tobacco farmers. Much more conservative than Golden LEAF. The Rural Center then followed suit. From both of them combined, we got $150,000 to spend exclusively on animals and processing. You need operating capital to start a business—so here was another hurdle for us. All the time we're thinking someone else is going to come in and own this—a grower co-operative, *someone*—we're just *testing* it. And Kellogg gave us money to hire me and hire Tina right out of business school. I needed someone with that financial advice. We knew that most businesses fail because they're undercapitalized. You need cash flow! You don't want to have customers and not have the capital to acquire animals or pay your processor.

Thank God for Kellogg. They were flexible, they could keep us going even as we're learning and trying to create a viable model. I realized, though, that there's nobody out there who believes in this—it becomes our vision. So in 2010 we incorporated, and Roger Crickenburger at NC State, part of CEFS—he was critical because he helped us figure out that we could get grant money to start a business. The grant couldn't go to *us*, but it could go to the Ag Foundation [the North Carolina Agricultural Foundation], which is affiliated with NC State, and we could be contractors to them.

The Ag Foundation was critical through the end of 2012. We hired Drew Brown, our chef, in fall 2010. That was when the grants came through. With friends and family money we bought the food truck. We launched that in fall 2010. And in March 2011 we went into the wholesale business—and the truck was just a brand-building opportunity. March 2015 will be four years in wholesale, and this week—October twenty-seventh is [when we will start] our fourth year in business.

It was probably fall of 2009 when Tina said to me, "I think you and I are gonna have to own this thing. We're just gonna need to do this, and we *can* do it."

BW: Why?

JC: She just didn't see anyone else out there. We need to bite the bullet and do it. That was both terrifying and thrilling. The more I got into it, and the more I realized the kind of impact you could have in the private sector, the more it started to feel totally right to me. And I could finally stop going to too many academic meetings! [Both laugh.] And we had $700,000 in sales in 2012 and passed $1 million in 2013.

For me it's been fabulous to be 100 percent in it—it's very dynamic. The business is always changing.

BW: Tell me a few ways in which even in four years things have changed.

JC: I think when we started it felt—this is going to sound hokey—a little bit blessed. We were the fourth food truck, the second savory truck[25] in Durham. We just latched onto something happening in Durham. That wasn't smart, it was just good luck. We were very worried about the impact this would have on small farmers. We needed to have so much goodwill—we needed to not be pissing them off. Because I knew all of these people, many of them were my friends. So we were very deliberate with each sales call that we did to *not* disrupt those existing supply chains. That was very strategic, and it worked. Over the course of three years some have handed us business, and we have done the same. We can send customers to other farmers when we couldn't supply a product. Some people wouldn't care, but we knew this is about relationships. Now I feel like most people understand what we're doing, at least in the local food sustainable ag[ricultural] community—they see what we're doing, they see our value, they're excited for our success. We have a lot of goodwill on our side.

The business advice we got was, "you are going to be supply strained, you're going to take off, and there won't be enough, and you are going to be pushed constantly to become the processor." You're going to be pushed because you're going to want to be able to control your quality and all the other things processors do. We said no, no, no, our mission is to work *with* these processors. We knew we'd be supply strained. And that is a challenge when we go out on a sales call, because you want to go to Charlotte and just sell the heck out of something, and you *can't* because you're not going to have it. We did just get a contract to sell beef to Guilford College—and still that scares the heck out of me, because I hope we'll have enough!

We are currently supply constrained in beef for reasons that have nothing to do with us. It has to do with the fact that the four companies that own all the beef in the world are buying up cattle at alarming rates—the prices are through the roof. I can't compete. And they're doing it to make their processing plants operational. And they own 80 percent of the beef in the world.

Over time our fears about competitive relationships with farmers did not become a hassle, but supply is still a problem, and processing is still a problem. We have developed good relationships with processors, but the costs are still really high, regardless of our volume. There's no tiered pricing for whether you have things all cut up into retail steaks or primals[26] for restaurants. You would think that would be two levels of pricing, but they're not. The costs for processing are really high, and when they make a mistake that's a huge cost to us, and it's infuriating.

What we did right was branding, for sure. I think that will serve us for a long time. This relationship that we developed with the co-op, the Natural Hog Growers Association—that was right. First I'm realizing, okay, I'm the supply side of the team. I'm going to supply from the co-op and a few farmers outside of the co-op mostly. Well, I learned fairly quickly that if I source from outside of the co-op, I'm going to mess things up for the co-op. They need me to be there every week so they can plan. But if someone [another livestock farmer] calls me, and they have finished animals and beg me to take them, I have tried to do that. We need to be exclusive with [the co-op], which is painful because I'm in the business of saying "yes" to every cattle farmer I can. So I have to let the co-op do that for me. But then again, can I trust them? Because they [the co-op] are going off to Whole Foods and other markets and restaurants. Our challenge this year is to get much more solid vendor agreements in place. I've had to school our processor in that. I'm like, "If you take on customers that are in our area [the Triangle], I'm not going to trust you." But he gets it. And in the end, the time we spend on relationships is worth it, but there isn't even time for that. I need to spend more time on sales. Because even with $1 million in sales, we're not at breakeven yet, we're still dependent on grants. We got a Small Business Innovation [Research] Grant—we wouldn't be here if we hadn't gotten those. We have about a year left to get to breakeven, and we're not there.

How do we address that? We upped our prices. We do the Meat Box,[27] which helps with cash flow, but isn't really a big money maker. It's really hard for us to cut costs, because 75 percent of our income goes back to farmers and processors. Yeah, we could cut our salaries, but then we're not motivated to keep with it. Beef is a business of pennies. There's more stuff you can do with pigs [that is, more of the pig can be used in restaurant dishes and related recipes], it doesn't take as long to raise them. Beef farmers are gamblers, and they will hold out for that highest price, and right now they're getting it!

I've had the most stress I've ever had with this business about beef lately. We went from eight beef customers, and now we've got twenty-five customers, but our margins in beef are like 10 percent. So we try to shore that up with higher prices, but you can't do that too much! All this time for 10 percent—so a little scary.

One thing we realized is that farmers need feedback, so that they can learn about bulls and boars.[28] We need to take a lot of time and show them a rib eye, show them their pork loin, and measuring, and documenting, and tasting, and grading, and sending that back to them. And that's information they need, and they value. But it takes a lot of time. I'm motivated by the relationships, I am. But they're really exhausting.

3

HERITAGE, HYBRIDS, BREEDS, AND BRANDS

In his excellent study of the evolutionary history of the Industrial Hog, Sam White describes the ways that Chinese breeding stock played a central role in the transformation of the English pig. The small, fat, black pigs from Asia, introduced[1] into Europe in the early eighteenth century, had been kept for centuries in China, where they converted household scraps and agricultural leavings—White calls the pigs "small-farm garbage disposals" (2011, 105)—into edible protein. It was this physiological capacity that made them so well suited to "improve" the rangy, hairy European hogs that fed primarily on forest mast (primarily beechnuts and acorns) as demographic pressures led, simultaneously, to rapid deforestation and an expansion of urban populations across Western Europe. By means of this hybridizing encounter, a burgeoning market in southeastern England for improved hogs raised in sties, trough fed, and fattened on peas and beans (when not scavenging in London's backyards) would be fed by farmers in the Midlands of Leicestershire and Lincolnshire.

This evolutionary transformation in the hybrid English pig was simultaneously a revolution in the pig's symbolic form. As Margaret Derry (2003) suggests, the expansion of English markets for pork facilitated by the presence of newfangled pigs raised on farms dedicated to their production was further facilitated by promoting specific and recognizable breeds of livestock, which allowed customers dispersed across England to identify the pigs with the distinctive characteristics they preferred. Citing Robert

Bakewell, a pioneer in the promotion of livestock breeds from the late eighteenth century, Derry argues that "the new idea of 'breed' was from the beginning nothing more than 'an ingenious marketing and publicity mechanism,'" as John Walton put it (1986, 152), and she finds that "the market . . . played a critical early role in formalized selective breeding" (Derry 2003, 4). Whether such ideas are ever "nothing more" than a marketing device is one of the questions this chapter pursues. Although I do not examine the historical evidence from England at this time, I think that the issues I raise for contemporary North Carolina may be relevant for reconsidering the relationship among selection, quality, and reproduction.

In any event, this concurrence of evolutionary, economic, and cultural transformation is all the more remarkable when we consider its longer-term consequences. What early adopters of these Chinese pigs facilitated was a proliferation of regional breeds across England. Yorkshire, Hampshire, Suffolk, and Berkshire pigs were all recognized as prize breeds by the end of the eighteenth century, and each of these breeds was the improved outcome of a breeding process that crossed Old English pigs with their distant Asian cousins.[2] But what these old English innovators could not have foreseen was the significant divergence in the future history of the hogs that they crossed. On the one hand, Hampshire, Durocs, and especially Yorkshire pigs—all traceable to early Chinese improvements—have become the quintessential Industrial Hogs that now thoroughly dominate the U.S. market. What is far more surprising is that a number of not too distantly related breeds of pig—the Berkshire, the Tamworth, and the Gloucestershire Old Spot among them—are highly prized in the U.S., British, and, increasingly, global markets today. In the United States and the United Kingdom, though, they are described not as industrially produced animals (like the conventional pigs raised in confinement operations) or the novel product of a market-driven hybridized breeding process, but as Heritage Breeds or Pedigree Breeds, respectively.[3] Thus, the pigs now intensively produced by Big Pork, as well as many of the pigs raised as niche-market alternatives to these industrial animals have a remarkably common genetic heritage, one that can be traced to early acts of selective hybridization and improved breeding in the enclosed and commercializing English countryside.

How some pig breeds end up as heritage breeds while others are relegated to the ignominy of industrial standardization is an intriguing historical question. In this chapter, however, I address a slightly different problem: What kind of thing is a heritage livestock breed? We might also ask why there are animal breeds at all. In other words, what is the purchase on variation in forms of life that is afforded to us by codifying animals into specific breeds? How are these specific qualities—especially semiotically charged attributes like heritage—manifested by breeds recognized and deployed in social action? Addressing such problems entails a consideration of the relationship between the production of livestock (especially heritage) breeds and concomitant efforts to market these animals and their meat. How might efforts to ascertain and reproduce these recognizable properties be translated into terms that can be disseminated among and appreciated by a consuming public—and is this relationship between livestock producers and consumers ever as straightforward as the one Derry and Walton suggest was present at the creation of English breeds of pigs? As I will demonstrate, animal production and marketing is also a recursive process, often laden with tension and contradiction, since the particular criteria to which livestock are bred may be transformed as discerning consumers seek different characteristics in the breed. In this way, breeds derive their significance from a network of diverse (often incommensurate) perspectives (Foster 2008), in whose terms the value of particular animals—alternatively as breeding stock, a source of meat, a niche-market product, or a form of heritage—is subject to continuous transformation or requalification along the lines of the model I outlined in the introduction. The ideas of qualification and of the incommensurate character of the perspectives that are able to participate in it are ones to which I will repeatedly return in describing the multidimensionality of animal breeds.

This recursivity, I will argue, is relevant to an understanding of social and cultural forms of typification (Palmié 2013), the practices by which categories are established and confirmed in social life. At the widest level, moreover, I will argue that this concern with categories and their elaboration is also a useful way to think about questions of materiality and immateriality. Breeds are concepts that reflect preferences, interests, and other conventional notions, all of which are contingent on a variety of contexts. At the same time, breeding animals to conform to these concepts is an intrinsically material process, requiring the skilled (Grasseni 2004; Ingold 2000) selection of animals possessed of specific attributes and a grasp of the wider husbandry practices, environmental conditions, and physiological well-being of particular animals that are all conducive to successful livestock reproduction. How might the materiality of this process—which includes not only the orchestrated biological reproduction of bodies, but also (and, arguably, centrally) the growth of desirable meat—inform the putative immateriality of conceptual types defined by breeds, and heritage breeds more specifically? What is it that is materialized in the category of breed? What concrete qualities are embodied in the creation of heritage breeds? One of the central arguments that I intend to make here is that the distinction between breeds as definitive types, or categories of life, and breeding, a process of selection and biosocial reproduction in animal husbandry, is characterized by a number of tensions and even contradictions. And it is precisely these tensions that inform the production of categories like specialty, pedigree, and particularly heritage (which is the focus of this chapter) and that have implications for the social conditions under which such animals are produced and circulate.

These questions about the material implications of prevalent, practical categories like breed are relevant for much wider cultural theory in the twenty-first century. Anthropological consideration of notions like "identity" and "heritage" has increasingly demonstrated the dualistic ways in which forms of "culture" are deployed and codified in a host of different domains—from policy makers who implement multicultural education programs and medical protocols designed to take cultural differences into account to touristic enterprises that promote cultural heritage or heritage foods. These contemporary invocations of culture seem explicitly to combine understandings of social constitution and biological givenness. "In its lived manifestations," note John and Jean Comaroff, "cultural identity appears evermore as two antithetical things at once; on the one hand, as a precipitate of inalienable natural essence, of genetics and biology, and, on the other, as a function of voluntary self-fashioning, often through serial acts of consumption" (Comaroff and Comaroff 2009, 40). The project of preserving our identity and heritage almost always entails deliberately making a commitment to promoting recognizable features of difference (for example, language, ritual, and cuisine), which are in turn seen to be unique and ineluctable dimensions of the being of those who possess these features (as in the biogenetic legacy of certain porcine life). As I show below, the distinction between breeds and breeding (and their complex intersections with hybrids) illuminate precisely this antithesis of "natural essence" and "voluntary self-fashioning." From this perspective, the problem of heritage breed pigs is relevant both to how and why culture has come to be grounded in both the social and the biological, and to how this potential contradiction can appear to be resolved in practice.

Ossabawness

In this account I focus on contemporary efforts to define, conserve, produce, and sell heritage breed pigs and their pork, again focusing on ethnographic findings from my work with farmers, conservationists, academics, chefs, and consumers in the Piedmont. Let me begin this exploration of the multiple links I have identified by considering the specific heritage breed of pig that I introduced in chapter 2 as a main character in this book: the Ossabaw Island Hog. As I noted there, Ossabaws are descendants of the Ibérico pig, or *pata negra* (black foot), abandoned on Ossabaw by Spanish colonial forces over four hundred years ago. Over these many generations the Ossabaws have developed the characteristic qualities of "insular dwarfism" (Prothero and Sereno 1982, 16–17), becoming smaller in overall size as well as a striking physiological capacity to store fat. Indeed, feral Ossabaw Island Hogs have the highest percentage of body fat of any nondomestic mammal (Watson 2004, 114). This remarkable ability, which some researchers have linked to the presence of a "thrifty gene" (Neel 1962, 353),[4] also produces a tendency to develop adult onset diabetes and cardiometabolic syndrome (Sturek et al. 2007). This propensity has made this insular herd of interest to medical researchers, who first began removing Ossabaw hogs from Ossabaw Island in 2002. Current medical research is promoted, for example, by the Ossabaw Swine Resource, a research group affiliated with Indiana University's School of Medicine and Purdue University that maintains "the only research and large-scale breeding colony of Ossabaw swine in the world that is certified to have a gene mutation, the metabolic syndrome, and heart disease" ("Ossabaw Swine Resource" n.d.).

The medical uses of the Ossabaw were facilitated, moreover, by the environmental impact of these hogs on their Ossabaw Island habitat. The porcine colony was making efficient use of the limited food supplies on the island by voraciously eating the eggs of such endangered species as the loggerhead sea turtle, any number of nesting birds, and assorted—often protected—reptiles and amphibians. For this reason, the Georgia Department of Natural Resources developed a management plan in 2000 that called for the eradication of the island's feral hog populations. Medical researchers, though, took an interest in the hogs, and were able to successfully export about one hundred pigs for animal experimentation. In recent years, the Department of Natural Resources has carefully managed the hog population on Ossabaw Island and has banned the export of any more animals as a safeguard against infecting domesticated herds ("The Ossabaw Pig" n.d.).

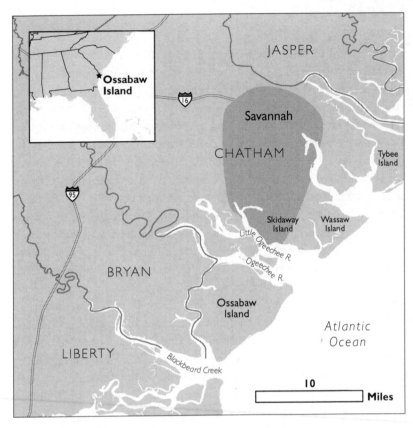

Map 3.1 Ossabaw Island (in proximity to Savannah, Georgia).

The selective breeding of Ossabaw Island Hogs (figure 3.1), then, is rooted in a complex history, one that extends from colonial expansion through environmental management to biomedical research. The development of this breed as agricultural livestock also has its origins in these medical projects, as well as a bit of culinary adventurism. As Peter Kaminsky, a food writer, describes in his compelling account, *Pig Perfect*, he identified the Ossabaw Island Hog as a likely descendant of the Spanish hogs that provided the *jamón ibérico de bellota* (ham from acorn-fed pigs) that he had come to love on various Mediterranean sojourns (2005, 135–41). Working with Charles Talbott, then the director of the Small-Scale Hog Producer project at North Carolina Agricultural and Technical State University (A&T), in 2003 Kaminsky found a group of twenty-three Ossabaw Island Hogs meant to be sacrificed in a National Institutes of Health re-

Fig. 3.1 Ossabaw Island Hogs and barn.

search study being carried out in Columbia, Missouri. Talbott and Kaminsky transported these hogs back to A&T, and this was the origin of the breeding stock that would be—and still are—raised in North Carolina, on Eliza MacLean's Cane Creek Farm.[5] Kaminsky also used his connections as a food writer for the *New York Times* to recruit chefs from New York to visit these pigs and offer them on the chefs' menus once the pigs had been "grown out" and processed. As has always been the case, livestock breeding is intertwined with meat marketing.

This little history is fascinating at any number of levels (and is a source of what often seems endless fascination to the many customers who purchase Ossabaw pork from Cane Creek Farm). In addition to demonstrating the historical connections between colonialism, livestock, and landscapes embodied by these "creatures of empire" (Anderson 2006), given the biomedical and culinary links already alluded to, the history of these hogs poses some problems for the study of breeds and, in particular, for the contemporary interest in heritage breeds that is my focus here. Note, for example, that the Ossabaw Island Hogs were (in all likelihood) deposited on Ossabaw Island in the mid-sixteenth century, well before the notion of distinct, recognizable livestock breeds was developed in Europe. What were the Iberian hogs, the pata negras, that landed up stranded on this island? In the course of four hundred years of inbreeding and environmental adaptation, the Ossabaw Island Hog developed phenotypic (and perhaps genotypic) characteristics that distinguished the Iberian pigs as a population, but it is entirely unclear that they had any such prior connections to one another. This fact makes a point that is obvious in some ways but by no means trivial: breeds, as such, are historical phenomena (and, moreover, possess a history that is bound to place in a concrete fashion). Yet the Ossabaw Island Hog presents the perhaps anomalous history of being a breed that was not selectively bred through techniques of careful livestock husbandry but left to evolve naturally through the pigs' abandonment in a resource-poor environment, a long-term process that generated animals that are both physiologically compromised (and thus prone to human-like metabolic ailments) and distinctively delicious.

Not only does the history of the breed date to an era prior to the development of modern breeds, but the genealogical stock of these pigs is also quite different from most heritage and pedigree pigs. The Ossabaw Island Hogs ended up in the New World well before the introduction in the early eighteenth century of Chinese pigs into the mix of improved pigs that would come to dominate the English and subsequently American markets for pork. Indeed, most Mediterranean strains of pig, even today, have not been improved by Asian stock (White 2011, 104). So these Ossabaws form a very odd breed indeed, with a very complex relationship to heritage. Removed from ongoing regimes of livestock selection and bearing little genealogical connection to the animals that have populated the American landscape—whatever the method of production—for more than four hundred years, the Ossabaw Island Hog is, nonetheless, extolled as a heritage breed, well suited to the ecology and management practices of the Piedmont of North Carolina and much of the American South. They seem to raise various questions: What makes a group of pigs a breed? How do their historical characteristics as a breed give them a discernible heritage? And how can we situate these historical characteristics, and the qualities of heritage, within the transformations in political economy, demography, and pig farming that we have seen sweep across the Piedmont in recent decades?

Something in the Breed

One way to pursue these questions is to look directly at the discourse and activities of the actors most interested in identifying and promoting heritage breeds of swine. The Livestock Conservancy (until 2013, the American Livestock Breed Conservancy), which is based in the North Carolina Piedmont, was founded in 1977. The organization is "working to conserve historic breeds and genetic diversity in livestock" (Livestock Conservancy 2015) by developing a range of programs, from marketing campaigns to educational programs, that aim to promote what it has identified as heritage or rare breeds of livestock, including breeds of poultry, horses, cattle, and swine. The Livestock Conservancy supports various breed associations (for example, the American Guinea Hog Association and the Piney Woods Cattle Registry and Breeders Association), organizes conferences for breed enthusiasts, develops initiatives for different forms of livestock (such as the Swine Initiative, begun in 2008), and produces a bimonthly newsletter for its members. In a wide-ranging discussion I had with two of the program managers, Jeannette Beranger and Steve Moize, at the Livestock Conservancy office in Pittsboro, North Carolina, we talked about the organization's mission and, in particular, the kind of work it does with farmers and breeders to identify heritage breeds and promote their breeding and marketing. In response to my questions about the particular challenges of breeding pigs, as opposed to other livestock, and what the newly funded swine initiative hoped to accomplish, Beranger said:

> One of the bigger things to tackle with the pigs is not just breeding them but breeding them correctly so that you've got good body type, good traditional body type, and [you're] not turning them into a commercial hog. For instance, with the Berkshire—the vast majority of them out there are *not* Berkshire. They've got Pietrain [another breed of pig, with Belgian origins] in them, and they're kind of *commercialized* at this point. Or Hampshires. And so getting people to understand that there's *something to* the old body types, and why that's important for the particular breeds. With the Swine Initiative we're hoping to create guidelines to help people understand—get people to understand, okay, *what are you looking at* when you look at the hog? What's a good back look like, what do good feet look like, *what qualities should you insist upon* [in] your breeders?
>
> Because—a lot of folks, because they're *getting premiums for breeder hogs*, they're selling everything as breeders, and they can't be doing that. But, you know, it's like "buyer beware" when you're buying hogs. We tell people, "do your homework. Know what a good hog looks like."

These comments disclose a range of interesting points, points that form a pattern in this ongoing discussion. First, there is a concern for discerning discrete kinds of pigs—the idea that Berkshires are different from Pietrains and Hampshires. This much would seem to be a minimum requirement for an agency dedicated to conserving breeds. Furthermore, when it comes to identifying specific breeds, Beranger emphasizes the ways in which particular breeds are characterized by particular qualities: "What's a good back look like, what do good feet look like?" Moreover, the notion of qualities is especially apt in this context, as it entails both recognizable characteristics and a hierarchical evaluation. That is, "good hogs" bred "correctly" are preferable in some recognizable ways to other pigs. "There's *something to* the old body types," as Beranger says. This theme of quality is an important one that resonates with the claims and practices of farmers—as well as chefs and consumers—working with pastured pigs and their pork.

Lastly, even these brief comments demonstrate the ways that breeds and breeding are complicated by marketing and commerce, an abiding theme, as we have seen, in the breeding of livestock. The real Berkshire is compromised by becoming a highly prized "commercial hog." Indeed, the entire process of careful selection on which breeding and conservation depend is challenged by the fact that heritage breeders demand a higher price than producers of standard breeds and hybrids. Beranger said that "because of the money involved, or the profitability of using that word 'heritage,'" many farmers are compromising their breeding stocks in ways that undermines the viability of breed conservation, even as efforts at conservation have promoted these commercial potentials. Not only does heritage breeding facilitate the discernment (in the sense spelled out in chapter 2) of desirable pork qualities for a specific market, but the marketability of heritage as a quality poses a risk to the success of such breeding. This complication points to the ways in which breeding is not simply an extension of market forces, pace Derry's claims about this process, but also marks a potential point of differentiation between heritage and commerce. This distinction—and such keywords (Williams 1985) as "heritage," "commerce," and "qualities" made use of in the discourse of experts like those at the Livestock Conservancy—speaks more broadly to questions of the relationship between the material and immaterial qualities of heritage breeds.

One way to comprehend the so-called risk to the breed that arises with indiscriminate or careless breeding (a problem created by market pressures) is to see this risk in the context of pig production in the United States, and specifically in North Carolina, that I have already discussed. One of the critical distinctions that activists for alternative food systems, like those at the Livestock Conservancy, deploy is that between commodity production and noncommodity forms. The terms for these noncommodity forms, as we have seen, are quite variable, including "artisanal," "local," "niche market," and, of course, "heritage." The significance of "heritage," then, needs to be grasped as a term of distinction (in all senses of the word) that offers a contrast to the industrialized production of pigs that dominates North Carolina—even as the term "heritage" also has market value that facilitates the production and productivity of "local" pigs as commodities. In this way, "heritage" carries with it the uneasiness of alternative practices that, nonetheless, depend on wider structures of practices to sustain them. Simply put, heritage pigs would have little value in the absence of their industrial counterparts.

Moreover, heritage as a specific quality clearly connotes the kind of temporal depth and historical legacy that I discussed in chapter 2 as relevant to the production of the Piedmont as a place. This sense of legacy, depth, and continuity, I suggest, is a rather surprising set of qualities to attribute to a breed of pig whose heritage status in North Carolina derives from the fact that it can trace its genealogical connections to Spain. How might these temporal and spatial attributes help us understand what a breed is? As I have suggested, the Livestock Conservancy is dedicated to conserving genetic diversity, and heritage breed certification is part of this mission. I asked Beranger how heritage breeds contributed to genetic diversity, and she suggested that such breeds were unique because they could not be selectively reproduced (that is, bred) from various other pigs if they were to become extinct. Most recognized commercial pigs are crosses of a range of breeds and so could be reproduced from that range of stock if a given population died out, but that is not the case with a distinctive breed. But maintaining a breed through genetic conservation required bloodline preservation. At this point I asked what the Livestock Conservancy was doing to support breeds like the Mangalitsa (the pigs mentioned in chapter 2). Beranger told me that "those aren't American breeds, so they are not our concern. They are doing a good job of preserving them in Hungary, we don't need to."

In this exchange it becomes clear that genetic diversity—and as a result, heritage as a quality of distinctive breeds—is always situated within a concrete social order (here, the United States, not Hungary). A heritage breed is relevant to someone's heritage, not simply to abstract continuity, traceability, or longevity. Insofar as a Spanish-derived Ossabaw Island Hog is evidence of this American heritage, then, it relates to the localized history of bloodline preserved in the historical development of the United States. Yet, as I have suggested, the pigs emerged as a recognizable breed in the absence of breeding as a feral population on an isolated island. Of course, not all heritage breeds have the same provenance. But the implication of heritage does entail the notion of bloodline preservation in a way that keeps this genetic legacy distinct from other (primarily commercial and, hence, mixed) populations. Pigs do not need to be feral to retain this distinction; their heritage can also be preserved through good breeding.

It should be clear that these kinds of claims about heritage breeds recall the duality of culture as both socially achieved in practice and inalienably present as an enduring (biological) essence. Here I would add two relevant points. First, the idea of bloodline preservation as a practice that distinguishes one heritage population from a commercial other population supports the values of authenticity that are central to the ways that heritage animals are marketed and that also motivate the farming, consuming, activist, and other practices of so many participants in this niche world. Such an unsullied line connotes a sense of what is uniquely real, and not modified or corrupted for commercial or commodified interests. Second, it should also be clear that, in addition to implying that remaining at a remove from the market constitutes these animals and husbandry practices as real, connecting Spanish (or other European, as most heritage breeds are held to be of English origin) ancestry through U.S. geography to contemporary Piedmont practitioners provides a different line of preservation, one also fictively rooted in blood. This lineage suggests the social distinctiveness of the people who inhabit this world, equipped to appreciate a heritage with which they can also affiliate themselves. In short, these attributes of a breed also provide an alibi, or a materialization of racial ideologies. I will return to this point below.

Performance

How do breeders and others interested in livestock breeding understand how the qualities that distinguish a heritage breed are embodied in these animals? Just what was this "something" that distinguished "the old body types"? Was it, I asked, just a question of conformation, the well-selected biophysical features of the animals' morphology? Beranger expounded on this notion a bit: "There are certain points in conformation that automatically equate to beneficial attributes within the animals. For example, [a] big thing with pigs is good feet. You don't have good feet, forget it. That's huge." But Moize was a bit more circumspect:

> Something you don't see in conformation maybe directly that plays into . . . any breed . . . is how the breed has been maintained for the last couple of generations. Because not only are we talking about heritage hogs, we're talking about heritage hogs in a sustainable pasture-based system. And they really haven't—some may not have been kept in that management model. Then you get like the Ossabaw, you're taking it from a feral population to a, technically a domesticated population, and they change. Even in that sense, if I was trying to conserve the Ossabaw as a domestic animal, we're changing it. There's variables there that aren't just conformation directly.

At this point I asked, "So there what you're conserving in effect is *genetics*— is that the idea? The Ossabaw's a great example, because it's a Spanish pig, feral pig, pastured pig?" Moize responded:

> Well, I think you are preserving the genetics. Part of my point was that in preserving a breed or the genetics of a breed we have to be mindful of the management style, or the way the breeding herd is maintained generation after generation, because that effects, positively or negatively *what we're selecting for*. We're not just selecting for conformation, we're selecting for *performance*. You know. Is it going to give you the muscling, or the fat, the back fat that you're looking for? Is it going to be *desirable by the end consumer chef*? There's a lot of variables there.

My clumsy efforts at characterizing breed qualities in terms of such mechanical terms as "conformation" and "genetics" yielded a much more anthropologically nuanced accounting.[6] The quality of breeds is rooted in biocultural processes of production and reproduction, as well as in the sociocultural purposes that these animals serve. The overall "performance" of the animal is the outcome of a process of selection that is carried out by certain management techniques. As a process of selection, breeds are phenomena that reveal themselves only over time, by maintaining the breed "generation after generation." Here is a direct link between the notion of a breed as a kind that can be recognized and differentiated from other groups of animals and the idea of breeding as the selective management style, suited both to an ecological context and the specific attributes of the animal, that is fulfilled in the ongoing reproduction—as well as transformation, as in the Ossabaw (figures 3.2 and 3.3)—of the well-maintained herd.

This biocultural process is clearly complex: "There's a lot of variables there," as Moize says. What I want to emphasize here is his argument that the process of selection, and the way breeds can be differentiated from one another, is best evaluated in terms of the "performance" of the animal. It is this performance that guides effective management—"we're selecting for performance." As a discursive term, "performance" has an interesting and relevant range of meanings. To begin with, the term is widely used in the livestock industry more generally. Animals are routinely subjected to "performance testing" by farmers and researchers. Cattle, in particular, are subjected to "feedlot performance" testing (for example, Johnson, Anderson, Meiske, and Dayton 1996). In industry usage, "performance" refers almost exclusively to weight gain—how much and how quickly an animal can put on weight in response to a range of variables. In heritage breed pigs, though, performance suggests something more. Performance certainly refers to pork, but the character of this pork has been used to differentiate varieties of pigs. Pigs have historically been described as either "lard hogs" or "bacon hogs." Lard varieties having more fat on their backs and legs, which allows them to be used for industrial purposes like the extraction of oil, grease, and biofuels (Blanchette n.d.). But lard hogs are also well suited to the long-term curing of hams and other pork pieces, as their thick back fat and intramuscular fat prevents the salted meat from drying out and facilitates a longer fermentation process. In contrast, lard hogs are not all that well suited to making sausages, because their excessive fat content causes the sausage mixture to smear rather than disperse throughout the meat when the sausage is ground. Bacon hogs, somewhat paradoxically, are leaner varieties of pig, not only preferable for bellies but also the foundation of the contemporary industrial hog that is meant to grow leaner and longer, and so produce a larger—and more profitable— loin from which pork chops and tenderloins can be cut (see chapter 5 for a further discussion).

All of these distinctions should be taken with a grain—or more— of salt, as the extremely lardy Ossabaw Island Hog not only produces a fine cured ham, similar to Spanish *jamon ibérico*, but it also provides sausages and super-fatty bacon that discerning—and well-educated— consumers and chefs can come to love. Note, however, that this understanding of performance, especially as Moize describes it, does not just refer to weight gain or volume of pork produced but also incorporates

Fig. 3.2 Ossabaw Island Hog. Photo by Ezra Weiss.

Fig. 3.3 Ossabaw Island Hogs eating.

a broader understanding of the quality of the pork: "Is it going to give you the muscling, or the fat, the back fat that you're looking for? Is it going to be desirable by the end consumer chef?" All of these attributes requalify the performance of heritage pigs and their pork. For example, the discernment of certain actors becomes a critical dimension of a pig's ultimate performance.[7]

These questions of performance are particularly important because they reveal the ways that management processes of selection are guided by the effort to produce—and reproduce—identifiable qualities, qualities that are simultaneously features of animals' lives ("old body types," "good feet," "muscling") and of these animals' performance as desirable, consumable meat. As I suggested in chapter 2, this concern with performance as a feature of breeding demonstrates that Wendell Berry's aphorism that "eating is an agricultural act" (1990, 153) can legitimately be inverted: agriculture (or animal husbandry) is a culinary act. Moreover, consideration of performance in this way allows us to situate breeding—as well as the wider value of heritage breeds and the practices by which that value is materialized—in a wider context of sociocultural activities. Seeing a breeding process as directed by a concern with what is most "desirable by the end consumer chef" allows us to incorporate the network of perspectives of chefs and consumers (Foster 2008), as well as those of pig farmers and breeders, into our understanding of what type of thing a heritage breed pig is. At the same time, the evaluative language that Moize and Beranger use—"good feet," for example—and, in some ways, the very notion of performance suggest an effort to carefully distinguish heritage from commodity forms, even as the central qualities of the heritage pig are realized when the pig becomes a consumable commodity. Given that the term "performance" is also used in the world of industrial livestock, using it in these ways creates a point of differentiation between commercial production and heritage breeding. In this way, performance is rather like bloodline preservation: it points to an effort to distinguish putatively real porcine character and quality from adulterated, commodified purposes. Performance, then, is a way to connect certain qualifications—those of chefs, discerning consumers, and selective breeders—while distancing these heritage breeds from the qualifications associated with commercial, industrial, and conventional animals. The idea of "performance" works as a kind of boundary quality, establishing a demarcation—both conceptual and material—that aims to differentiate real pigs from their commercial cousins.[8]

The range of "variables" that Moize refers to in discussing the characteristics of heritage breeds confirms, in many ways, Cristina Grasseni's claims about how breed characteristics are identified and selected. She points out that, as much as there is a quest for genetic markers in breed definition, the techniques of the breeder and the apprentices he or she trains are paramount in this process. These techniques entail the cultivation of embodied, sensory understandings of how to differentiate between "objects that are commonly available to generalised perception" (2004, 49), such as pigs: "Specific sensibilities and capacities—including the symbolic pre-eminence of certain senses—are engendered through the active socialisation of apprentices into structured and shared contexts of practice" (48). In her discussion of Bergamont cattle breeders, Grasseni describes these "specific sensibilities" as a "skilled vision" and examines "the actual process by which the breeders' perception and strategies for action, together with the relevant aesthetic and moral sensibilities, become embodied through training" (49). Beranger alluded to a similar concern with sensory understanding, telling me, for example, that the preeminent features of a pig's "performance" could be "seen by the breeder"—unlike chickens, where it was necessary for "you to get your hands on them" to identify them by breed.

Maternal Hogs

My research with pig breeders is not nearly as extensive as Grasseni's work with cattle breeders in the Bergamont; indeed, the number of heritage pig breeders in the United States is still rather small. In part, this reflects the very different understandings of heritage and local origin in European and North American contexts (Grasseni 2004; Rodríguez Gómez 2004; Trubek and Bowen 2008). But I do have evidence of ways that various participants in the production and productivity of heritage breed pigs—farmers, chefs, and consumers—evaluate the qualities they are looking for in these animals, and their performance as pork (or as potentially pork). Let me begin with a story.

In the spring of 2010, I met two friends of mine at a restaurant for lunch. One was Ross Flynn, an aspiring farmer and butcher, and the other was Sam Suchoff, a young chef on the verge of opening his own restaurant, The Pig. On the menu that day was barbecued pulled pork belly, which we all sampled. Ross, who worked at the time at nearby Cane Creek Farm, said to me, "You know this belly comes from Ursula." I told Ross that I did.

I had been selling Cane Creek Farm pork at the Carrboro Farmers' Market the previous Saturday, where we sold her other belly, or side. "Yeah," said Ross, "you know she was that bitch." I asked him which pig she was. "That weird looking pig," he said. "She looked like a Martian." I tried to remember which sow she was from my time working at Cane Creek, and I asked what breed she was. Was she an Old Spot? Or some Berkshire mix? Surely not an Ossabaw. Ross was not certain, but he was pretty sure she was a Farmer's Hybrid, an "old-timey" hearty cross that is extremely popular in efforts to revitalize pastured pork across the Carolinas and beyond (a point to which I will return below). "Wait a minute," I said, "was she the pig in the garden pen, who was really ornery"—to the point of regularly attacking the staff? Ross affirmed that she was the one who was impossible.

Ursula was one of the first sows I met when I started field research at Cane Creek Farm. In the course of doing chores, the daily feeding and watering of animals, I could not help but notice the piglets—called "pigs" on a farm—that were free to roam more or less wherever they liked on the farm.[9] In the course of feeding sows in the large "garden pen," in my utter inexperience and frank stupidity, I grabbed a small calico pig as it snuck under a fence in front of me, picked it up by its hind leg, and held it up to look at it while it squealed and screamed bloody murder in my face. Within a few milliseconds the sow that was this pig's mother barreled toward me, and had I not leaped out of the way and up onto the fence, she easily would have got her jaws around my knee and snapped my leg in half. I didn't make it back into that pen again for several weeks, and every time I did walk past the pen, the sow—Ursula—would take a good long look at me and often rush toward me to back me off.

When I had asked if Ursula were part Berkshire, Sam had asked, "Aren't Berkshires bad mothers?" Ross was not sure about that, but he did say that part of what makes any sow a really good mother is equally what makes her really lousy to raise and handle on the farm. And, indeed, it became increasingly impossible to try to get Ursula's pigs away from her, to "grow them out," castrate them (the fate of all market boars, henceforth barrows), or otherwise make them independent of her so that they could be raised up for the market. So Ursula was taken off to slaughter—not, as was the case with other sows I knew, because she had proved incapable of further farrowing (that is, of reproducing again), but rather because she was such a good mother that she was far too dangerous to keep on the farm without doing damage to the staff and so the farm as a whole.

This anecdote highlights a number of problems that are relevant here. First, it demonstrates the extent to which pigs contribute to their own domestication and their own selection for breeding. That is, pigs' abilities to be good mothers are not just the natural attributes of a particular breed, they are part of the behavior that pigs can exhibit relative to the kinds of farm work and labor that are needed to see the sow through the processes of reproducing and raising her offspring up for market. Maternal qualities are the outcome of a biocultural process through which pigs are selected and bred for attributes that contribute to their management. Being a good mother means being well suited to raising pigs that can be grown out for slaughter; this is the minimal criterion for successful breed performance. From the perspective of the breeder, then, selection and marketing are again conjoined in the processes that constitute a breed. This connection between selection and marketing should also be defined as a skill, a practice inculcated into the breeder "in a richly structured environment" (Ingold 2000, 5). But there are some additional points to make. First, this is one of the few places in this book where I am able (at least to some extent) to incorporate the perspective of a pig on the selection and breeding process. From Ursula's point of view, breeding is a process that actually undermines her interests as a pig. Her maternal skills, though they may allow her to produce offspring and care for them, are antithetical to the process of breeding as the farmer pursues this endeavor.[10] These skills— like the qualities of commodity pork that are at odds with the Livestock Conservancy's understanding of breeding—are excluded or even suppressed in the economy of qualities that generate heritage breeds. This is a crucial point, building on the ideas of performance that demonstrate that networks of perspectives are not simply empirical chains of requalification. They also depend on differentiation and forms of exclusion. In many respects, the critical question to ask of any such network, then, is how do certain perspectives (like those of Ursula, or perhaps those of farmers who do not participate in direct marketing and so do not typically make use of such discourses of heritage in their practices) get excluded from the perspectives that come to dominate this economy of qualities? Which perspectives, and so which qualities, count?

I would also note that the "richly structured environment" of which Tim Ingold writes is also profoundly historical. This is true not only because of the long-standing processes of selection that create this structured environment, the organism, and the breeder (as the history described by White illuminates), but also because of the connections between reproducing pigs and marketing pork and the wide possibilities that exist for transforming this nexus over time—as in the development of both industrial and heritage hogs in the late twentieth century. By historical, then, I mean the sense of both having a past and continuously contributing to the future. These historical possibilities, grounded in the material potentiality of pigs and their pork, can be usefully articulated with the social and cultural environment that is laden with skilled practice, to pursue further the question of what is materialized in a heritage breed of animal.

Hybrids: Value-Added Pigs

Let me return to the Ossabaw Island Hog as an exemplary heritage breed to describe in a bit more detail the kind of performance farmers, chefs, and consumers can expect of it. This focus on performance is meant to help us grasp the historical potential of a heritage breed (in the sense I just described) as realized within the network of perspectives (those of farming, breeding, cooking, and consuming) that are brought to bear on the Ossabaw. To begin with, let us return to some of the material conditions of Ossabaw life. As an insular breed, the Ossabaw Hog not only stores (delicious) fat very efficiently, but it also grows very slowly. A full-size Ossabaw Hog may not reach 250 pounds by two years of age, at which point conventional breeds or even such heritage breeds as Berkshires, Old Spots, and Red Wattles routinely reach 400 to 600 pounds (at the low end) in the same time. These material limitations clearly have direct implications for the performance of the Ossabaw as a breeding hog and—most important—a source of meat. Small hogs may eat less than larger ones, but if they take longer to raise to a weight at which they can be viably slaughtered, processed, and sold (often up to eighteen months, compared to six to seven months for other conventional and heritage breeds), the costs of keeping these animals can be prohibitive. The solutions to this challenge vary. At the level of marketing, a farmer can try to sell Ossabaw pork for a premium price to recapture the costs of raising this breed. Here, of course, is one of the ways that we would anticipate that heritage breeds are materialized, in the work that the notion of "heritage" does to produce knowledge that is of interest to discerning customers willing to pay more for a prestige food. And as the Bourdieuvian model would have it, the heritage of pigs thereby becomes materialized in the distinction that accrues to those who consume their meat (Bourdieu 1984; but see chapter 6 for a different reading of distinction in pork tastes).

A parallel practice aimed at a discerning consumer clientele can be found in the value-added dimension of pork marketing. In the case of the Ossabaw hogs raised at Cane Creek Farm, this has led to the production of a line of cured ham that is made exclusively from Ossabaw pork. Recall that part of the motivation for domesticating the feral Ossabaw herd was Kaminsky's quest for the New World equivalent of the jamon from the pigs he had eaten in Spain. In pursuit of this premium culinary treat, Eliza MacLean sought a meat-curing facility that could create this product from her Ossabaws. In 2010, she found a ham processor in a neighboring county (several hours from the farm), a family-run business that had been producing what is known in North Carolina and across much of the South as "country ham" for nearly a century. The most recent heir to this company had been approached by a number of hog purveyors from across the country who were looking to create a premium, value-added, cured (or, better, "artisanal") ham from their (generally) heritage breed pigs. So he was receptive to Eliza's efforts to work with him to cure Ossabaw hams.

Here, again, the value-added process of curing ham raises the price that MacLean can get for her expensive-to-raise Ossabaws. Moreover, it adds a premium quality to the performance of the Ossabaws' pork and so contributes to the distinction of the customers as well as the livestock breed. The artisanal ham from these Ossabaws is cured for twenty-four months and sold in the Piedmont today as prosciutto for $40 per pound. The development of this product materializes the heritage of the Ossabaw in a range of complex ways. The term "prosciutto" instantiates a framework that locates the Ossabaw in a region that (somehow) connects the Piedmont to an Old World habitus, one meant to evoke the tastes and techniques of artisanship, care, and quality that customers imagine (or, in some instances, recall from their own experience) is embedded in the form of this food. For a very few discerning customers, real afficionados of charcuterie, this cured ham is often described as a jamon ("more like a Serrano than an Iberico," noted one of our tasters at the Carrboro Farmers' Market), thereby completing the circuit initiated by Kaminsky. I should also note that this product is labeled simply as "ham," as European Union regulations restrict the use of the prosciutto or jamon denomination to cured meats produced in the region of Europe that retain proprietary rights to produce and market these comestibles. Nonetheless, this product is known and ordered as prosciutto by Carolina consumers, confirming again their interest in situating this product (and their tastes) in the region that links the Piedmont to the Mediterranean. Here we also see part of the historical potential of the heritage breed, for it is the Ossabaw that permits this transregional (and temporal) framework to be maintained. This is so not because the Ossabaw is really genetically descended from Spanish pata negra (a great many consumers of prosciutto have no knowledge of breeds, nor are they even aware of breeds' relationship to particular foods), but because the interest in heritage breeds confirms the network of perspectives among connoisseurs, farmers, chefs, and the like that locates the desirability of the breed in its performance—here, in the tasty, "funky"-flavored ham it provides. In this way, fine prosciutto is a correlate to the maternal qualities of sows. It is a way of appreciating pigs, and one of their material properties whose significances derives from the nexus of marketing and breeding livestock. This nexus confirms the potential for imagining new possibilities—country ham reinvented as artisanal charcuterie—for the breed.

Charging higher prices for value-added, or premium, cuts of slow-growing Ossabaw hogs is only one way to recoup the costs of breeding this livestock. Beyond modifying the market in this way, or managing their consumers, farmers also modify the animals. In the case of Cane Creek Farm, this process entails crossing Ossabaw Island Hogs with other breeds of pigs to produce a faster-growing and larger pig. In part, this kind of move embodies the concern with commercializing the "old body" types that gives the Livestock Conservancy pause. In this particular case, though, there is no attempt to deny the presence of non-Ossabaw genetics in the livestock that are produced or to suggest, somehow, that a new form of heritage breed has been crafted in the process. Rather, MacLean and other farmers raising Ossabaws recognize that the viability of the Ossabaw as a commercial form of livestock—an animal bred for the performance of its pork—depends on their know-how in expanding the potential of the heritage breed. At Cane Creek Farm, the pig of choice with which to cross the Ossabaw is the Farmer's Hybrid (figures 3.4 and 3.5). The Farmer's Hybrid has specific qualities that suit it to crossing with the Ossabaw. The fact that the crossbred pigs are larger animals than pure Ossabaw Island Hogs means that they will produce cuts of meat that can be sold more profitably. In particular, their tender premium loins are larger, which means that consumers can purchase pork chops of a size that conforms more to their expectations of what this premium cut should look like. Furthermore, the Farmer's Hybrid is a rather fat and hairy pig, and these qualities also contribute to the quality of the meat that is produced by the resultant Ossabaw Cross (also known as the Crossabaw), discussed in the

Fig. 3.4 Farmer's Hybrid pigs eating.

Fig. 3.5 Farmer's Hybrid pigs. Photo by Ezra Weiss.

previous chapter. A good amount of fat back and a thick, tawny coat ensure that these pigs can be raised outdoors successfully in environments that are equally suited to the Ossabaw. Yet the Farmer's Hybrid is large enough that the fat is distributed on the animal in such a way that it will not make for excessively fatty pork (as would be the case if Ossabaws were bred to fat, dark-haired Berkshires, for example).

Moreover, the Farmer's Hybrid is of much wider importance in national efforts to revitalize natural and pasture-raised pork production. Originally developed as a line of livestock by the Farmer's Hybrid Company in Des Moines, Iowa, the Farmer's Hybrid pig is, as the name makes plain, a hybrid line derived from a combination of different breeds (Duroc, Hampshire, Yorkshire, Chester White, and Poland China). The Farmer's Hybrid Company developed this line in the 1940s as a way to improve these breeds and produce livestock that were suited to the grueling winter environments of the prairie states (Iowa, Illinois, and Minnesota) where pig production would be dominant in the United States from the period after World War II down to the present. The Farmer's Hybrid pig, however, would be pushed out of favor with the rapid industrialization of the hog in the 1980s (Blanchette n.d.), as the vertical and horizontal integration of production (described in chapter 1) demanded distinct new body types for confined animal feeding operations (CAFOs). Long, lean, pink pigs replaced fat, hairy Farmer's Hybrid, pigs which were ill suited to indoor production. In time, though, opposition to the perceived economic, social, labor, and environmental degradations of the CAFO system sparked a renewed interest in the Farmer's Hybrid. Paul Willis (discussed in chapter 1), who had grown up raising Farmer's Hybrid pigs on his farm in Thornton, Iowa, began raising them again in the 1990s and recruited many of his neighbors to form a "free range" pork cooperative. In 1998, Willis began selling his hogs through the Niman Ranch, which was then marketing meats for the San Francisco Bay Area (Grey 2000, 144). The Niman Ranch took a great interest in the quality of Willis's pork, and he became the manager of the Niman Ranch Pork Company, which is now a national consortium of several hundred independent livestock farmers that market their meat under the label, and according to the specifications, of the Niman brand. The Farmer's Hybrid was critical to the development of the Niman brand as it promoted the adoption of this line of pig to ensure quality control and uniform standards among the far-flung pig farmers that the company worked with.[11]

The significance of the Farmer's Hybrid pig as a model for promoting natural pastured pork cannot be underestimated. As I described in chapter 1,

Niman Ranch not only worked with farmers in various regions—including the Piedmont—to promote pastured pork production, but it also sought to develop markets through retailers like Whole Foods and marketed its products directly to chefs to develop a commercially viable naturally raised hog industry. In this way, the Farmer's Hybrid also provided vital support for the promotion of heritage breed farming, as breeders of heritage livestock depended on the wide network of perspectives that the Farmer's Hybrid Company and Niman promoted. This network includes a discerning set of chefs, retail outlets with well-heeled clienteles, and farmers familiar with outdoor hog production practices. Each of these and all of them in concert are vital to the plausibility of raising heritage breeds of pigs in a commercially viable fashion. Even if Farmer's Hybrid pigs are not actually crossbred with these heritage breeds, then, their presence is already built into the material conditions that make such breeds possible.

It might seem ironic that a hybrid hog has been absolutely critical to American farmers' efforts to conserve and promote heritage breed pigs. Of course, this situation is not unique. The original hybrids (and the origin of the term "hybrid") were the offspring of domesticated ancient Roman gilts bred to wild boars to enhance the vitality of the herd. We have already seen that crossing Asian pigs with their distant English kin is what allowed improved hog breeds to come into being in the eighteenth century. The hybrid undoubtedly precedes the breed. Both the history and practice of breeding suggest that successful performance is the critical quality of breed management and that the capacity to recognize good performance in the pig (the "something" in the "something to the old body types") is central to breed recognition. A Berkshire is a bad mother only with respect to the performance of her pigs—can they be raised into proper pork chops? These skilled orientations toward viable performance have long shaped the selective process of breeding these livestock. This is what gives them their historical potential. So it is only once the definitive characteristics of properly performing animals has been materialized that the breed of the animal can be known. A breed is the product of hybridization.[12]

Breeds and the Antibrand

In characterizing what is materialized in heritage breeds, I have drawn on the notion that breeding is oriented toward the performance (itself a discursive term that is part of the qualification process under investigation here) of the breed. This performance can further be described in terms of a network of perspectives that incorporates such diverse criteria and interests as the behavior of sows, crossbred hybrids, value-added meat products, and discerning chefs and consumers. Heritage breed pork is inconceivable in the absence of this range of concerns and commitments. When we ask what kind of a thing a breed is, or how it is possible to think of types of life, we need to situate the making of kinds in this nexus that links pigs, pork, and the markets to which they contribute. At the same time, it is important to point out that this network, and the breeds it sustains, cannot simply be reduced to a marketing device. The particular qualities that constitute performance and that permit breeds to be distinguished from one another as kinds can be evaluated in ways that are not strictly selected for according to the economic viability of the livestock. Breeds are certainly commodity forms, but—as the activities and discourse of groups like the Livestock Conservancy repeatedly reveal—their status as breeds is also made vulnerable by their commodifiable potential. Breeds, and perhaps especially heritage breeds, are both integrated into and at odds with the market interests that enfold them.

One way to put this simultaneous connections and conflict among husbandry practices, the phenotypic characteristics of animals, the qualities of the meat they exhibit, and the strictures of a niche market was suggested to me by Mike Jones, a farmer. Jones is described by many of the other farmers and food activists I work with as one of the best hog farmers around. He has an academic background in animal husbandry and extensive experience in both industrial and pastured production, and he has worked as an extension agent for a major university, training novice pig farmers. He also helped develop the marketing scheme for North Carolina on behalf of Niman Ranch when the company sought to expand their production network in North Carolina. When I first visited Jones's farm, I had recently been to a farm that had begun raising Berkshire pig, and adding them to the mix of its breeding stock in response to inquiries from a chef who had extolled the virtues of Berkshire pork. So, as Jones and I looked at his pigs, I tried to guess what breeds he was raising. These were big, high-backed, sleek, but clearly fat hogs. Were they Hampshires, I guessed, or mostly Farmer's Hybrids? In response to my guesses, Jones told me about his customers. "My customers know that they can count on my products," he reported. The customers are looking for particular attributes in terms of flavor and quality—as well as in the health of the meat they are feeding to their children. But Jones is also looking for particular attributes that will contribute to the lives of his animals—that will ensure that they can survive outdoors, that sows can be bred without "breaking down" under the weight of a massive boar, and that they have feet that are sturdy and well positioned so that the pigs can easily endure the long walks necessary for moving them around to different pastures. To achieve these qualities that made both his customers and his pigs happy, Jones had calculated the kind of mixed ancestry he was looking for—Hampshire pigs for stature, Durocs for disposition, Farmer's Hybrids for endurance, and Berkshires for marbling—and tweaked the breeding of each generation to achieve the successful blend. Finally, he noted in response to my question about what breeds he used: "A breed is really a brand."

To think about breeds as brands, as Jones suggests, we must find some way to develop an understanding of brand that entails very specific material qualities (from animal vitality, to health benefits and delectable pleasures) and that clarifies how these are embedded in and signified by such breeds as brands. One useful way to think about pig breeding as evidenced by the practices of farmers, chefs, and customers and the material links between the genetic diversity, animal husbandry, skilled practice, and the marketable performance of quality meat might be to think of breeding and the production of specific breeds (which is not the same thing as breeding) as a form of brand management. I have demonstrated how the significance of breeds can be understood to incorporate a network of perspectives (among farmers, chefs, and consumers, among other interested parties) across which these breeds move, their values transformed and requalified (as maternal success becomes artisanal prosciutto, which generates an Old World taste, as well as $40 per pound) in the process. In Robert Foster's (2008) terms, a brand is a mode of capitalist appropriation (Arvidsson 2006; Mazzarella 2003), a means of extracting value that works by aligning the qualifications—that is, the attributions of significance—that consumers and producers (and many other actors involved in the circulation of brands and brand-name goods) apply to commodities. According to Foster, brands are managed through efforts to promote—and regiment—strong attachments between consumers and producers. Such an approach to brands cuts across the semiotic and ideological distinction between brands and products, exemplified by this statement by Jing Wang: "a product is made in a factory; a brand is bought by a consumer" (quoted in Manning 2010, 36).

Classic marketing accounts extol the immateriality of the brand, as though it were both epiphenomenal and entirely conceptual, in contrast to the real materiality of production. If, instead, brands are seen to operate as icons of the processes through which they are produced, then they can be understood to possess substantive qualities (the "something" in the "old body types," from "good feet," hairy coats, and well-marbled muscle to bloodlines and "funky" flavors), which are subject to requalification as the animal-carcass-primal cut-product shifts positions across the network. In a felicitous transaction (like the purchase of some fine charcuterie) a sought-after breed, worthy of conservation and tasty to boot, can embody the alignment of perspectives that is characteristic of a well-managed brand.

Paul Manning notes both the notorious difficulty of offering any coherent definition of "what brand is or means" (2010, 34), as well as the tendency toward "dematerialization" (Moore 2003, 333), so that a brand comes to seem to be "an immaterial form of mediation essentially identical to semiosis as such" (Manning 2010, 36). My argument jibes with Manning's efforts to resist this dematerialization. I have asserted that saying "a breed is really a brand" invokes the very way in which industrial commodities circulate the qualities of that production process. I thereby demonstrate how alternative processes (for example, careful breeding selection, compassionate concern for animal welfare, and artisanal production of value-added products) of food production can equally be materialized and embedded in the foods themselves and circulate as part of their value (Munn 1986). To offer pork from a heritage breed of pig is not, therefore, simply a tactic meant to improve one's market position. Rather, it is a means of asserting an alternative praxis to industrial production, one governed by a distinct set of values (for example, concern for animal welfare, artisanship, and local community relations) and exemplified in a set of sensible, material qualities (hairy pigs living out on pasture, producing slowly fermented ham with a funky taste)—all of which exemplify the core values of the direct connections among farmers, animals, and the consumers who acquire their meat through the direct relations they make in niche markets. As Krisztina Fehérváry discusses in the parallel case of socialist Hungary, "transparency and truth" in the direct, functional, and unadorned ways that consumer goods were designed, promoted, and displayed served as a kind of socialist brand in contrast to the implicit deception of capitalist commodities (2009, 438). Like socialist brands, then, heritage breeds invoke directness, honesty, and substantiality—providing the quintessential "real food" as I have described it—and materialize these in the form of the products they promote. As both metasemiotic objects and practices, heritage breeds (and other niche-market pigs that sustain those breeds' production) challenge the perils of industrial pork, calling into question the ideological distinction between products and brands, and thereby serve to qualify the authenticity of the processes that produce them.

Conclusion

Heritage pigs are a contemporary innovation with the potential—and the purpose—of forging a viable future. Grounded in an entangled history of improved breeding techniques, they simultaneously confirm and challenge the impetus to develop a commercial industry in livestock. Their heritage is critical to their niche standing. But this value-added position may also render them vulnerable (Keane 2003; Moore 2003), for the temptation to commercialize the breed through the specialized value that heritage status commands may lead to the loss of the genetic profile that defines the heritage breed. At the same time, even if carefully selected for, the qualities that characterize the heritage breed extend beyond these biogenetic markers to incorporate a wide network of perspectives of breeders, farmers, chefs, consumers, and other advocates for livestock breeds. In this chapter, I have highlighted certain key nodes through which heritage breeds are materialized in this network. The importance of performance in a breed provides the opportunity for a series of qualifications, as physiological and anatomical features of a breed can be selected for. In turn, these features will permit the qualification (here, the selection and processing) of particular kinds of products—bacon, loins, fat, and so on— that can then be requalified via, for example, value-added processing, tasting, charcuterie, and cooking. Each of these different acts of qualification provides a reflexive opportunity for confirming both the significance of the heritage breed as a valued form and the value of (for example) the breeder's expertise in husbandry, the chef's culinary artisanship, or the consumer's connoisseurship. In addition to performance, the role of hybrids in livestock husbandry reveals how the commercial viability of niche markets in heritage breeds is underwritten by an ongoing history of improvement and transformation (and not simply preservation and continuity). The economic success of almost all pasture-raised pork depends on the success of this hybridization, as does the performance of these animals, both on the ground and in the market. Finally, the notion of breeds as brands provides a means of both articulating and concretizing—that is, rendering material—the values of direct, forthright forms of social

Fig. 3.6

practice that provide an alternative to the industrial food system. The care and craft of the livestock breeder—indeed, the honest labor of an actual farmer you can meet and look in the eye—are conveyed in the way that heritage breeds (like the Ossabaws in figure 3.6) serve to brand the authenticity of these tactile encounters.

In all of these ways, heritage breeds materialize a wider world of values and interests and provide a concrete form—and an opportunity—for these values to be aligned and transformed. The heritage breed is therefore a critical feature of ongoing efforts to reform American meat production. Given these points, we might still ask, why are there breeds of animals, per se? Why is livestock variation codified in distinctive breeds? And why might this be of such pressing interest today? In his recent critique of "hybridity talk," Stephan Palmié challenges contemporary anthropology's all-too-easy embrace of the ideas of hybridity, mixture, and syncretism as though these social forms necessarily (and productively) destabilize the presumed fixities of systems of classification (2013). Unsettled by this unexamined endorsement of unsettling, Palmié argues not simply that the hybrid implies the pure, but that coherent praxis—in both social life and social analysis—requires the marshalling of classificatory infrastructures. This does not mean that categories are fixed and intelligible, but that they are made to be so. The proper question for anthropology, therefore, is "not *what is* a hybrid . . . but *when*." Furthermore, "under what socially and historically specifiable conditions do any of them emerge, become ratified or contested, and eventually normalized, suppressed or transformed, with all the potential violence any of these options may imply?" (472). What's good for the hybrid is good for the breed (since they literally produce one another). So we might ask "what socially and historically specifiable conditions" ratify these animal forms?

In her assessment of Charles Darwin's interest in the domestication of pigeons as an apt illustration of the "conditions of life" that provide a model for natural selection, and the production of "well-defined species," Gillian Feeley-Harnik demonstrates how this interest suggests that "classifications in contemporary natural history [are] part of larger patterns of social interaction" (2007, 148). Her analysis of Darwin's research into pigeons, therefore, shows that domestication is part of a much broader pattern of human-animal relations, and it also draws attention to the social and working lives of the men in London who bred pigeons in the mid-nineteenth century. Feeley-Harnik offers a fascinating account, with great depth and nuance, of the Spitalfields weavers, denizens of what had become one of the poorest slums just outside of central London, partly in the East End. Feeley-Harnik shows how the "conditions of life" that fostered the domestication of pigeons were an objectification of the conditions by which these craftsmen domesticated themselves. The reproduction of the laboring lives of the weavers was ensured not only through the familial inheritance of the tools of their trade but also through the inculcation of a habitus that was attuned to varieties of color, pattern, and texture. This "weaver's eye" of the Spitalfields handloom craftsmen was materialized not only in the "figured" and "fancy" silks they wove but also in the plumage, color, and iridescence of the pigeons they kept and bred (164). Here, the "conditions of life" that generate animal varieties and types include the socially oriented, laboring bodies of artisanal craftsmen, each species coproducing their domestication.

The North Carolina Piedmont is no Spitalfields. Most important, the kinship connections, so vital to the laboring and domesticated lives of those skilled English artisans, are configured very differently in contemporary North Carolina. Where London households once reproduced themselves in the habitus exemplified by a refined aesthetic judgment, in the Piedmont, the farmers, chefs, and consumers most committed to heritage breeds are pointedly not reproducing the conditions of life into which they were born. Rather, in carefully selecting and qualifying the livestock they husband and the meat they consume, they exemplify the conditions of cosmopolitan mobility that have so dramatically transformed the region (especially the Triangle) in the last two generations (a point to which I return throughout this book). Of the dozen farmers who sell pastured pork at farmers' markets in the region, only one—an African American man who lives on a farm founded a hundred years ago—grew up raising hogs. One other hog farmer raises pigs on land that he told me has been in his family for over three hundred years, but that was used to raise tobacco almost exclusively until the 1990s. The rest of the hog farmers are first-generation farmers, almost all of whom moved to North Carolina from points north. Not surprisingly, they describe their interest in using hogs in their farming operations as part of their commitment to the innovative values that they bring to their endeavor. They want to support sustainable operations, promote ecological well-being, and offer an alternative to the industrial agriculture that has devastated so many small farmers in the state. For such first-generation farmers, the promise of heritage breed pigs is the kind of historical potential they possess, the capacity to present an alternative and so to introduce the possibility of transforming the conditions of life in the region.

I am substantially in sympathy with their efforts. My work with many of these farmers, chefs, and others often ventures into advocacy and routinely helps farmers like these expand their markets and develop productive alternatives to the ubiquity of industrial pork. At the same time, the demographic shifts I have alluded to here, and the preference for heritage breed pork among many of these farmers, consumers, and others committed to innovation should also recall, as I noted above, the ways that heritage status works to provide a kind of narrative of realness and un-adulterated intentions. The temporal depth and sense of enduring place sought by these largely inmigrating innovators, and readily encountered in these porcine lives, highlights the way that such breeds embody a desire for preservation amid displacement. They also indicate (in spite of the uniformly progressive politics and socially conscious intentions of these innovators) the exclusionary potential of such racializing semiotic and material processes as the ascription of preserved bloodlines or the notion of an ineffable "something" that distinguishes crass commercial creatures from those that are worthy of distinction.

In both of these respects, it is only a slight exaggeration to suggest that today's farmers, chefs, and consumers of these widely prized newfangled old-fashioned pigs most resemble the Ossabaw Island Hogs—both are sources of innovative practice and modes of sociosemiotic differentiation. Transplanted into new territories, their exceptional qualities can be recognized and cultivated as they introduce new possibilities for remaking the local order. Bearing cultural commitments (swine with heritage, entrepreneurial farmers with local sustainability, locavores as ethical consumers) they craft an innovative future.

PROFILE: Will Cramer

—

Will Cramer is a twenty-seven-year-old farmer who works at Ever Laughter Farm, outside of Hillsborough, North Carolina. Will started the farm in 2008 in collaboration with Sam Hummel. Today, it uses sustainable methods to grow a wide variety of vegetables that are featured at restaurants in the Triangle and available at the Durham and Chapel Hill farmers' markets. I met Will in 2010 at the Chapel Hill market and worked in a Crop Mob[13] and a bit on my own at Ever Laughter in 2010 and 2011. We had this conversation in early October 2014.

BW: How did you become a farmer?

WC: The reason . . . that I started doing it, and I loved doing it, and I wanted to continue to do it is I was looking for something that I would be interested in when I was in high school. I had some service-learning hours that I needed to do (a requirement of Chapel Hill schools), so I volunteered on a farm the summer before my senior year and really enjoyed it. And from the get-go I knew that it was what I wanted to do. I didn't grow up gardening and didn't grow up with pets even! After high school I continued to work on farms, and studied at Carolina Central Community College, and did some internships, and then continued on. In the fourth summer that I was working on farms, I did the Plant at Breeze[14] incubator program. From there, I was looking to have my own farm. What landed me at Ever Laughter is that I was commuting about forty-five to fifty minutes from Chapel Hill up to Breeze Farms, which is really unsustainable for a quarter-acre incubator farm garden plot.

Before I started at Breeze I worked at Shady Grove Farm, which is now Heritage Acres Farm. That was Steve Moize's farm. It grew all kinds of

Fig. 3.7 Will Cramer.

vegetables, and he had fruit, and they had a lot of animals, and a lot of layer chickens as about half their operation.

BW: What got you so excited about it?

WC: Being outside, growing food, creating something. I was especially interested in sustainable farming and having a job that is enriching to the environment rather than destructive to the environment. That was my big concern, and it continues to be a concern. The impact we have on the world just passively by being a member of society made me pursue farming instead of a career that might have been wiser, or more popular. Before farming I thought I might be a musician. I was inexperienced and young and don't blame myself for not having a business plan at the time. I haven't had time to play music as much since I became a farmer.

The other farms I worked on were mostly produce farms. One in Pittsboro that is no longer there. And then I did a summer where I

WWOOFed[15] in New York and Pennsylvania, just to try to get more of a quick study of a lot of different operations. It was interesting but sort of self-selected for the type of farms that look for WWOOFers, which are not necessarily economically viable farms. But Breeze was the first time I ever managed a garden on any scale. There I first began to learn how to sequence things and make plans. It's what I'm still learning in my seventh year of farming!

So I started learning—experiencing—how to make plans and think about having things for the entire season. I certainly was not successful that first year, but it was a first step, and that's the point of Breeze. I sold produce in a little CSA [community-supported agriculture] to family and friends and at the Orange County farmers' market, which is now the Eno River market. I remember I had a lot of squash, tomatoes, and cucumbers and then a lot of sweet potatoes. I didn't have any data to draw on after that year, but what I really got out of the Breeze program was the chance to connect with Sam Hummel. Sam had just bought this piece of property outside of Hillsborough with a house, and he was looking for a housemate and for someone to turn this property back into farmland. And he had less experience and training than I did with farming. But he had a lot of smart insights from other experiences as well as being a clever person. At the time that he moved out to the farm he was doing IT [information technology] work for an organization that promotes sustainability in higher education. Besides IT work, he was involved in the content of what they were trying to do. So it was a good connection. I was looking for a place to farm, also to not be as far away from the Breeze Farm, and he was looking for both of those things. So I moved out there in August 2008.

BW: What was the biggest challenge scaling up from Breeze to Ever Laughter?

WC: I can think of a lot of things now. I can see things now that I didn't see then. We knew that we had a lack of infrastructure. We just built that up year by year, but we didn't have a lot of money to do that. I didn't have experience with equipment—it was missing in my training. It would be great if there were a class in how to run a tractor.

In our initial discussion we talked about a plan, knowing that I was going to do most of the farming and Sam was only going to be doing it half-time, and that it was mostly produce. We knew we wanted to have some chickens. And we started just looking on Craigslist and finding free chickens where they were available. We started out with a chicken tractor, something you drag on the ground, where chickens sit right on the ground, so the birds have access to the ground. We've seen improvement, certainly. We've become more efficient in some of our methods. We've gotten a tractor—we also got a second property with some investors, ten acres eight minutes away.

BW: What are the wider challenges, not just to you, but to sustainable agriculture? What limits farming?

WC: There is more unpredictability than any other industry. We're not in a building with a closed loop, we're working with the sun and the rain and insects and disease. *That's* why it's hard to farm. That's why industrial farming has been an attractive *short*-term option for so many people.

BW: What policies might help alleviate these problems? What can we do?

WC: The other problem is we live in a society that does not recognize the cost of food. There are customers that are willing to pay what we ask for it. But there are a hundred times, a thousand times more people in the location we're selling our products that are used to the convenience and the prices of going to the grocery store. And it's hard for them to see the incentive to get up early on a Saturday morning to pay more for our product. Even though we never hear "yours looks less fresh" or "your stuff is less flavorful" or "your stuff is so bland compared to the super-market!" It's totally the other way around.

BW: Could you sell more product from Ever Laughter? You have so much acreage, you have a certain price point you need to make. Are there people you're not reaching that you could reach with your production capacity?

WC: At this point, we could be more efficient. And more responsive to weather or disease. More experienced farmers will have seen more it-erations of different conditions and patterns. An example of a mistake based on my limited experience is that I have a field that doesn't drain that well which I grew cover crop[16] on. And then I intended to plant spring root [crop]s in it, including potatoes, onions, and carrots. I did the same thing in another field where I'd been able to kill my cover crop and plant the vegetables—but in this field I couldn't kill the cover crop, and I didn't know why I hadn't killed it. The soil was all turned up, it looked like soil I was used to planting in, we planted potatoes, and we put our onion plants in the ground—and three weeks later it was just grass. And there was no way I could weed it—this was a whole quarter-acre. The soil had never dried enough for the cover crop to die, but I didn't see that because the soil was different to what I was more accustomed to. So it was a total loss. Going forward, I've tried to grow a cover crop that a cold winter will kill, but that would require me to plant something far enough in advance to make sure the crop could get hold of the soil. And then it has to be a cold enough winter to kill and break down the cover crop before I want to work the soil. A conventional way of doing things is to just leave the soil bare, but that's not what we want to do. It's possible we will leave rows bare, or put down plastic. So I've learned to not plant spring roots after a lush winter cover crop.

This all goes to say that we could be producing more, in part by learning from mistakes and becoming more efficient. And hopefully we will be able to sell it all when we do.

BW: I know your farm was originally an African American homestead, and your neighbors are relatives of those farmers. What's your relationship like with your neighbors now?

WC: It was a farm until about thirty years ago, and before that for forty to fifty years. Whenever we get into a conversation with the older generation, they actually seem happy to share stories about how they worked the farm when they were kids. A lot of them tell us, "Yeah, we worked the farm when we were kids, that's why we're not doing it now!" But I feel like there's a connection for us to that generation. The younger generation, some of them are curious about what we're doing, but they don't have the experience of having farmed, and they don't have a strong interest in going into it.

We haven't really had any conflicts. And I've tried to be conscious of it. I try not to have an eyesore or stuff that really smells bad. I'm sure that to some, some of our projects have been an eyesore! I'm sure it's something they notice. We have one neighbor that used to mow what is now our garden as part of his lawn. And he still loves mowing the two acres of grass he has two or three times a week, keeping it an inch tall. So I'm sure he notices that we don't mow very often, and we have a lot of weeds in the yard, because we're busy farming. And we try to make it not look terrible. I've seen farms that look worse. But it is an active farm, and we don't have the budget or time to mow. I felt a little bad about it, and I was talking to him this summer, and he said, "To each his own."

BW: Pigs! When I met you in 2010 you had had pigs for a little more than a year. How did you end up with pigs?

WC: What got us into pigs was that Sam was seeing that in our first year of production we could benefit by diversifying our income sources. There was an idea that in order to be sustainable we want to be producing manure on the farm. Those are the main reasons. It was not because we love pigs, or we love pork. What is ironic about it is that Sam was a vegetarian, and I was raised kosher. So it was weird in the first place. We got them in October. We got three pigs from Bobby Tucker down at Okfuskee Farm in Silk Hope. The first batch was half Tamworth and half Gloucestershire Old Spot. And it seemed like those were highly regarded breeds, and we just happened to be friends of the breeders. We went to other farms over time looking for heritage breeds, preferably trying to support a farm that was raising rare or endangered breeds— but that's not easy to find, by definition.

When we first moved in we had the whole field plowed up and put into cover crop. There were still a lot of perennial weeds that would have a lot of roots on them. So we put the pigs on that field, and as it got into summer we gave them access to the woods. I know people think of pigs as little tractors, but I'm not really sure they work the field the way you'd want. They made the field all muddy, but there was still wiregrass. And they dig out pits, and we didn't have a tractor, so I had to fill the wallows in without a tractor.

We knew Bobby and learned stuff from him. We started with three at a time. After six or seven months, we got another three. And then we saw, "Oh, wait we're going to be running out of pork in two months," so we needed to be raising four batches of three so that every three months we take some in. Three pigs every three months. But when you go to pick up a pig from a small farm, there might be four pigs, and you don't want to just leave one by itself. Or you think, "We could make a little more money, why not just get an extra one?" But then the other thing that was different—once we had them staggered like that, it was difficult to rotate them that way. And we only had one set of fencing. We found . . . that when they were weaners, or feeders, like ten weeks old, they would stay in a little enclosure of pig panels for two months until they were ready to go into a larger paddock. But then we did have to deal with having pigs that are two feet tall, and some pigs that are three feet tall. There were complications doing that.

BW: How did you market your pork?

WC: We sampled a lot. We did pork chops and sausages. We always had Boston butts. We went between Acre Station and Matkins [processors]. We had some restaurant customers, but we were only doing three pigs, and we could sell some at the Chapel Hill market and then the Durham market. Among those customers, we could sell all the premium cuts and sausage.

BW: And four years into raising pigs, you give it up! What happened?

WC: I guess what went into the decision was, for one thing, Sam was getting less and less involved in the farm. He wasn't doing too much of the big tasks. The work with pigs is not a big thing each day. But the big things are getting the pigs, and then getting them to the slaughter-house, and then going to get the meat a week later. As he became less available I started doing more of that, but it was not good for the rest of the farm for me to spend so much time away from the gardens. The other thing is that it was Sam's instigation to raise pigs, and my heart was never in it so much as his. I was really happy to do it. But I guess—raising animals for me, the biggest part that I didn't like was taking them to the processor. The other thing is that I felt bad about not feeling more bad about it, if that makes any sense. It was very easy for me to get into treating these animals like animals and not like living beings. And they do have personality, and you can have some sort of connection, or you can see that they have connections with each other that make it different than raising vegetables. And I don't have any moral qualms about raising a carrot. Obviously I eat meat,[17] which I only started doing after being vegetarian for many years as I started farming. I thought mammals were a little too close to home. That sort of went out the window when I started raising pigs.

The other issue was economic. We could see from the numbers, especially with the meat, it's easy to see how we could make money with pigs, rather than vegetables. There are disease risks for sure with pigs, but in our experience there was less uncertainty about the animals than the vegetables. Because we were getting them when they were ten weeks old, and we had to keep them alive for six months. And just check them, make sure they're all right. If it rained, they went in their hut. They have legs, they move if they need to. Looking at the numbers, we could see that for the amount that we were making, we could make more money raising pigs than vegetables. Even though there are big investments of time, those were only every so often in a six-month period. What we could make per hour was a lot more with pigs than vegetables.

BW: And yet you still gave it up.

WC: Well, we could see that the way to make more than $3,000 every six months was to scale up with pigs. And then I'm not vegetable farming anymore because I'm not just spending thirty minutes on chores[18] every day, not only going to the processor every six months, I'm going every week. I'm spending all day worrying about tons of animals. That was really the big thing. I could see that at the scale we were doing, I didn't want to spend the time doing it at the scale we were doing it. And the only way I could make it worth doing for the amount of headache that I was already getting was to do it even more, and that was just not attractive to me. And I really like vegetables. We had crept up. The last two or three batches were six pigs, and it was scaling up, and it meant writing a check to the processor for thousands every three months. And I felt anxious about having freezers full of meat that could go bad if something happened. I could have kept at it longer to see if I could make it more efficient, but my heart wasn't in it. And then Sam wasn't there to put the time into it.

It's hard to imagine going back to raising pigs, especially now that I have a new partner who is a committed vegetarian. Although she never said, "Oh, you shouldn't raise pigs," she's now come on as the new partner, since Sam left to move to Durham. Sam still owns the property and we're leasing it from him.

BW: What do you see going forward?

WC: We need to be growing more than we are right now, and we need [to be] selling more than we are right now, and we need to find the markets, whether at the [farmers'] market or wholesale. We have restaurants, but especially this year we've fallen off on being able to cater to restaurant orders. So it's mostly been chefs coming to the market.

Yeah, the farmers' market is a huge drain of time, but it's the way to sell it in the most pure way, to sell it to the person that's going to eat it, not the person that's going to cook it for someone else that's going to eat it. It is still really meaningful, and it's fun, and it's fun to be there with all the other farmers, and it's hard to imagine giving it up.

PROFILE: Ross Flynn

—

Ross Flynn was raised in northeastern Ohio and came to North Carolina in September 2008 to work on the farm of his friend Eliza Sydnor. He has worked as a farmhand, on and off more recently, on Braeburn Farm and Cane Creek Farm since then. In the fall of 2014, he opened Left Bank Butchery in Saxapahaw. Saxapahaw is about twelve miles northwest of Chapel Hill and has grown up around the Rivermill, a residential and commercial complex that was built in what had been the Saxapahaw Cotton Mill for 150 years before it closed after a tornado. Ross and I met the week that I started doing research at Cane Creek Farm in 2008. We had this conversation in Saxapahaw as he was in the final stages of preparing to open Left Bank Butchery.

BW: How did you get the bug for meat?

RF: I left New York as the economy tanked. I came to North Carolina to work on a friend's farm. I had never really raised animals before. They liked me, and I liked the work. This is what got me to Cane Creek and Braeburn Farms.

I had some experience on the plant side. But I got to be outside with my friends every day, and it was beautiful—maybe if I'd shown up in January I would have decided to keep on going! It was supposed to be a couple weeks. And I was working there five years later, and working on how to open up a butcher shop that I bought from those two farms.

BW: And when did you know that you liked the animals—or was it meat?

RF: I knew that I wanted to be in agriculture, and I knew that I didn't want to be a farmer in the sense that I didn't want to rely on that as my sole income. I got to know farmers well enough that . . . [the problem is] being a small business owner, and being in an industry where the cards are stacked against you, or stacked for the big guys. And then you add that on to the fact that you're farming, so you're completely dependent on the weather—complete chance, fluctuating markets all the time that are really out of your control. Price of feed wants to double one year, you can't do anything about that. And then to boot you're dealing with

Fig. 3.8 Ross Flynn.

animals, which are just one more variable. And it just struck me as this crazy lifestyle. Which I totally respect, and so many of my friends do it. But just to be reliant on that for an income is gonna take years off my life. So I decided that I wanted to stay in food, and I had just taken a knack for butchery and the value-added side.

Also I decided to open up a butcher shop *here* in this town with these farms. I don't think I'd want to open up a butcher shop somewhere else, I don't want to work with other farms—this is my contribution to those farms and those friends and their way of farming. There have been a lot of butcher shops that have strayed away from their standards and look for lesser meat and don't tell their customers. And I *know* I won't do that, and the reason I won't be doing that is because—at the end of the day—that means I'm just cutting meat. Which is the day I could be working at a grocery store. Which is to say, I don't know the person that raised it, I don't know how they raise their animals. I just don't like cutting meat *that* much! To be bloody and sore from cutting something that you don't believe in? Well, that sounds miserable to me!

BW: When did the butchery present itself as a possibility?

RF: This was an attempt to control one of those variables I talked about. Everybody who's in the small-meat world knows that the processors are the bottleneck. It's not their fault, I don't blame them at all. It's a tough thing, and they've mostly been run out of business, but there's a truth that we've asked the same people to kill as to cut, and so the quality of the cutting suffers. So that's one variable.

And another thing is you raise this animal for a long time, you take it to the processor, pay all your processing fees, and then you go put it in the freezer and hope you sell it in six months. There's a lot of money that goes out, so our whole goal is: how do we sell every part of the animal? And how do we do it immediately, so that you don't add on more time. That, on top of the fact that we were often frustrated with the quality of the cuts and having to discount product for chefs all the time. I came and told the chef here in Saxapahaw, "I'll cut this animal. I don't *exactly* know what I'm doing, but I know the animal really well in my head, and I can do as good a job for you as what you're getting now." The first time I did it, I worked the first couple of days at the farm, came into the kitchen, cut it up. Did, actually, a really good job, and then I went back and worked the last two days of the week at the farm. And that was kind of a cool balance. And then at some point, one day in the kitchen became, "Well, you butcher this day and then make sausage this day—and then you start curing," and you start to have fun with it. And then I realized that, as much as I love being outside, my knack is more in taking the meat from the farmer and turning it into something good. I'm no charcuterie master, but I like handing it off to the kitchen and saying, here, turn this into something great.

How does the farmer take this awesome animal, get it to a chef who wants it ready to turn into a finished plate? And it's that middle process. It's kinda weird 'cause it doesn't sound very sexy, but I sort of like that middle. And I saw that step needs more emphasis.

You know, for the cows we raised it was sort of heartbreaking. You're raising its mother and then it's got this calf, and then you raise it for almost two and a half years. And it gets killed and it gets hung for three weeks, and then they cut it *terribly*. It was just so frustrating. I know it's a tough line of work.

BW: So you realize that there's this middle ground that needs to be developed—then what?

RF: The local food resurgence has definitely been dependent on cities— highly educated professionals in cities, let's be honest, with disposable income. That's very true, but there was also a part of me, when I worked at the farm and I delivered all this food to chefs—I wasn't frustrated that I had to drive to Raleigh; I knew that was necessary. But I also kept driving through Saxapahaw—this was my town, this was a farming town. It wasn't that I resented anybody else, it was that this food wasn't as accessible to the community that was raising it as I wished. You know, I get the question several times a week, "Why are you doing this in Saxapahaw? A whole-animal butchery? Who knows? I may eat my words here. Chapel Hill doesn't have this, Raleigh doesn't have this, Greensboro, Winston-Salem. It gets back to . . . I don't want to cut meat in a city. I want my farms to be my neighbors. I just wouldn't be rewarded enough to do this in a town. Those other places have a Whole Foods. And Whole Foods, you know, does a good job.

But I want to have this butcher shop for the rest of my life, and I want my kids to come to the shop after school and do their homework. If anybody ever wants to take over the butcher shop, I want people to come here and say, "That's where my dad used to buy his meat." That's the kind of business I want to have. I want people to say, "I don't know what I'm cooking!" and I can sit down with them and show 'em some recipes and talk to them, and say, "Well, this didn't work and this did. I had to start learning about the cuts if I was going to sell at the farmers' market. And a friend recommended the *River Cottage Meat Book* [Fearnley-Whittingstall 2004]. And it was the first food book I ever read that was written by somebody who understood how animals were raised. This was a book that said, "What are all the parts of these animals?" And then I had to start experimenting in my own kitchen. And it so happened that the meat I was able to get for free was beef tongue and ox tail and pork liver.

BW: But you never wanted to be a chef?

RF: Working on a line seems like some sort of misery! It's not just the lifestyle; I actually don't like restaurants. Which is not to say I don't go to restaurants or know wonderful people that run restaurants. But my big hang-up about a restaurant is that you sit at a table with somebody who's eating a different meal than you are. And to me, so much of food is about that *shared* experience. That's why your grandmother's lasagna is the best lasagna you've ever had. It's that shared experience that we have with it, and restaurants don't allow for that. Much as I love food, I want people to take home things to cook around their own house. And we'll also do ready-to-eat meals. But it's just one meal. So you can take it home, eat it in your pajamas, talk about school and do whatever you want to do because that's the way that food makes sense to me.

Restaurants are so limited in the cooking techniques that they can use. That's what I'm always telling people: you have so many more cooking techniques available to you than a restaurant does, because they have to have something that's ready to serve in ten minutes. Which means it needs to be 90 percent done before it's ordered. When I cook at home, no pressure!

BW: What are the nut and bolts of running a butchery in terms of getting it up and running?

RF: It falls under the same regulations as the restaurant here, so a lot of it I just got to know at the pub. I got to know so much about the sourcing side by just working at the farm. I'm guessing what sort of things people want in a butcher's shop. We're not going to have the abundance of a Whole Foods, and I don't want it. Because they throw away a lot of stuff. Too many options is not a good thing. So we're limiting this, hopefully making really personal connections. To me so much of what is fun about food is the personal connections to it.

BW: What about the space itself?

RF: We'd always kind of talked about putting a butchery here. It had to be in the building—there's just the one building in town! And it was connected to the restaurant, so that satisfied a lot of regulations. We have that restaurant partner, which is nice.

BW: How will you know that you've been successful?

RF: When people said, "Have you written a business plan?" And we have. It's tough because what we're doing is not being done. I don't know of another whole-animal butcher shop in America that can look across the street and say, "My cows are *right there.*" Everything we're doing is going to be different. We have the mobile unit.[19] There really isn't a script. But I'm willing to stay very late and come in very early. The nice thing about doing this in a community where I've lived for a while, I feel like I do have a lot of support. I know that it's going to take a whole lot more than my friends to keep the shop afloat, but I have so many friends that have helped make this happen. The friend who's a welder has done some welding for me, and the friend who's an architect is consulting on this. To me it makes me think that if we're going to create a different food system, it does wind up becoming a community endeavor. It makes it pretty rewarding, because at the end of the day you're still cutting meat, so you've got to be making a larger connection. Well, *I* need to.

Opening a business means learning new stuff every day, more stuff about things you knew nothing about. Every day you need to learn something you never knew. It wasn't quite a year ago that we smashed out a wall! But the whole project has been about a year and a half [in the works]. The construction has actually gone pretty smoothly.

BW: What do you know about Rose's?[20]

RF: I really like what they're doing. I do. I mean, our shop will have a different feel. Their shop strikes me more as like shops I've been to in New York City, California, Chicago. They do a good job! The quality is there; the shop is beautiful. But I want a little different feel here. I want people hanging out here, I want people talking about *agriculture*. That's something I can do. I know exactly how these animals are raised. That's gonna make for kind of a different experience. But they do a really good job!

I mean this really truthfully. I want people to have a really good experience when they go there. I mean, what are we going to do, squabble over the 1 percent of people that actually go to a butcher shop? Or are we going to say, "Hey, there's a real value in our line of work!" When people have good experiences there, I'm happy about that.

We have the pub, the mobile unit, a meat CSA—we'll use the mobile unit to go offsite to cross-fit gyms. When you're a whole-animal butcher shop and you're down to your last three sirloin steaks, it's not like there are more primals[21] back there that you can use to fill up your deli case. You're down to three. So, okay, let's vacuum seal them, put them in a CSA box, maybe slightly discount them. But the key to my shop is there should be really zero waste. Ideally, first someone buys it fresh over the counter; second, the mobile unit; third, the meat CSA; fourth, maybe the pub. But there's no reason to be grinding sirloins down.

What's really important for me is that when my farmers show up, I will write a check then and there. They've already put the feed costs into that pig. A farmer doesn't need a thirty-day net[22]—screw that! If you respect a farmer . . . we've asked Eliza to raise a pig that takes twice as long to raise as other pigs—pay her on delivery! That always bothered me. Our farm isn't some big Cisco!

We'll have other products. Some cheese, but we're going to have *four* kinds of cheese, that's it! And some fish that we may smoke. We'll do some lamb and goat. I'll have a backup—Firsthand Foods—for deli things. If we're going through a side a week, there's not enough of that for pastrami—so we'll tack on a couple of things that way. There's not enough belly for what people want, and bacon, so we'll supplement. They're doing a great job, Firsthand. They've made it so much more accessible for so many more restaurants. I really like what they're doing.

BW: What do you do about questions of scale?

RF: Every time diesel goes up, it affects beef prices. What we do differently, what we are doing is very connected. I'm committing to a farmer. We want to have the same farmers for years. Right now beef is at an all-time high, and I know that Doc [Sydnor, of Braeburn Farm] can sell those cows for top dollar. But he's committed to me, I'm committed to him, and that's not to say that prices won't go up. But somebody who comes along and says, "I'll sell you these hogs for half the price that Eliza does"—my commitment is to Eliza. I know exactly how she raises them, and I've told her, "I'm going to buy the pigs from *you*. Now if you can't provide me with all I need, I'll start adding to it. But I'm committed to your pigs." That is something that the free market doesn't respect. Without these relationships, it all gets on a really loose foundation.

4

PIGS IN PARTS

In the chapter on how a sense of place is developed through food, and how participants in alternative food systems come to think of their practices as oriented toward the local, I noted that locality itself comes to be an attribute, or a quality, that operates in this world. Locality can motivate actors, guide policy, and be engendered in concrete forms and institutions, as when farmers' markets limit their sales to producers who come within a certain distance from the market. One of the ways that these various actors often describe their desire for a more effective food system, and especially the way they understand these desires to be embedded in qualities of the local, is in terms of an interest in realizing a more powerful connection between themselves and the sources of their food. This notion of "connection" is one of the critical terms used by the locavores with whom I have worked as I developed my ethnographic project in the Piedmont of North Carolina, but it is plainly a global concern as well. The pursuit of meaningful connections is manifest in people's concerns and claims about the linkages between taste and place; cuisine and heritage; farmers and their market customers; and those who are included in and those who are excluded from communities of food production, provisioning, preparation, and consumption, as the evidence presented in this book clearly shows. In this chapter, I want to change the focus of this question by turning again to the problem of connections, this time considering associations between animals and connoisseurs (here I consider connoisseurship to encompass artisanal producers as well as their discerning publics) and, more pointedly and concretely, the relationships among the lives of animals, the meat they yield, and the craft that brings about that transformation. In exploring these relationships, I hope to interrogate, at the level of the particular, what qualities of connection are manifest in the discerning appreciation of the transformation of animal flesh into cuts of meat and to ask the general question of why connection should be such a privileged focus at this cultural moment.

A number of celebrated farmers and chefs have talked about the value of innovative slaughter and butchery processes to their enterprises. One of the central tableaux in Michael Pollan's *The Omnivore's Dilemma* is Joel Salatin's open-air slaughter facility, the "glass abbatoir" in which Salatin claims to demonstrate the value of transparency and integrity in the humane slaughter of his chickens (Pollan 2007, 226). Dario Cecchini, a Tuscan butcher who is much sought after by food activists as a speaker, extolls the moral virtues of proper animal slaughter and butchery (figure 4.1).[1] The ethnographic content of my discussion of processing and butchery draws on a particular kind of contemporary practice that is increasingly popular among enthusiasts of local meats—namely, artisanal butchery programs that offer clients an opportunity to see how cuts of meat are derived from an animal carcass and often to participate in the butchery. These activities can be usefully assessed by closely examining the performative dimensions of these events.

For example, I hope to show that questions about the participatory framework developed in these performances can reveal dimensions of ways that various social actors are not only situated in these contexts but also are qualified as participants to evaluate and appreciate the performance. These qualifications have implications far beyond the immediate context of the butchery events because they entail recognition of the kinds of qualities that are relevant for the various participants in the world (For example, what makes "good" meat? What motivates home cooks or chefs to seek out this kind of instruction? What is an effective demonstration?) and a grasp of the wider social context of which such performances are a part (for example, how artisanship differs from industrialization and how discernment is established, acknowledged, and challenged in social institutions). Attention to these innovative programs as cultural performances can, I suggest, provide us with a perspective from which to consider how particular modes and qualities of artisanship are involved in wider transformations of social and economic systems of value production.

Fig. 4.1 Performing butchery.

In addition to my attention to the performative features of these events, the nature of the questions they raise about enacting relationships between animals and people, *techne* and nature, and knowledge and practice, among other dialectical categories invokes a range of other anthropological concerns. Today, many commentators are drawn to the posthumanist dimensions of these relationships and of the entanglements of nature and culture and to the ethical implications these entail (Haraway 2008; Kohn 2013). But an older anthropology might frame these problems in terms of a different set of practices and ask, for example, how butchering animals can be grasped as a technology of social reorganization, or how food preferences can be assessed as a means of embodying an abstract order of socially relevant categories. These frameworks, of course, are equally concerned with ethical matters (White 2011). My intention is not to adjudicate among these approaches but to suggest ways in which contemporary problems are a part of abiding anthropological interests.

This chapter, then, has a series of nested ambitions. At the most concrete level I want to illustrate an interesting ethnographic phenomenon that speaks to a widespread, contemporary social movement. Furthermore, I want to show how considering the events I discuss here as a kind of cultural performance can illuminate some of the wider values at stake in this alternative food movement. And finally, I want to think reflexively about how changes in anthropological theory draw our attention to different possibilities in our ethnographic accounts. Overall, then, my hope is to reveal how our current commitments to an alternative food system both creates and depends on a particular set of sociocultural values.

Meat, the Carcass

The butchery programs I am interested in, with a paying clientele that has come for training as well as provisioning, are increasingly widespread, especially among clients and producers who are interested in local pasture-raised meat. Butchers, farmers, and processors offer programs that serve to promote their enterprises and educate consumers in a discerning practice.[2] I have detailed evidence from three rather different kinds of butchery performances that I will consider here. The first and most recent (2012) was the most straightforward of the three. It involved a single, two-hour demonstration of how to "break down" (that is, cut up) half a pig carcass into a variety of different cuts, carried out by a butcher looking to open a butcher shop in the community. The second (2011) was in some ways the most complicated of the three. It was a complex, multiform event undertaken over a few days as part of a meat conference that brought together farmers, chefs, activists, and educators interested in promoting pasture-raised and niche-market meats. The butchery programs at the conference included both hands-on activities, in which participants worked in teams with individual animal carcasses (figure 4.2), guided by experienced butchers; and a series of demonstrations led by one renowned chef who has developed his skills as both a butcher and a master of charcuterie. Finally, the earliest (2009) and most unusual of the three events did not involve a butcher at all, but rather a worker with over twenty years of experience at a small meat-processing facility who runs his own home-based butchery shop, which he uses primarily for processing deer brought to him by hunters. This event involved breaking down half a pig carcass into the principal primal cuts in which pork is routinely sold to retailers. One pig was used for two more or less identical demonstrations on consecutive days. What

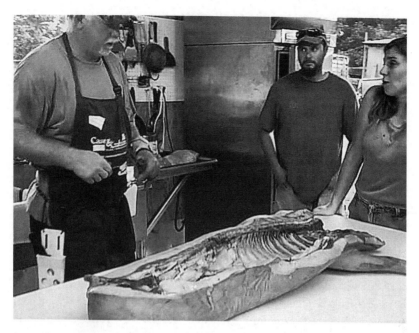

Fig. 4.2 Encountering the carcass.

added complexity to this otherwise straightforward demonstration was the fact that the first day's demonstration began with the slaughter of a live pig that was then "dressed" (that is, scraped and eviscerated) to be roasted as a whole-hog barbecue. In addition to the butchery demonstrations, each of these events also included snacks for the participants, which are not just ancillary enjoyments but, in fact, a demonstration of the wider ethos that joins farmers, processors, butchers, and consumers together in a farm-to-fork totality (see chapter 6). Furthermore, each of these events was a commodified form of instruction and entertainment, as what I will call the audience consisted of participants who had paid a fee for the opportunity to learn about butchery and to take home a sizable portion of meat from the animals being butchered. Indeed, these kinds of events, with a paying audience whose members have come for training as well as provisioning, are increasingly widespread for a public interested in enriching their understanding of meat.

To note an obvious point, all of these butchery demonstrations begin with an encounter with a pig carcass. Obvious though it may be, this moment is never just self-evident, and it entails some awkwardness or confusion on the part of the participants. At one event, the pig carcass that was meant for butchering that night had yet to arrive from the refrigerated facility where it had been kept overnight, so the crowd—snacking and chatting—anticipated its arrival for a few more minutes than they had expected. Aside from this uncertainty, the encounter with the carcass immediately clarifies differences between participants' expectations and the reality of the demonstration of the butcher's skills and the form of the animals in question. For example, in all of these cases the carcass of the pig that was to be butchered was presented as already "transitioned"—that is, as half a carcass, scraped clean of hair, eviscerated, and without a head.[3] Why no heads? Most small processors, like the ones who had killed the pigs used in these programs, stun the animals that are to be slaughtered with a single shot from a .22 to the head, and the U.S. Department of Agriculture does not permit animal parts contaminated by lead shot to be publicly sold. In any event, having the transition already done is a necessary dimension of the butchery event because the animal carcass cannot be successfully butchered until the meat has been allowed to rest and cool sufficiently. So these programs' participants always confront a day-old carcass, ready for cutting. What this encounter with the carcass reveals is a kind of hybrid (Latour 2012; Lock 2002), neither fully meat nor wholly animal, and this hybrid form leads to interactions that attempt to resolve this ambiguity. For example, the problem of moving the carcass to begin the demonstration was noteworthy and challenging. In the 2009 case, the carcass had to be lifted by two audience members (who had to figure out how to handle the eighty-five-pound half carcass) in its plastic sheeting and then laid out on the butcher's table for the audience to observe. At the conference facility in 2011, the half carcasses were laid out on separate tables before the audience members arrived, but even then, to demonstrate their butchery techniques, participants in the event had to lift and flip the carcasses. In all of these cases, then, the tactile encounter with the pig carcass was confounding and physically awkward for the participants.

There is certainly nothing surprising in this awkwardness for American consumers of meat who are rarely afforded the opportunity to observe the connections between animal life and the portions of meat they purchase, even at farmers' markets, let alone the typical grocery store. But of course it is precisely this absent connection that is the point of this kind of event. Participants are interested in hosting and attending these programs because they are committed to seeing for themselves how the transition from animal to meat occurs. Butchers promote these events because they see their skills as a method for educating a public that will learn to appreciate the craft and skill that they exhibit in demonstrating and con-firming that connection for their clientele. Consumers, on the whole, are hoping to get an improved understanding of what they are eating, where their food comes from, and how they might themselves learn to embody some of the skills that allow them to realize the connection between animal and meat. Yet the initial encounter with an already processed but not yet edible pig carcass produces not this fulfilling sense of skill and understanding but—in the primary tacit, embodied, tactile qualities of this performance—a sense of uncertainty. How do we handle a fresh (or day-old), cold, heavy carcass? How do we position it to begin converting the carcass into cuts of pork? Where can we touch the flesh so that we can recognize where the cuts should be made and avoid rendering the meat less desirable for aesthetic or hygienic reasons? The participants produce and enact for themselves a sense of the disorientation that is characteristic of the wider experience they have of meat that motivates them to attend these events in the first place. This fleshly discomfit invokes the very absence they al-ready know, and in this way it confirms a premise of these events—we do not know our meat, and we need to be shown what we need to know about it.

The conversations that accompany these encounters both confirm the uneasiness that can be observed in these embodied interactions and reveal more of its significance. In all of the examples I witnessed, the au-dience not only demonstrated some clumsiness around the carcass, but they also expressed some befuddlement about the pig and its carcass. For example, many people asked where the head of the animal was, since the heads had all been removed before the carcass was presented. One friend of mine wondered whether the blood had been saved during the slaughter-ing process, as he hoped to use it for a dish he had in mind. Other people wondered about how the pink, fleshy carcass had been produced from the mottled, hairy pigs they had seen pictured on websites and brochures for the local pigs these demonstrations were using. At the 2012 event, the pro-cessing of the animal was discussed in this way:

AUDIENCE MEMBER: So when you picked up the pig from the slaughter-house, were you able to get all the innards?

ZACH FRANKLIN[4]: They didn't give 'em to me. I didn't even ask. They ob-viously took the brain out . . . the liver's not too hard to get. . . . It's funny, because in California, when we would get whole pigs in, the kidneys would be attached . . . and we'd just get a bag of other stuff. Sometimes blood. . . . If you all had seen the meat that was going into that bucket that just said "inedibles"—it was kind of like a metaphor, I think in a way, when I looked at it. Like the amount of meat—

AUDIENCE MEMBER: You'd cry.

ZACH: Yeah! Like it was just getting *thrown out*—I don't know where it was going to end up, but it was unbelievable that these half-way skilled workers were just throwing it out.

At the event in 2009 at which a live pig was slaughtered and dressed for a whole-hog barbecue, the context of a similar conversation was a little different—the audience could actually see what was happening to the head, blood, hair, and so on of the animal—but the conversation nonetheless reflected the theme of uncertainty about how the animal is processed into a usable carcass more generally. Once the pig was scraped and eviscerated, people began to ask about various pig parts:

AUDIENCE MEMBER: Frank,[5] is there any offal there that, uh—got anything else that we should want?

FRANK: Well, here's his kidneys, 'at's his lungs.

FRANK'S RELATIVE: Where's the lights at?

FRANK: Right here.

AUDIENCE MEMBER: You ever eat any of them?

FRANK'S RELATIVE: Are they good? What [about] the lungs?

FRANK: The lights, yeah, the lungs, same thing.

FRANK'S RELATIVE: You just boil 'em till they get done and they're poofy. . . . Me and my momma used to love 'em.

The conversation turned to the pig's spleen and liver, chitterlings and casings processed from its intestines, and so forth.

Again, for a discussion of the disposition of the pig's body to occur at a butchery presentation is probably not surprising. But note how this discussion complements and amplifies the enacted uneasiness with the already processed animal carcass. Rather than asking, for example, about what techniques were used to slaughter the pig, how large the processing facility was, where it was located, or what the working conditions of the plant were like; or perhaps what farm the particular pig had come from, how it had been raised, or the environmental impact of the animal husbandry techniques that brought the animal to market—all questions, I should point out, that are routinely asked by consumers and chefs at the farmers' markets, high-end grocery stores, restaurants, and other venues that feature pastured pork for sale—the participants' performance and concurrent discussion focus on the carcass of the pig and its missing bodily form. In actions and words, the participants struggle to reinvent the whole hog, imagining its physical presence in its totality to fulfill the completed transition of the animal from living pig to edible meat.

Moreover, the commentary on the missing bits of the pigs is not just abstract questioning about porcine anatomy; rather, it focuses on the pig as food. Note, that is, how questions about the pig's lungs are tied specifically to the edibility of the pig—indeed, to particular means of preparing the parts of the pig (parts that, in fact, aren't generally available) for eating. One audience participant in 2012 joked about how he had been looking forward to trying pork shanks, but every time he went to Whole Foods they never had them—which led him to ask if they were purchasing only pigs that had no shanks! If their confusion about the presence of the carcass enacts their motivation to know where their food comes from, the discursive practice of these participants both confirms this need to know and supplements it by imagining a set of procedures that would unify the incomplete pig. This moves both backward to the missing elements of the pig carcass (the head, blood, and offal) and forward to the dishes that could be prepared from these missing elements (spongy lights, headcheese, and blood sausage). In this way, a completed process of transitioning from the living animal to its rendered flesh, cooked and eaten in its entirety, is envisioned. This imagining provides a kind of model in sentiment (a term whose significance I will return to) for the butchery demonstration as a whole—even prior to beginning the process of breaking the carcass down—as the audience and butcher together recreate the integral pig and, more importantly, for their mutual commitments to grasping the life, transition, breaking down, cooking, and eating of that whole animal as a unified procedure.

I might suggest, as well, that the anticipation of the pig as a totality also works reflexively on the participants in these programs. That is, their understandings of the pig also provide a way to characterize themselves as a kind of totalizing subject, one who does not just encounter the vacuum-packed piece of pork in a grocery store. Here the subject is engaged now in butchery, now in cooking, now in considering their appetite, and now in performing his or her inclusion in the network of other discerning actors. In short, there is a kind of utopian vision of overcoming alienated consumption that participants evoke in their experience of the program and, indeed, in their initial encounter with the pig.[6]

Conveying Vitality

Thus far my discussion has anticipated some of the argument I will make in chapter 6, which explores snout-to-tail cookery. There I will suggest that using all the flesh of a well-cared-for pastured pig exemplifies a deep concern with authenticity, a value that derives from what is conceived of as a direct, unmediated, and uncommodified experience of one's food. Those pursuing such authenticity find in the whole animal an icon of these productive practices. Certainly, the participants in the butchery programs I have been discussing in this chapter share this commitment to authenticity and understand it, again, in terms of the unmediated connections that are forged between the concrete animal, the skilled butcher, and the discerning consumer. Here, though, I want to develop a somewhat different perspective on these sociocultural forms of authentic values, and whole beasts. What is displayed in the performance of the butchery demonstration is not just the realness of the food or the seamless integrity of the ties between productive farmer and discerning consumer (as we have already seen, the processed carcass reveals gaps in this chain), but a particular experience of the vitality of the animal—indeed, a quite visceral sense of animal life. This vitality is also quite critical to the form and meanings of the connections that are made available to participants in these interactions.

Consider the way the butchers present themselves in each of these events. Each is equipped with an identifiable kit: an apron, a set of knives, and (almost always) a chain-mail safety glove. It is also not unusual to see butchers wearing a billed gimme (or baseball) cap (figure 4.3). It might be suggested that this apparel is strictly utilitarian—it protects butchers from dirtying their clothes with animal tissue and keeps their hair out of their eyes and out of the meat. If you have ever sliced your finger open while cutting meat, you do not need to be persuaded of the merits of a well-made chain-mail glove. But although I am not in any way undermining the legitimacy of its practical value, the kit's utilitarian nature is clearly part of the performative character of the butchery program. What is demonstrated is a particular manner of being put to use, practical, and handy. We see that both Frank and Erika[7] carry their knives in a holster made of either polyurethane or aluminum, which they affix to their hips by means of a heavy chain belt. Zach and Craig Diehl did not wear holsters but carried their sets of sharpened knives and sharpening steel (like the kind wielded by Frank) in a roll with compartments suited for the purpose of carrying these tools (figure 4.4). All of these elements of the kit, with their weight, durability, and sheer physicality, work to embody and convey the practical and engaged character of the skills of butchery. In the same way that a physician's white coat represents a kind of neutral detachment and lack of aesthetic flourish, which also works to connote authority and a dedication to an objectified biomedical truth (Goffman 1959, 200), the heavy metal of the butcher's presentation displays a dynamic, active body capable of withstanding—and inflicting—great force. From this perspective, even the ubiquitous gimme cap worn indoors suggests focused force.

I want to explore this sense of a physically active body further, moving from the butchers' apparel to their bodily motility (Merleau-Ponty 1962) to suggest a framework for thinking through relevant ideas about vitality and the human-animal relations that are in play in these demonstrations. We see Erika demonstrating the main muscle groups into which a pig is divided, groups called primals, through the use of her own body (figure 4.5). She turns away from the audience to show her back as the location of a pig's loin, the region from which pork chops and baby back ribs are taken. We also see the way that the butchers use their hands with the pig carcass, not only for purposes of demonstrating to the audience how to manipulate the carcass but also to show them how to know where the cuts of pork in the pig carcass can be found (figures 4.6 and 4.7). "I'm cutting the shoulder, I like to go—like four ribs," says Frank, counting down each rib with his gloved left thumb to guide his bone saw (figure 4.8). Zach shows us where loin chops separate from shoulder chops by feeling with his thumbs along the notches of the pig's vertebrae; Erika demonstrates the shoulder primal that includes the picnic and the butt (each cuts from the pig shoulder) in this shot and measures out the pork hock on the carcass. In each of these cases, the knowledge of what makes a recognizable and desirable cut of pork is an embodied skill (Grasseni 2004; Ingold 2000).

But the skill embodied by the butcher is not just a feature of the craftsman's body or experience per se. It is realized in the world and, quite concretely, in the body's engagement with its object. As the class talked with Frank about the different kinds of tools he had available to him in his job at the processing plant as opposed to in his home shop, he mentioned the

Fig. 4.3 The butcher's kit.

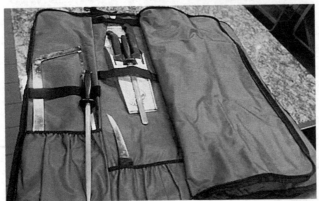

Fig. 4.4 Tools of the trade.

Fig. 4.5 Erika finding the loin.

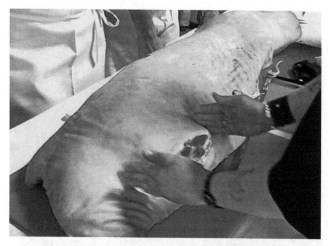

Fig. 4.6
Hands-on
demonstration.

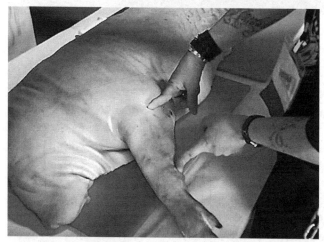

Fig. 4.7
Demonstrating
a pork shank.

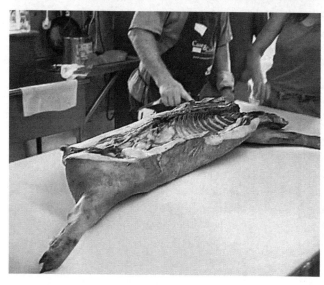

Fig. 4.8 Frank
demonstrates
where a
shoulder
begins.

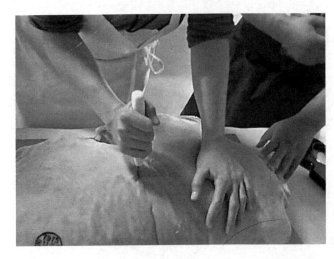

Fig. 4.9
A student
performs the
butcher's grip.

enormous pulley-operated Butcherboy bandsaw that was used for bisecting pig carcasses. After he told us that he was the only one at work qualified to do the job, I asked him how he knew where to butterfly (or halve) a pig carcass properly. "When you got the whole hog together," Frank told us, "you can see where it's a *crease* in its back, just like every one of us has got one—you can see the crease right down the back." That is what he uses to guide his saw. The program that Erika led was the only one I attended in which the audience participated, not just by watching and questioning the butcher at work on a single demonstration pig, but also by handling their own animal carcasses (we cut pig primals and boned out a whole chicken). To facilitate our learning, Erika instructed us in the technique of breaking down a carcass in a number of ways. She had everyone feel where the cuts were to be made ("we can see the knee right here—if everyone wants to feel that"), and she showed us how to handle a knife in a "butcher's grip," making a stabbing motion that produces a long, straight, clean cut (figure 4.9).

"When you're cutting large animals," she told us, butchers "use their shoulders more than their wrist, [but] make sure your hands are far away because, if you're using that weight, you could really cut your finger off." As she instructed us in this technique, it was hard not to notice that she was cutting through the shoulder of the carcass, and that the strength and weight of this large muscle was palpably present in both the pig's and her own (vulnerable) flesh, as well as in her dexterous motion.

What these examples and Erika's demonstration of the position of a pork loin by referring to her own spine demonstrate are the ways that the embodied skill of butchery emerges out of its encounter with the animal body. These butchers' techniques are incorporated into their habitus, but, just as significantly, the butchers come to grasp their own bodies as exemplars of the modes of skill that they command. In this way, the body of the pig shapes their own bodily form and motility. Like the physicality and directed potential demonstrated in the butchers' kit, the motion, technique, and activity of their craft bespeaks a forceful command of one's own body, the body of the animal, and one's own body as an animal body.[8] This reflexivity—the way that the body of the pig derives from the body of the butcher, itself understood through its tactile, heavy contact with the pig—suggests a framework for thinking about such butchery demonstration as ways of articulating a wider concern with vitalism. The liveliness of the animal and its capacity for generative production—for bringing forth potent forms, not only of nutritive substance or mere flesh, but also of creative, active strength and vigor—are revealed in the kinds of mutual constitution that inform the butchering and porcine body.

This vital potential, for example, informs the way that the carcass is understood to yield cuts. The butcher does not follow Plato's image of a roast that is to be carved up at the joints in keeping with the natural divisions of the animal's body,[9] although a certain image of the animal's body does inform the cutting process. In general, all of these programs follow standard U.S. practice and nomenclature. They begin with the premise that a carcass is made up of primals—typically, four large sections: shoulder (foreleg), loin, belly (or middles) and ham (rear leg). Occasionally the primals are expanded to include two more, with the shoulder divided into the butt and picnic and the middle divided into the belly and ribs. The invitation to the 2012 program I attended told customers they would "learn why using whole animals is not only more economical, but also how it benefits you and the farmer. We will be breaking down half a hog from primals down to sub-primals, which are more manageable to work with." What makes a particular part a primal, then? Even this little, slightly confusing invitation contains clues to the category. A primal creates a "benefit" shared by the farmer and the consumer, and it is the foundation for cooking the meat derived from the primal.

When butchers describe to their audiences the process of "breaking down" a hog they emphasize two pairs of *qualia* (Chumley and Harkness 2013; Munn 1986), perceptible potentials that guide much of the butchery process: toughness and tenderness, and slow as opposed to quick cooking techniques. What makes for a tough or tender primal? The shoulder is the quintessential tough cut. As Zach described this primal, he talked about separating the butt from the picnic and said of the picnic: "The best use for this is because—since it moves around so much, this is really good for sausage and stewing. It has a lot of collagen and different—moving tissue that has more flavor, but it's not as tender."

Note, then, that there are different features of the primal that contribute to its toughness. First is the substance of the shoulder, since it contains collagen and "different" tissue. Chefs and farmers at market often talk about tough primals and subprimals as having a lot of connective tissue that defines the character of the cut. This substance is further derived from the activity of the animal, since a muscle that moves repetitively and bears a great deal of the animal's weight—like a shoulder or a ham—develops both the distinctive tough substance of the primal and—this is crucial—the flavor of the meat. In significant measure, then, toughness derives from the life of the animal—the use of its muscles transforms their substance and texture, creating a distinctive anatomical feature that is then registered (in the body of consumers) in the flavorful or rich taste of this meat. For this vital connection between pig and person to be created via flavor, the primal has to be prepared in a certain fashion, either ground into sausage, cooked slowly in a stew, or perhaps smoked. Thus, the primal is constituted by a set of integrated relationships among animal movement, bodily substance, culinary practice, and sensory quality.

I must admit that I have been selling (and cooking and growing) tender pork chops and rich pork butt, or ribs laden with connective tissue to Piedmont customers for so long that writing this account occasionally feels as though I am simply stating the obvious. Shoulder is tough and needs to be slow cooked, so it yields succulent meat; loin is tender and should be cooked quickly, so its intramuscular fat retains the juiciness of the meat. It takes some comparative work to recognize that these are not just transcendent porcine truths but learned techniques of discernment. But comparison—even relatively close to home—shows there is more than one way to slice a pig. To begin with, one of the most revered of pork preparations in the Carolinas is whole-hog barbecue, in which an entire (dressed) pig is slowly cooked over smoldering embers in a shallow pit or in a large steel drum, which produces the same result. The distinctions between the tough and the tender are obviated here, since everything is cooked slowly and chopped into a mound of meaty goodness (for a further discussion of this process, see the profile of Sam Suchoff below). Moreover, virtually any feature of the pig's body can be cooked quickly and appreciated for its tenderness if it is butchered differently. As Alex Blanchette (n.d.) points out, much of the industrial pork production system in the United States has been transformed by the Japanese predilection for thinly sliced pork shoulder that can be quickly sautéed or grilled. A friend of mine who had trained as a chef in Spain told me how he had used a Berkshire hog shoulder that he had had specially shipped to him from the farm where it was raised in Missouri (in preference to the local pork he could get in Carrboro), because these whole shoulders could be broken down to yield the celebrated Spanish cuts of *secreto*, *presa*, and *pluma*—tender cuts that come from the shoulder or the spinal column that joins the loin to the shoulder. Belly, a characteristically tough primal, also yields (as everyone knows, right?) bacon, which may not be tender but is certainly quick cooking (not that slowly braised pork belly is not fantastic).

What this comparative evidence suggests is not that tough and tender cuts or slow and quick cooking techniques are merely symbolic forms, or that primals are simply cultural categories—or worse, that they are merely artifacts of the butchery performance. In fact, these are plainly material qualities, as inextricably a part of the meat and muscle of the carcass—when butchered into primals as these cuts are understood—as lard and bone. But it is equally true that they acquire their value as qualities (that is, tenderness or toughness becomes accessible and desirable) by being incorporated into the primals in the fashion that these butchery programs emphasize.

To push this point further, I would also note that the relative values of these different qualities are weighted differently in ways that reveal interesting points about how and why meat—and especially pastured pork—is desired in the ways that it is today. It was a bit surprising to find that the members of the audience at the butchery demonstration run by Frank much preferred to take home not the tender cuts but the tough ones of belly, shanks, jowls, and even heads to prepare for a fund-raising potluck that the program was intended to support. The members repeatedly passed over the export rack—a length of ten pork chops that incorporates the loin and tenderloin cut from the lean and tender lower back of the pig (and so is significantly more expensive than any other cut of pork sold)—until someone (who had already claimed some belly) agreed to try to make something with it. Indeed, in both the program run by Zach and the one run by Erika, we were instructed in the merits of slow cooking, braising, and low and slow roasting the cuts of pork that were less likely to be found in supermarkets. Just as the collagen-rich tissue from the shoulder that has more flavor, tougher cuts were seen as iconic of the benefit shared by the consumer and farmer. The butcher's knowing practice produced knowing customers, who could be both discerning of quality and economizing in their culinary practice, complex qualities that are most ably captured in the toughest primal cuts of the pig carcass.

I hasten to point out that toughness as a quality of the meat as performed in the butchery class is the same quality that is performed in the butcher's kit and in the ways butchers use their bodies—in a butcher's grip and their routinely referring to their own bodies as flesh. That is, toughness is a quality—or, more accurately, a qualisign (Chumley and Harkness 2013; Munn 1986; Peirce 1955) that is not only bodied forth in these performances but also serves to create a point of contact between the butchers and the pigs they both act on and realize for their audiences. This quality is clearly a primary feature of the vitality of the human or animal under consideration, a way in which the very life of the pig becomes featured in these butchery performances.

It is also interesting to note how closely these qualia of toughness and tenderness track to the gendered characteristics of these performances. My point is not that the practices are especially masculinist; in fact, just the inverse may be true. As my discussions with Jennifer Curtis and Sarah Blacklin (profiled above) indicate, it is remarkable how women in farming have taken especially to livestock production. For many women, working with animals is, as some put it to me, a way of showing their commitment to caring about the well-being of animals and the health of other people who will eat the meat from their livestock. And the burgeoning interest of women in meat often goes beyond agricultural practices to include butchery—many programs have been developed that target women who want to develop their butchery skills. Toughness, then, might be seen as a quality that suggests overcoming the initial challenge to conventional gender expectation that butchery might connote. As Blacklin notes, many women become interested in livestock, meat, and butchery precisely because they want to overcome these conventional expectations, and toughness—which many women embody through their skills, discernment, and tastes—is precisely the quality that concretizes this challenge to expectations.

Respect Your Meat

This vital correlation between human and nonhuman animals provides a means for realizing the ways that performative settings like these butchery programs (and farmers' markets, tastings, cookery demonstrations, and so on) are integrated into a wider set of concerns that have to do with the sociopolitical implications of food provisioning in the United States. If we look at how these butchers emphasize the moral implications of their actions—how butchery creates benefits for consumers and farmers and, more generally, is intended to promote the marketing and consumption of niche-market meats—we can see their interest in vitality as of a piece with their ethical commitments. Performing the vital qualities of the meat they both purvey and demonstrate for their audiences allows these butchers to materialize the ethical force of their work. These performances thus make manifest the health of the animals, as well as of the consumers who will eat their meat; the well-being of the farmers whose work is revealed in the fine animal carcasses they produce; and the flavorful character of meat derived from animals that move around and come in the more interesting varieties of specialty breeds. Vitality, in part, derives its significance from the encompassing context of industrial agriculture and confined animal feeding operations that, as we have seen, dominate the American meat provisioning system, especially in North Carolina. At the same time, attention to this vitality can alert us to several related questions: why has meat suddenly captured the imagination of food activists of all sorts (from committed vegans to old-timer barbecue pit masters), and why has butchery become a form of interactive entertainment? What—to use a classic idiom—makes meat so good to think (and play) with?

To address these matters, I want to take a slightly different approach to this ethnographic context, one that is less typically associated with the contemporary study of food and the political economy of things culinary. In a recent article on hunting and its epistemic and ontological implications in a First Nations community in the Canadian Yukon, Paul Nadasdy encourages us to take literally the extremely well-known claims of peoples in these and historically related communities to the effect that nonhuman animals are engaged in relationships of sociality, communication, and exchange with their human counterparts. Rather than dismiss such claims as mere approximations of "scientific" understandings or reduce them to "cultural constructions" of Western "others," we might strive to "build a theoretical framework that can accommodate the possibility that there might be some literal truth to what hunters tell us" (Nadasdy 2007, 37). While my concern here is not necessarily to develop either epistemological or ontological models that can legitimate the kinds of uncanny claims about animals that First Nations hunters—and Nadasdy himself—make, I am interested in the substance of these claims about animal sociality and what implications they have for the decidedly Western concerns with meat, butchery, and cuisine that I have focused on here.

For the hunting communities in question, animals are often claimed (and seen) to engage in relationships of reciprocity with their hunters. As one of Nadasdy's neighbors told him, one should never feel bad about the unnecessary suffering of one's prey. Rather, the "proper reaction . . . is simply to say a prayer of thanks to the animal. It is disrespectful to think about an animal's suffering when you kill it" (2007, 27). Another told him that hunting is "like at a potlatch": "If someone gives you a gift at a potlatch, it is disrespectful to say or even think anything bad about the gift or to imply that there is some reason why they should not have given it to you" (27). Taking animal life, then, engages a hunter in relations of reciprocity with animals. Their very lives are "given" to the hunter, and they must be properly thanked to show respect for this gift.

This formulation of prey as gift—or "the gift in the animal," as Nadasdy puts it—casts an interesting light on the contemporary U.S. phenomena I am examining here. To begin with, I am always struck by the language that is used to describe chefs' and butchers' relationship with animals and their interests in niche-market meats. For example: "Not long ago, chefs got credit simply for knowing the breed of the pigs or chickens they served. Pork from Berkshire pigs was the must-have meat status symbol, and chefs engaged in nose-to-tail competition to use the most parts of the animal. Now, it seems, intimacy with the animals during their life—and preferably, their death—is required" (Moskin 2008). Or consider this post from Butcher's Grip, at the time an anonymous blog tied to an underground charcuterie program and now affiliated with the (no longer blogging) Butcher & Larder shop in Chicago. Why, the blogger and butcher asks, does a customer seek out one-on-one butchery instruction? "It is about respect. Respect for the animals. Respect for the farmers. Respect for the little guys like me that will try and convince you to trust me when, while I may be out of the skirt steak you need for your fajita party, the sirloin flap will do just as well . . . and cost you a little less. And respect for herself" (Butcher's Grip: December 6, 2010). I have dozens of ethnographic and media accounts of how participating in animal butchery and slaughter produces a valuable relationship with the animal that allows the chef, butcher, or consumer to demonstrate his or her "respect for the animal world" (quoted in Hanel 2013). Plainly, there is a way in which taking the life of an animal—and knowing how to carefully and properly convert its flesh into food—is grasped as an ethical practice that entails an appreciation of the sociality of animal actors whose lives demand respect and are exemplars of a wider world of respectful things. In other words, the animals are moral beings in a moral universe.

This notion of "respect" seems to invoke the spirit of the gift that Mauss (1954) identified in his celebrated essay, and that generations of scholars trolling in his wake have referred to. It is critical to note, in the butchery context, as many others have in different contexts, that this "spirit" is not simply an abstract sociological principle, the obligation of reciprocity. The spirit of the gift is not a metaphorical projection from human relations onto extrahuman forms (Nadasdy 2007); rather, it is iconic of the qualities at stake in the transaction (Gell 1977; Munn 1986). That is, the moral characteristics of respect that these hunters, butchers, and connoisseurs demonstrate is something that inheres in the animal and their treatment of it. In this regard, respect is iconic in the further sense that it resembles the processes through which it is produced (Munn 1986; Turner 1968). The respect for animal life that both orients these actions and is generated by them is manifest in the careful attention to the welfare of the animal; the knowledge of the connections among the farmer, animal, butcher, cut, and cooking that these programs cultivate; and the intimacy of appreciation of the animal that derives from attending to its death. In each of these dimensions, respect is a kind of value that runs parallel to the concrete forms of vitality that I have described as materialized in the butchery performance in the same way that transcendence, for example, is a value that is manifest in concrete aesthetic forms, like perfume (Gell 1977) or that fame is a value that is materialized in the ordering of relationships across spatial and temporal orders (Munn 1986). What is especially useful about considering respect as a kind of value and vitality as its material underpinning is that it allows us to see how vitality is a product of social relationships between humans and nonhumans. Vitality is not simply a given feature of life itself; rather, it is a quality that has to be (re)-infused into the animal-as-food (something that advocates of animal welfare feel that industrial confined animal feeding operations undermine) so that meat can become once again a medium of moral integration and thereby an expression of well-being and legitimacy.[10] In these ways, animal vitality is an especially apt focus for the process of revitalizing what many see to be a corrupt and degraded food system, so it follows that meat has captured our imaginations and become especially good to think with.

That said, I want to offer a slightly amended version of this framework to clarify the nature of the moral force entailed, the forms of sociality that produce this force, and the qualities that are materialized in the practices of butchering and preparing good meat, all of which are promoted by this complex of activities. If we accept the fact that these practices permit one to demonstrate respect for the life of the animal, then it must also be noted that butchery, like hunting, is clearly a way of taking the life of that animal. We can think of this respectful taking as generating a form of reciprocity; but I think it is more useful to think of taking the life of the animal as an act that is understood to entail and generate certain moral obligations. Once the animal's life is taken, it is not entirely clear who bears the obligation to make a return on that gift, and to whom.[11] It might, then, be helpful to examine other modes of life taking that are understood to demonstrate and create a moral force—to wit, sacrifice—to both comprehend the ties across these diverse practices and specify the nature of the values, especially the moral obligations, that are created by events like butchery programs for the food cognoscenti.

It is telling that the spirit of these gifts is most fully revealed in the death (and butchery and consumption) of the animal. Making death the prerequisite for experiencing intimacy with an animal and thereby demonstrating one's respect for it fetishizes death in the Marxian sense—that is, it renders it as a transcendent force that both ably represents certain features of animals' social life and obscures and mystifies other features of it (Marx 1977; see also Comaroff and Comaroff 1990). Thus, respectfully taking the life of the animal (through hunting or processing) becomes an alibi for the well-being of the animal, but also for ecological sustainability, and humane considerations more generally.[12] It is not hard to see that what might be obscured in this focus on death is the wider biological-cum-social life of the animal. By that I mean the processes of breeding, husbandry, and so on that involve caring for the animal before its death; but also, quite crucially, the social conditions of this animal care and the welfare of the labor that sustains this husbandry,[13] as well as the strictures that exclude a great many participants from sharing in the values of the humanely slaughtered and expertly butchered pasture-raised pig—that is, the price of such meat.

The ways that animal death draws our attention both to what is illuminated and what is obscured in animal life, and the ways this process of value production can be grasped as a social technology of including and giving authority to certain social participants while excluding others, nicely situates these butchery programs[14] in the arena of sacrifice. Valerio Valeri calls sacrifice "an efficacious representation," one in which those making the offering (the "sacrifier") produces a mimetic image—an icon—of "what the sacrifer wants to obtain and of the condition for its realization" (1985, 67; see also Loisy 1920). Sacrifice, then, is a form of effective symbolic action, one in which participants create an image of the conditions they confront and then act on that image to produce an experience that transforms those conditions (and thus reflexively see themselves as the agents of that transformation). In Godfrey Lienhardt's work (which directly influenced Valeri's model) symbolic action, as Lienhardt puts it, produces a "model" of its agents' conditions (their hopes, ambitions, intentions, and so on) that can then be acted on to control "a set of moral and mental dispositions" (1961, 283). Symbolic action, and sacrifice in particular, constitutes a transformation in the world—it does not merely represent it—because it brings about a change in the moral condition and mutual obligations of the participants in the rites and, therefore, in the experience of the participants as capable of undertaking effective action (291).

Above, I described the various ways that the totality of the living animal is imagined in these butchery programs as a process that creates what I called a model in sentiment. This model is also iconic, in the sense proposed by Valeri. It is meant to resemble the living form of the butchered animal in a host of ways that evoke the overall vitality of the pig that the participants aspire "to obtain and . . . the condition[s] for its realization." What is crucial, then, is that this model is an expression of the moral commitments of the participants, of their hopes of bringing about a transformation in the industrial system of food production that they aim to confront and of making a powerful, knowledgeable connection to local farmers, butchers, and food. Like all sacrificial acts of expiation, then, these butchery programs are not performed as oblations to otiose beings, but they do perform a moral violation (i.e., killing) to affirm the truth of an envisioned wider moral universe (Hubert and Mauss 1964). That is, to affirm their commitments to animal vitality as a moral force, the attendees have gathered together to properly, thoughtfully, and carefully, engage with the violence that is done to a living pig to turn it into pork worthy of respect. They act on the model in sentiment of animal vitality that they create to define and qualify themselves as full participants in this vitality—as capable, responsible, ethical consumers whose respect for animal life is affirmed in their control of the moral dimensions of this consuming experience.

Conclusion

By characterizing these classes as performances and using a rather classic anthropological framework of sacrifice to analyze them, I in no way intend to dismiss or denigrate the commitments that bring these participants to such programs. It should be clear that I have participated in these programs, and my conversations with other participants have generally revealed that we have many of the same commitments to animal welfare and environmental stewardship, as well as a well-braised pork belly. At the same time, I think that these analyses should alert us, as I have indicated, to some of the mystified character of these values, and that point brings me to some historical and sociological considerations. To begin with, the notion that this concern with vital connections is a revitalization of traditional techniques of animal husbandry and food provisioning—a claim that is widespread among many advocates of these alternative food systems—is problematic. It is not hard to demonstrate that any number of heritage breeds or old-time farming methods are contemporary innovations. It is also true that communal hog killing that uses every last bit of a pig has been—and is still—practiced in eastern North Carolina for generations, while artisanal butchery is an invented tradition. My discussion of heritage in chapter 3 demonstrates that these practices are less continuous with a forgotten vein of ongoing practice than they are with ways of valorizing the idea of continuity as a means of confronting pressing contemporary political concerns. This group of connoisseurs' search for the vitality of animals as the ground for offering respect to them in the ways they are killed, butchered, and eaten strikes me as all but unimaginable in the absence of a history of land, labor, and animal degradation that is so strongly felt by many in this region and around the world. But that history has transpired, and I think there is little value in pointing out, merely for the sake of doing so, that claims of heritage and renaissance are largely baseless. If this is an effective strategy for countering the effects of financialized agricultural production and animal confinement operations, then perhaps we should say only: more power to it.

Of course, this raises other questions: Is it an effective strategy? Or do the same interests that promote the transformation of the regional political economy in the so-called New South also promote the modes of ethical consumption that buttress these niche markets? Certainly, many of the strongest supporters—the most loyal customers and many of the new breed of farmers—of these niche markets are products of the demographic shift in North Carolina that has made high-tech Big Pharma, banking, and insurance leading industries in the state. It is too facile, though, to say that pastured meat is an elitist delicacy relevant only to those that can afford it. The same activists who promote grass-fed beef and heritage hogs also point out that U.S. food policy maintains low food prices by hiding the real price of food, privatizing the profit on cheap food while spreading the costs in environmental destruction and human health (see, for example, the profiles of Jennifer Curtis and John O'Sullivan above).

How does this relate to the butchery programs at hand? Plainly, these activities are not, and cannot be, for everyone. But do performances like these work to turn communities of shared interest into self-secured enclaves, transforming the political into the personal at the expense of direct political engagement? Or might they be ways of formulating problems—creating efficacious representations of moral commitments—that offer ways of modeling more dynamic and inclusive action? Even if this is the case, could such models of action become so inclusive and so widely disseminated that they might effectively confront the enormous social, political, and economic interests[15] that are so pervasively powerful in the food system today? What alternatives do we have? What strikes me about these performances, as I suggest here and throughout this discussion of porcine matters in the Piedmont, is that they extoll the virtues of connection and felt and shared experience, yet they turn a blind eye to (or perhaps mystify) questions of just what counts as a connection and what does not. Who is connected? And who might be excluded by the practices of connection performed here? Clearly these are persistent questions for the niche market in meat and for this book. If the commitment to knowing your food that motivates so many endeavors is limited to intimacy with the life of the animal held in the butcher's grip, then the possibilities of generalizing the potency that is generated in these demonstrations are rather slim. If they can be harnessed to reframing our moral commitments to wider forms of social vitality, then perhaps there is room for optimism.

PROFILE: Kevin Callaghan

—

Kevin Callaghan is the owner of and chef at Acme, in Carrboro, North Carolina. I met Kevin through my work at the Carrboro Farmers' Market, where he is a weekly fixture. We had this conversation at the bar of Acme one morning in August 2010.

BW: What do you think motivates the changes we've seen in food in recent years?

KC: I think that one of the things that we all do is we project out a future that we want to be a part of, and then we work in that direction. And in food I feel like that's something that you see happening. You see people making those decisions. For so many people the essential pieces of their lives seem out of control. But food is now something they can rein in—like, "Oh, I can actually control this and feel sane about this"—because so many other things that you do are so insane. I think food is a very central place where people can grab hold of something. Also the idea integrates with a feeling that people are reconnecting with. I'm sure grocery stores once had that kind of feeling, that they were small. And people like my grandmother's generation, they wanted desperately to get away from that. They wanted to go into the really clean store. It is all about how you imagine your future. For us it's become about feeling that we've lost something, that something is missing. But at one point the idea was I want to be as progressive as I possibly can. And frozen food is going to be the most progressive, easiest, and it also makes me the most advanced, cosmopolitan person I can be.

There's this thing that occurs in the United States—we want to grab onto so many pieces. And it's a thing you *can* do. You know somebody who wants to change a tomato so that you don't have to use Roundup on it. We can't say, "No, that's bad!" We're having this conversation because technology has made it possible to talk about these things. I get frustrated by people who want to make farmers, or restaurants, or whatever "quaint." I think it's because it's the only model available, because as Americans we only look backward. I think there are these esoteric ends of arguments that occur because we're in this bubble. I think with food, what we think about a lot in the restaurant—our responsibility is like a river of culture that's running. You're continuing a

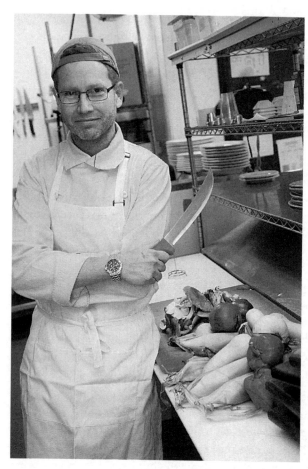

Fig. 4.10 Kevin Callaghan.

tradition, because sometimes restaurants say they're more important than the culture and that sort of narcissism can be wildly successful for a *while*. But restaurants—and this is what we really think about a lot—restaurants are changing. Twenty years ago restaurants were formal. Sure, there was fast food, but people did not go out to eat at the range of restaurants. I think that restaurants are benefiting from the fact that people are reevaluating where they're spending money. And they're thinking, "Gosh, my money is better spent going to dinner, because I'd rather spend my energy doing *my job*."

BW: Isn't there a way that restaurants benefit from knowing about cooking?

KC: Those people may be the leaders; they're the people that other people talk to. But I think by and large the nonelitist clientele that you want to cater to are the ones that feel like they are getting a good deal. And this has to do with why cheaper cuts of meat are coming back, too. People can feel that they don't have to spend a gazillion dollars. And that's what chefs are supposed to do. It's silly for restaurants to buy expensive cuts at farmers' markets—chops, hams. I mean, you can, but those chops can be sold on a retail level—but restaurant customers shouldn't want to pay that price. I mean that's part of the game, and that's fine for me. Our job is to provide local food in a way that makes sense. Okay, now we're starting to make that bridge and that connection that we really want to do, but in a thoughtful way. Because a lot of people want to do it and go, "Dammit, it's local—you should eat it!" But local has to be *better*, or it's going to fail. We used to get a certain type of burger, and then we switched to an all-natural product, but people didn't like it. And we got immediate feedback. Since we switched to Braeburn [Farm's beef] there's been none of that. So obviously the flavor profile was good.

BW: How do you deal with inconsistency in a product?

KC: You can't do anything about it, but you have to be aware of it. It's curious, there's this low maintenance phenomenon. Somehow there's this notion that human action is bad. If nature does it, it's fine. There are these natural wines—they're really expensive, and they're just not good. A lot of people who have intellectualized the process get really into this. This low maintenance thing really interests me, because if you're in a restaurant you're all about the human piece. So let's bring our human values to bear on it.

One of the things that I experience in the restaurant—and it's a big cultural movement, and I haven't really figured out how to embrace it—there's a lot of young people that come to work for me who are vegetarian or vegan, which is great, but it's almost as if they are ashamed of that part of themselves. They don't want to make a footprint. Sometimes they're making their choices as an attempt to say, "I'm not bad!" We've created this idea that human action is just a danger. And we just moralize everything now!

Another piece of this Slow Food thing is that by and large in Europe you have old family land. And money making *is* a huge piece of this movement. For a restaurant to make money you have to get a lot of things right, and then get lucky, and then push and push and push. In low-margin businesses, like restaurants or farms it's a cash flow issue. And once your restaurant crosses a certain level, all of a sudden you're making money.

And I really appreciate how that works for farmers. The thing that I had to learn is you have to pay all of your bills immediately. In a small town you need to pay as you go. Because there's this tendency of restaurants to glom their integrity off of their farmers: "Look how good we are because we are talking to this person!" My integrity is that I pay you. That's my responsibility. I know that's my number one job. There was one time—this guy was delivering blackberries to me. For whatever reason, there was no next time, and I owed him like 100 bucks. That's the sort of thing that makes me crazy. When you do that, then you begin to sort of . . . connect. I pay everyone as we go.

BW: As chef, why do you think pork and the pig seemed to take off?

KC: It's really adaptable to lots of applications. It's relatively easy, and that's a big deal. And I think, too, there's a tradition of slaughtering that hasn't gone away. I also think that it's delicious. I think that people love fat. Pork, especially heirloom varietals, have all of this intramuscular fat that's really yummy. We serve goat at the restaurant. My mother will never order goat—are you kidding me? People have disconnected from that. People are much more open to pork. It's one of those things that was labeled bad for people, and now they eat it and it's delicious. Pork just sells, sells, sells, sells. Somehow or another it seems less primal than beef. It seems *more* than chicken.

BW: That's interesting. It tells me what kind of restaurant you are. Because I have talked to chefs at more "white table cloth" restaurants where pork doesn't sell that well. The idea is, "If I'm going to spend $35 on an entrée, I am not going to get a pork chop!"

KC: Yes, we experience that with our specials. What's interesting for me is what I can do [to sell a dish]. I have like three thousand e-mail addresses, so if I have specials, I can let everybody know. It's the *personal* thing that people want, when I'm connecting with them or with a farmer I'm telling people I'm standing behind *this*. Because sometimes you get things that *aren't* better products. People in the restaurant business refuse to recognize that. You know, Outback Steakhouse is very successful. If we're not better than they are, they're gonna eat our lunch. We have to be better every night.

There are certain ingredients that I call pass-through ingredients, which are things that the quality I get walking through the back door will translate directly to the plate. Like Braeburn hamburger: just get it out the door, just don't mess with it. Crabs that I serve are crabs that were living that morning. Then there are other things that we make that are not that at all. I really love pickling things, and that's another way of doing work . . . take an inexpensive item, add labor to it, and that's a way of translating the product directly to the plate.

One of the things that I believe—and it's an old, old idea: restaurants should look better on the inside than they do on the outside, the food should look better than it reads [on the menu] and should taste better than it looks. Every step inward has to be better. Places get that wrong. I remember as a kid eating at a restaurant in Charleston and seeing onion rings on the menu. And then they showed up, and there were two! I'm like, "That's not onion rings!" Restaurants have to be generous.

BW: So, if you can tell me this, what makes pork delicious?

KC: It depends on what the piece is. There's a slow-cooked type of pork flavor that I really love, and that I think I can easily translate to people. With a pork chop, I want that juiciness that comes from—you grill it and it stays juicy inside, and there's a flavor profile that's there that I always associate with pork. There's a sweet-salt thing that goes that's not in other cuts of meat. Well, I guess duck has it, to some degree. It's interesting me where you're able to add fruit to a cut of meat, that's a sure sign of that meat having sweetness in it. You put a plum sauce on a steak—no! There's something about that that's clearly inside of pork.

I want pork to have a sear. The fat when it cooks correctly is ridiculous. When you have a shoulder and there's this cap of fat, the most amazing thing that I love is, in that cap of fat there's always one vein of meat—I don't know what it is or does—but you pull that meat out and it's just ridiculous. On some level to me pork is about fat. And you want that to be highlighted. That's the wonder of chicken. And that's why chicken succeeds as a fried meat, because it isn't very fat.

Shanks are maybe not a hard sell, but the way I want to serve them is not necessarily a Southern application, which is a big thing [here at Acme]. If I were really to do shanks the way I like them, they would be part of a stew with collards and rice. And then have it in that broth, where you pull the meat off the bone and eat it almost like a soup.

There's a Portuguese dish called *caldo verde*, which is essentially collard greens. I've been very successful with shanks at things like wine dinners. There's this weird thing that happens in the restaurant world where you serve food that's different. And people love it: "Oh, it's so good! You should have it on the menu!" And then okay, great, it's on the menu and no one buys it. Because when you're *choosing* something, people go to their comfort zone, but if they're forced to eat something different they love it.

If staff gets behind something, that clearly connects to the customer. And that's something. I think the local movement succeeded once servers began to get it. Because that connects to the customer. Even if the first time you hear it, you're like, "huh?" And once you start hearing about it—"local food, local food"—you start to see it *everywhere*. I feel like we're in the middle of something.

BW: How'd you end up cooking?

KC: Good question. I'm from Charlotte. I got a scholarship to come to Carolina [the University of North Carolina at Chapel Hill]. Then out of college I wanted to write, and during the day I could write, and at night I could work in restaurants. I wrote for magazines, I was working on fiction, all sorts of stuff, trying to make ends meet. At the end of the day, I liked restaurants, liked working in them, and that was something I could actually do. My father had polio, couldn't walk, so he and I couldn't bond over playing football, but we could bond over a pork chop. The experience of sitting around the dining-room table was a big thing for our family. We sat there for hours and debated politics and whatever. And I think it informs a lot of this restaurant. I want this restaurant to be that kind of place, where people come to enjoy themselves and have that kind of experience. That's really the most important thing. I see the food as an excuse for having a good conversation.

So I wanted to open a restaurant. And I looked at buying a place. I worked at Crooks. And Bill Neil, who ran Crooks at the time—he was tough, but he and I agreed that the restaurant's number one job was to make people happy. And food participates in that. You're paying for food, but you're buying something else. You're buying the experience, and I think that's something that I really took to heart.

I'm also very anti–food-as-art. Food is a craft, it's a thing. There's been this overromanticization of the people that make food. Like we're gonna do this thing in October. My grandmother's birthday is October 7, she

would be 109. My grandfather was the first person [ever] to get a graduate degree from Clemson [University] in education. She helped put him
through grad school by making pies, and she sold them for, I think, 25
cents or 50 cents. So we're going to do all her pies on her birthday, and
they're going to be 50 cents a slice. See, that's the kind of thing that I
love. Because food connects to all of us, we all have stories about food,
and we can remember things. I'm not really interested in food as art
because it's not that good! We went to this restaurant in Charleston.
And it was a good meal, but every drop of food on the plate was perfect.
And because of that it wasn't hot. And it lacked, like *wow*. To me the
wow should be the easy part. Have you ever been to the taco truck at
Johnny's? They have this lamb stew, and it's full of cilantro, and then
I add this green salsa to it. And you get a quart for about $3. It's *soooo*
good. Here's $3 of absolute deliciousness. I always use that as my barom-
eter. It's like, in Charleston this plate of food was $38. And it was very
good. But it didn't jump ahead. I would have been just as happy with
that lamb soup.

All of a sudden, I become more aware of what I'm spending on a piece
of food and the experience. Maybe that's an issue of my own resources.
Because I always think about that. You know—$38, that's a lot of money!
People who have a lot of money, maybe they don't think about that. But
that's something I think that restaurants need to be aware of. I always
think, you can't be more expensive than like a large pizza, you know, you
really shouldn't be. When people order our food to *take out*? I think I can
get you a rocking pizza for a third of the price, why do you want to do
that? So we try to be aware of that.

I really feel like restaurants need to provide an opportunity for people
that don't have as much money. If I wanted to make money by marketing this place, then you either have to have a big press thing, and make
that work for you, or you have to be in a big town. I'm interested in
making a business that works. I've been here twelve years. I've always
wanted to be here forever.

5

A TASTE FOR FAT

In the late 1980s the National Pork Producers Council inaugurated its campaign to promote pork as "The Other White Meat." What is this "other" white meat? Why is it "white"? What are its material qualities? And what might "white meat" that is also pork taste like? One way we might think of this American campaign is that it is designed to make pork appealing on the basis not of taste but of other valued qualities: lightness, simplicity, healthfulness, or convenience. Pork is extolled, in fact, as a ready analogue to the ubiquitous chicken breast.[1] It is worth noting that this campaign also invokes the materiality of pork in very specific ways. The "whiteness" of this "other" meat not only promotes an association with chicken breasts, but it also depends on the physical and biological remaking of pork and pigs. To turn pork into "white meat," pigs must be raised to be long and lean, with as little fat as possible in their tender high-priced loins, the cut most often marketed as "white."

This well-known advertising campaign encapsulates many of the themes addressed in this chapter. To begin with, the ambiguous materiality of fat is, in many ways, the object of the National Pork Producers Council's advertising. As the organization itself puts it, "the goal of the campaign was to increase consumer demand for pork and to dispel pork's reputation as a fatty protein" (National Pork Producers Council 2012, 2). This attempt to recast pork as "white" focuses on the persistent conception of pork as something problematic and locates that problem in pork's fattiness.

Moreover, this concern with the "reputation" of a protein and the attempt to address this problem by reclassifying pork as "white," using descriptive terms reserved (in the American vernacular) for poultry, suggest that fat is not simply a physiological feature of pigs and their undesirable meat, but that it is also a social and cultural symbolic form.

In this chapter I consider pork fat as a symbolic form. I also ask how we might describe the materiality of taste. Taste, in both its prescriptive and descriptive versions, is often assessed primarily as a discursive form. There are all sorts of ways that taste can be understood as a representation, a commentary, or a moralized point of reference for securing the bonds of commensality or demonstrating potent sources of social distinction. In many critical assessments "taste," as Carolyn Korsmeyer puts it, "invites philosophical interest" (1999, 144) when it is situated within what she calls "narratives of eating." Such approaches to taste (for a few examples, see Appadurai 1981; Bourdieu 1984; Korsmeyer 1999; Smith 1972; Stoller 1989) raise a host of compelling questions and have cast remarkable light on the significance of food as a sociocultural form. But at a perceptual level, taste has its own specific qualities, which are not just narratable or referential but felt. And it is these felt qualities in lived experience that merit consideration. Such a consideration of pork fat as a symbolic matter with sensible and sensuous properties leads me to understand the fat in terms of the qualisigns it exhibits. The model of qualification I have developed throughout this book draws on Charles Sanders Peirce's (1932) discussion of qualisigns, which argues that qualities are primary experiences, feelings, or immediate sensory characteristics (for example, whiteness, redness, heaviness, and lightness). These properties have the potential to convey significance and so to serve as qualisigns across the different material forms in which similar qualities are embodied. Thus, the fattiness of pork has the potential to suggest, for example, unctuousness of character, smugness, and immoderation, but also humility, sincerity, and modesty. How these various qualisigns convey any of these actual meanings is an open question that can be determined only in specific contexts of practice and discourse (Keane 2003, 419).

Critical attention to fat in these terms is warranted, in part, because the felt qualities of taste so frequently motivate people to pursue particular foods and, in pursuit of them, to engage in a host of social projects. Fat, in particular, can evoke questions of health and well-being, as well as socioeconomic deprivation, so it has been especially central to food activists' efforts to develop alternative food systems.[2] Yet the taste of fat is generally assumed to be intrinsically desirable and satisfying, perhaps because it is—according to many—simply a cheap source of caloric content.[3] So questions remain very much open: What is taste, and how do we recognize those distinctive qualities that make it a discernible phenomenon that is not simply reducible, or equivalent, to the discursive meanings of "consumption," "dining," or "cuisine"? While taste is undoubtedly a dimension of each of these, the vocabulary that we need to describe taste itself[4] and the perceptual qualities particular to it deserve further inquiry.

I argue that the taste of pork fat and fatty pork is critical to understanding different registers of value that are available when eating pork. The taste of fat is occasionally defined as a distinctly different basic taste worthy of the same primacy of importance as salty, sweet, bitter, sour, and the fifth taste, umami. I will address these claims in my discussion of contemporary meat science. But my primary focus, even in consideration of these scientific assessments, is on how these reveal certain phenomenological as well as political economic qualities embedded in pork fat. These qualities can be discerned when we put them back in the context of this ethnography and ask how they relate to contemporary social movements in the Piedmont that are attempting to transform the way that pork is produced and brought to the public and working to advance alternative models—embraced as simultaneously new and old-fashioned methods of animal husbandry—of meat production. These alternative models, and the kinds of pigs they promote, often privilege the taste of fat as a critical feature of that innovative social and cultural practice. Taste is framed in these efforts as something both gustatory and political, and thus a more nuanced appreciation of what taste actually is might reveal matters of broad relevance to contemporary social practice.

A Sense of Memory: Anthropological Approaches to Taste

Taste is evanescent, seeming to be available to us only when we have tactile contact with some material form, yet it can elicit nostalgic reminiscence of bygone days. Seeing is believing; a touchstone is something we can get our hands on that confirms the concrete presence of the world; and the aromatic stimulates the erotic. The place of taste (to turn terroir on its ear) in this array of associations—its place in the taxonomy of senses—is its complex evocation of memory. In the course of this chapter I ask what taste is (or can be) and how we can know it (or at least make shared, meaningful claims about it). Evocation, recollection, and nostalgia are the canonical modes of remembrance allied to tasting. More specifically, in asking about the relationship between taste and memory, I am interested in the various ways that gustation can formulate relations between the past, present, and future. In keeping with Karl Marx's enigmatic assertion that "the forming of the five senses is a labor of the entire history of the world down to the present" (1968, 139), I explore the historical possibilities of gustatory tastes by examining a particular taste's history.

The evocative character of taste has been noted often in the anthropological literature. David Sutton's (2001) celebrated account of alimentary practice in the Aegean offers a cogent theoretical and ethnographic illustration of a Proustian anthropology's efforts to capture cuisine's ability to formulate and incite recollection, commemoration, and nostalgia. In his recent review of the literature, Jon Holtzman (2009) demonstrates that memory is often the implicit subtext of ethnographic examinations of food and shows how considerations of such memory-constructing processes as commodification, urbanization, and ethnogenesis can fix on things culinary as apt illustrations of social transformation. He also makes the provocative point that the scholarship on food often celebrates the interconnection of cuisine and remembrance as a sensuous mode of fond recollections, while it overlooks the ways that meals—both bitter and insipid—can recall hardship, illness, and—of course—hunger.

C. Nadia Seremetakis's notable invocation of the peach known as "the breast of Aphrodite" (1994, 1) offers a well-known illustration of the characteristic mode of capturing memory through taste (and the senses more generally). Her work highlights "the complicity of history and the senses" (4). But what is truly critical in Seremetakis's work is less a concern with what that peach tastes like—her entire description of its taste is "a bit sour and a bit sweet, it exuded a distinct fragrance" (1)—than an interest in contemporary Greek nostalgia for the peach, which is no longer grown, it seems, anywhere in Greece. The peach itself is not remarkable for its (perhaps indescribable) taste as much as for its absence: "The absent peach became narrative" (2). The absence of the peach, then, becomes a way of recalling and therefore of remembering history. Its taste remains strangely inaccessible.

Judith Farquhar's magisterial account of post-Maoist banquets in China describes opulent feasts in which newly wealthy businessmen and bureaucrats indulge in newfangled appetites in highly poetic ways. At one banquet, amid the dishes of three-in-one duck, artfully carved root vegetables, and barrels of white liquor that grace any such affair, are an assortment of mossy plants with fried and roasted insects—the foods of hunger that barely sustained these eaters during the depths of the Cultural Revolution (2002, 134). Here Farquhar shows the complexities of memory in relation to shifting ethical demands in a society where it has become "glorious to get rich," as contemporary Chinese subjects keep alive their recollections of collective immiseration by transforming them into modes of exquisite refinement and, of course, distinction.

These anthropological assessments are valuable touchstones for exploring the taste of fat and its connections to history and memory in this book. In the specific history that I discuss here there is, as we shall see, a discourse of tastes that are lost and so subject to being found, revitalized, and reproduced in the present. What intrigues me most about this formulation is that, like Farquhar's exquisite banquets, these ways of grasping tastes do not merely register the passage of time, they posit its trajectory; they comprehend a past from which the present has not just emerged but has deviated, even declined. Such taste claims, then, are (as we saw was the case with heritage breeds) ways of evaluating temporality, and—insofar as values induce strong feelings, motivate subjects, and compel action— attention to these claims might allow us to understand taste as a means of making history. The following section offers an overview of taste as a phenomenon and is a prelude to my more ethnographically focused discussion of how this perception is relevant to understanding how pork has been remade in the Piedmont.

Toward an Understanding of the Significance of Taste

It is interesting to note, in respect to these questions, a kind of paradox in Aristotle's hierarchy of the senses. If taste is a quintessential "proximal sense" (1986, 2.10) that can encounter and confirm its object only in the intimate interiors of the body (which makes it less noble and more bestial in Aristotle's view), our accounts of taste characteristically make reference to locations distant in place and time. This is as true for classical tastes of foods whose concrete qualities are grounded in the humoral stuff of the universe itself (Shapin n.d.), as it is for contemporary claims about the bacterial profile of cheeses and their molecular counterparts in grassy hillsides and thistled pastures. The Tanzanians I have eaten with routinely describe the tastes of stewed plantains as heavy, satisfying, and wet, like a farm replete with vegetation; and the cassava porridge they consume only in the absence of plantains as dry and pallid like the exposed grassland where it grows. A food of hunger, then, tastes like the social condition itself. Indeed, the general amenability of taste to connote potent memories and, as I'll suggest, to call forth others suggests that taste's so-called proximity belies its eminently social character. Again, the evaluative efforts of food artisans of all stripes puts food into the making of history, recuperating what has been lost and calling forth new ways of tasting.

To ask the question again: What is taste (for example, the taste of tasty pork)? Is our ability to attribute a temporal character to tastes, such as the nostalgia or commemoration regularly invoked in anthropological accounts of taste, akin to the temporality of other modes of perception—as when we offer a new vision for the future or capture the ancient tones of a musical genre? My premise is that taste is not just a sensation, the product of a stimulus formulated by various flavor precursors targeted to human receptors, but a mode of perception and so a form of being in the world. Taste is simultaneously part of who we are, in body and mind; it is both an opening to and an embedding in reality for us. It is, then, a way of both making and acting on existence, of inhabiting the world.

Consider a comprehensive review essay titled "The Taste of Fat." It offers a summary of how meat scientists characteristically understand taste, or "gustatory mechanisms": "Gustation (informally often referred to as 'taste' or 'flavor perception') is a form of direct chemoreception in the taste bud that is bathed in saliva. The taste bud is composed of sensory taste cells surrounding a central pore, and has several layers of support cells on the outer region of the taste bud. . . . The superior laryngeal branch of the vagus nerve innovates the epiglottis and larynx and the posterior one-third of the tongue. Different sensory signals from ortho-nasal, retro-nasal odour and gustatory receptors may integrate in the higher centers to give 'flavor' cognition" (Dransfield 2008, 38). Evaluation of the taste of fat, so critical to meat flavor, requires attention to this chemoreceptive process, the coordination of lipid-derived volatile compounds, saliva, sensory cells, and neural innovation. But note that this essay begins with the observation that the perception of fat, and therefore meat quality, is not entirely comprehended by these mechanisms: "The evaluation of fat by the consumer comprises elements of the fat itself (its amount and quality), as well as the consumer's sensory capacities, cultural background and concerns about environmental and ethical considerations in meat production" (37).

This characteristic divide between object and subject (and, we might add, between nature and culture) has provided a methodological agenda for meat scientists in the field, and a spate of recent studies (Meinert et al. 2008; Moeller et al. 2010) has investigated the difference in flavor between meat from pasture-raised as opposed to that from convention-ally raised animals. Not surprisingly, given the ties of meat science pro-grams to industrial producers, these studies often attempt to discredit the claim that, for example, grass-fed beef tastes better than grain-fed beef, or to attribute such claims to subjective biases or cultural factors like the consumer's country of origin. I have no reason to doubt the validity of physiological claims about chemoreception, the levels of linoleic acid in consumer-preferred meats, or the role of fatty acid transport proteins in the mechanics of taste. But it remains an open question as to how these mechanisms are articulated as the experience of taste; or why, for example, the mere presence of these acids, proteins, and physiological structures should register not just as a flavor sensation but be evaluated as, say, toothsome and rich, rather than cloying and heavy. These ques-tions about evaluation and quality, to say nothing of the role of "cultural background and concerns about environmental and ethical considerations in meat production" in consumer preferences, indicate that taste is a feature of how we make our worlds.

Giorgio Agamben offers an apposite and characteristically eccentric dis-cussion of what taste might be through the illustrative example of what taste is not in the *Umwelt*, or environment-world, of a tick (2003, 45–47). Here he relies on the ecologist Jakob von Uexküll's notion of an environment-world, characterized as a welter of what Uexküll calls "carriers of signifi-cance" that form an integrated system of features that correspond to the bodily receptors of the organism that inhabits this world. There is, then, no objective environment with fixed features or abstract body with discrete sensory capacities. Rather, Uexküll describes the correspondence between "carriers of significance" and bodily reception as a musical unity, "like two notes 'of the keyboard on which nature performs the supratemporal and extraspatial symphony of signification'" (quoted in Agamben 2003, 41).

And what of the tick? The tick, says Uexküll, has an environment-world with three carriers of significance: (1) the smell of mammalian sweat that attracts it, (2) the hairy surface of the mammalian body to which it clings, and (3) the temperature of 37° C that corresponds to the blood of mammals. The life of a tick is united to these three elements; indeed, says Agamben, the tick is the relationship among these elements. And it is no ca-sual observation to note that what is not present as a carrier of significance in the environment-world of the tick is the taste of blood. Indeed, Uexküll observes that the tick can carry out the fullness of its existence without benefit of the taste of blood, for ticks will attach themselves to any suitable surface and absorb any liquid beneath that surface at the proper temperature (picture warm, hairy water balloons). Agamben moves on from this observation, but it raises interesting questions for me about the possibilities of taste as a kind of attuned engagement (to follow his musical metaphor) in the world, and what it might mean to have it. What kind of "carrier of significance" is taste, and how do we attribute significance to it?

The questions derived from this perspective on engagement, in my view, raise problems for the standard models of stimulus and response that inform much discussion of taste perception, and the perspectives and protocols of meat science intended to disclose the machinery of taste. If taste is a carrier of significance to which we are attuned, it would not seem readily reducible to any such mechanistic framework. In what follows I elaborate an understanding of how this process of significance unfolds and is expressed in affect, language, and memory. Meat science often offers some clues to this signifying process, for it both proposes and records the words used to describe the taste of meat in sensory panels. "Flavor," reports one respected article, "was the attribute that the focus groups discussed the most and found relatively hard to describe" (Meinert et al. 2008, 312). Indeed, it is notable how wide-ranging accounts of taste are when they are offered in reports on tasting panels. A given meat sample, for example, can be described in identical terms (such as "intensive" and "acidic") but preferred or rejected for those very attributes (for example, one panelist might report "good flavor, a little acidic" while another says, "sour, a little boring in flavor") or, conversely, can be described in opposite terms (such as "very meaty taste" and "not really meat flavor") (312). Rather than saying that there is simply no accounting for taste, we might look directly at some of the language used in sensory analysis of pork. Consider the table 5.1 as a not atypical example of how sensory attributes are described in pork tasting. The series of replications across these categories—the "roasted nut" quality that smells like "roasted nut aroma" as found in "roasted walnuts"—suggests, at a minimum, the challenge of disarticulating perception, objects, and language when it comes to taste. In spite of the mechanical reduction of taste to chemoreception and volatile compounds in meat science, things in the world (or perhaps in the world of meat) seem to be what they are in our ability both to taste them and to express the qualities of those taste perceptions. This isomorphism between language, subject, and object on matters of taste was further suggested to

TABLE 5.1 **Vocabulary of the Sensory Attributes Used in the Descriptive Sensory Analysis of Pork Semimembranosus**

Sensory attributes	Description	Reference
ODOR		
Fried meat	Fried pork aroma	Fried pork schnitzel
Burned	Charred pork crust aroma	Well-done fried pork schnitzel
Roasted nut	Roasted nut aroma	Roasted walnuts
Piggy	Piggy aroma	Melted pork fat
Acidic	Acidic aroma	Leavened fresh milk
FLAVOR		
Fried meat	Fried pork flavor	Fried pork schnitzel
Burned	Charred pork crust flavor	Well-done fried pork schnitzel
Sweet	Sweet taste	Sucrose (1%)
Acidic	Acidic taste	Citric acid (0.1%)
Salty	Salty taste	NaCl solution (0.001%)
Piggy	Piggy flavor	Melted pork fat
Metallic	Metallic taste	Copper coin

Adapted from Lene Meinert, Kaja Tikk, Meelis Tikk, Per B. Brockhoff, Camilla Bejerholm, and Margit D. Aaslyng 2008, 252.

me in a conversation I had with a chef about the breed of chicken she was using at her restaurant. The tasting panel she had convened had preferred an organically raised free-range local bird for the "really deep flavor" it had. "It really tasted like something," she said. And what, I asked, did it taste like? "It tasted like chicken!"

What implications might this wedding together of world, perception, and language with respect to taste have for the pronounced associations of taste and memory and, in particular, for the notion of pork having a lost taste that could be recuperated? Consider one of the more intriguing sensory attributes from these meat-tasting descriptors: pork that smells and tastes "piggy." At one level, this looks like the perfect example of the unity of subjective and objective characteristics of taste—a taste that is the quintessence of the thing in itself. At the same time, this clearly is not what is entailed in the category of "piggy," which implies a certain "off" characteristic, or an excessively intense flavor and odor. "The distinct pork-like or piggy flavor noticeable in lard or cracklings and in some pork," according to the textbook *Food Chemistry*, "is caused by p-[para]cresol and isovaleric acid that are produced from microbial conversions of corresponding amino acids in the lower gut of swine" (Fennema 1996, 674). The use of terms "porklike" and "piggy" as mere signifiers might seem evidence of the inadequacy of language to express the complexity of taste, but as sociolinguistic elements in a community of speakers, they are terms that can have specific meanings. Therefore, they are available for diverse meanings as those communities change over time and across space.

My examination of the meat science literature and the tasting panels convened by meat scientists indicates that "piggy" is a quality solicited and reported primarily (but not exclusively) by Danish researchers. The Danish Meat Association extolls industrial farms by reporting that chops from pigs fed a completely organic diet have a more piggy and metallic odor than chops from conventionally fed pigs (Søltoft-Jensen 2007). Given the facts that pork is truly pervasive in Danish cuisine (Buckser 1999) and that Denmark regularly competes with Canada and the United States to be the world's leading pork exporter, it is perhaps not surprising to find a general public in Denmark that can discern such flavors as the aggressiveness of pork that is too piggy or porklike. But note that pigginess is a flavor that is increasingly being promoted by advocates and connoisseurs of pastured, local, or heritage breed pork. In a taste comparison of artisanal British charcuterie, the *Guardian* critics described one brand of *coppa* (air-dried ham) as "oversalted, not enough piggy flavour" and "strong, dry, piggy, not bad" ("Taste Test: British Charcuterie" 2010). In the *Times*, a pork pie is extolled as being "full of piggy flavour," while a Vietnamese *banh mi* luncheon meat is dismissed for lacking "the true Viet depth of sticky, piggy flavour" (O'Laughlin 2010). In such instances, pigginess is celebrated as an esteemed "deep" feature of real pork.

I do not think that the taste of pigginess as it is used by these British advocates of pork is identical to the Danish perception of pigginess, though given the vagaries of the lexicon, I am not really certain of this distinction. What matters, though, is that the perception of taste is elicited in identical language that can be valorized in opposing ways. In each instance, pigginess, the taste that confirms the presence of the thing in itself, is a carrier of significance that conveys the intensity and force of the animal in question. But is that quality of intensity a form of overpowering excess or evidence of the authentic character of the animal, well cared for and naturally raised? As a tangential, but not unrelated point, I would note that male pigs raised for meat as opposed to for breeding are almost uniformly castrated in both conventional and pastured farming in the United States, which prevents their meat from acquiring what is called a boar's taint. However, I have spoken with a very few consumers who have eaten "intact" boar's meat and have a preference for this "tainted," flavor which they describe, in a parallel fashion, as "aggressive," "deep," or simply "strong." This evaluation of "depth" or "intensity" as a signifier with a range of available meanings is also, as I hope to show, an indication of how tastes can be lost and found.

Piedmont Pigs and Pork Fat: A Regional Taste History

One of the intriguing things about pork (especially in the United States in recent years) is that it has not always been obvious that pork has a taste—or, perhaps, that taste is the quality most relevant for pork producers and consumers. In the Piedmont of North Carolina I can show how the taste of pork—and fatty pork, at that—has come to be relevant to and, in many ways, exemplary of flavor and taste, more generally. It further seems iconic of the potent, robust pleasures of eating for the locavores, artisans, and foodies who have embraced pastured pork production in this region and across the country.

At the same time, appeals to taste, like those made by advocates of local foods and the virtues of terroir—or a taste of place (discussed in chapter 2)—are ways of evaluating temporality, so paying attention to taste affords us an important (perhaps even privileged) perspective on processes of making history. And making history through fat pigs is very much what many food activists, chefs, farmers, and consumers have in mind in the contemporary United States.

You might note that the massive industrialization I described in chapter 1 coincided with the National Pork Producers Council's campaign to promote "The Other White Meat," described at the beginning of this chapter. This national campaign (1987–2005) was surprisingly unsuccessful in many ways. While the Economic Research Service of the U.S. Department of Agriculture suggests that pork sales rose by 20 percent in the first five years of this campaign, longer-term assessments indicate that pork consumption in the United States has remained at a relatively stable level since the 1910s. Moreover, since 1998 production of live animals has been unprofitable. In 2009, hog farmers who marketed their pork in the United States were losing about $20 per pig (National Pork Producers Council 2009). Industrial pork, like most American industrial agriculture since the

1970s, survives through tax breaks and direct subsidies (Blanchette n.d.). Nonetheless, the model of vertical integration based on the consolidations for economies of scale continues apace. These industrial processes, as I indicated above, radically transform the biology of pigs and the taste of pork. The industrial process breeds a long and lean hog, which maximizes the marginal returns available to pork growers and encourages the sale of such innovative and higher-priced products as lean bacon and tenderloin (as opposed to simply tenderized loins, or other cuts of pork) which are notably free of fat and quintessentially exemplify "the Other White Meat."

In a host of ways, these historical transformations in North Carolina offer a microcosm of wider rumblings in the American food system. These dramatic changes have attracted the attention of a wide range of critics who decry all aspects of this intensified process of industrialization, from the cruelties inflicted on pigs through the confinement system, through the environmental degradations wrought by the industry, to the dangerous and often criminal nature of labor exploitation in factory farms and processing facilities (Kaminsky 2005; Kenner 2009; Morgan 1998; Niman 2009). Critics of such industrial agriculture also often lament the tastes of the food it produces, and with respect to pigs and pork, it is the absence of fat that is generally decried. Indeed, bringing fat back into pork has been one of the ways that advocates for change in the industrial system have both worked to bring about transformations and demonstrated the clear superiority (in their view) of alternative production methods. In an interview I conducted with one chef committed to promoting these alternative methods, I asked him what qualities he was looking for in the "local pork" that he featured at his restaurant. Was it some specific breed of pig, I wondered, or perhaps healthier meat derived from a pig raised outdoors and unconfined? He told me simply: "I was looking for a pig with some fat on it." No "Other White Meat" for him! One of the most popular pork products sold at the farmers' markets throughout the Piedmont, provided by farmers dedicated to methods of animal husbandry that today are embraced as both innovative and old-fashioned—that is, raising pigs outdoors in unconfined pastures—is bacon. Bacon procured from a "pig with some fat on it," which such pastured animals inevitably are, is no ordinary bacon, for it is self-evidently exceptionally fat. In fact, it is so fat that at the market stall where I worked each weekend, my coworkers and I made sure to tell each of our new customers to cook their bacon at a low heat (preferably in the oven at 325 degrees for fifteen minutes) lest its fat burn up in the pan. Indeed, these fatty bellies are found on restaurant menus across the Piedmont.

The Cane Creek Farm stall in the Carrboro Farmers' Market has customers who come each week asking for what one of them calls the farm's "life-changing bacon." This term (while somewhat idiosyncratic) and the general popularity of bacon (which, at $13 a pound, is roughly two to three times the price of industrially produced bacon) suggest that bacon as a cut of pork—an especially fatty one at that—is iconic (in the classic Peircean sense) of this alternative food movement. That is, not only are the pigs raised by techniques that oppose the perils of confinement operations, but also the fatty bacon they produce has characteristics that exhibit the virtues of—and in this way resemble (like all iconic signs, Peirce 1932, 101)—this transformed production process. In other words, with its distinctive fattiness bacon possesses the qualisigns of value (Meneley 2008; Munn 1986) of artisanal, pasture-raised, healthy pig production that counteract the qualisignificance of industrially produced, confined, "inhumane" processed pork that is best embodied in what is marketed as "healthy," white, lean meat. Bacon and loins are each icons of the productive processes that generate them (pastured and industrial, respectively), and their distinctive qualisigns of fat and lean are bodied forth in materially meaty form.[5]

To elaborate on how this fattiness is regenerated in pigs, and with what consequences for the taste of pork, the phenomenology of memory, and political economy, I will draw, once again, on the history of the Ossabaw Island Hog. This pig was literally revitalized as a heritage breed by virtue of its exceptional and excessive fat. In the early 1990s, as I discussed above, Charles (known to all as Chuck) Talbott, an animal scientist at North Carolina A&T who was dismayed by the devastating effects of confined animal feeding operations on both the animals and the farmers who are increasingly ensnared by this production system, began to look for alternatives to this system of pig production. By his own account, Talbott is driven primarily by economic concern for farmers no longer able to operate under the onerous terms of the pork contracts in the system. His concern stems not from some nostalgic appeal to a disappearing way of life, but from issues of food security and environmental degradation. And it was only later, toward the end of the 1990s, that he hit on the idea that taste might be a significant factor in farmers' ability to market pork raised on pasture rather than in confinement.

As I explained in chapter 1, Talbott became interested in changing consumers' tastes in pasture-raised pork when he read an article that profiled

Paul Willis, a farmer in northern Iowa who was committed to raising his pigs outdoors, in straw and hoop houses, even as outdoor pig production declined precipitously in Iowa through the 1970s and 1980s. The article, by Edward Behr, paid particular attention to the fact that pigs raised in this fashion produce delectable pork. Behr's first experience eating Willis's pork had been when he ate a "thick chop . . . roasted before a wood fire" at Chez Panisse in California, which inspired his pilgrimage to Iowa (Behr 1999, 9). In his article, Behr offered a thorough survey of the techniques of outdoor production and its advantages over confinement for both the health of the pig, and the environment, a point he made repeatedly by referring to the horrific stench of confined animal feeding operations. His discussion of Willis's farming expertise focuses on the taste of the pork produced. As Willis puts it, "if something tastes good . . . I think it reflects the health of whatever it is you're eating. Allowing the pig to behave as naturally as possible is enhancing the eating quality" (12). "It tastes like the pork I had when I was a little kid," says one of Willis's neighbors (18).

After reading Behr's article, Talbott contacted Willis about how to promote the same production practices, and cultivate consumers and markets more generally, across North Carolina. This began Talbott's relationship with Niman that I described in chapter 1. The set of material and institutional arrangements that the Niman project incorporated—from marginal farmers, through capitalization from the tobacco buyout, to a branded network of high-end meat producers and the scientific expertise in swine husbandry at A&T—fundamentally reshaped the market for pasture-raised pork in central North Carolina. Here it is especially important to recognize the vital role that taste played in motivating these actors. According to one of the agricultural extension officers who worked on this project, Talbott became, in effect, a meat scientist, driven by an interest in the ways that pasturage, feed, and behavior of animals produced the taste attributes prized by discerning consumers. In pursuit of these discerning consumers and the pigs they preferred, Talbott traveled across southern Europe, looking at varieties of pigs that were, as he put it in a conversation with me, "part of the whole way of life" in little towns and villages where pork production and provisioning is integrated into the seasonal round, what members of the Slow Food movement call the Ark of Taste. After returning to North Carolina, Talbott found the insular group of pigs with ancestral ties to Iberian pata negra pigs on Ossabaw Island about to be culled by the Georgia Department of Natural Resources, as I described in chapter 3. It was these Ossabaw Island Hogs' ties to the celebrated Ibérico pigs that Talbott had encountered in Spain—and notably to their exquisite taste—that made Talbott and the swine husbandry team at A&T become extremely excited about the prospects of raising a herd of Ossabaws as a niche-market heritage breed. So today, the Ossabaw Island Hog, the breed described in detail in chapter 3, is raised by a small but growing number of farmers along the eastern seaboard and in a few places in the Midwest.

It is also important to recall that the Ossabaw—and other types of pig that have been revitalized as heritage breeds—are materially different from industrial hogs in ways that go beyond their production techniques. In addition to the ancestral connection of Ossabaws to Ibérico pigs, for example, the physiological adaptations the Ossabaw Island Hog had made through four hundred years of island life are also important to their viability and materiality. What makes the Ossabaw Island Hog especially suited to pork production is the unique biochemical system of fat metabolism the breed developed. The hog's metabolism enables it to store a larger proportion of fat than any other hog. Indeed, Ossabaws have the highest percentage of body fat of any nondomestic mammal (Watson 2004, 114).

Telling the Taste of Fat

But what is the taste of the Ossabaw and its characteristic fat? How does its taste connect it to the Spanish pata negra with which it shares ancestry or to other heritage breeds raised by similar methods of swine husbandry across the Piedmont and elsewhere? How might this taste be implicated in the complex and varied narratives—of heritage, adaptation, cultivation, ecology, and connoisseurship—through which this domesticated American breed came to be? This chronicle is further informed by more general claims about the lost taste of pork, where fat replaces lean, and the capacity of these animals not just to taste good but to recuperate taste. I will show that such recuperation is also a form of innovation that brings with it, not surprisingly, a new taste of pork.

How can such tastes be told? Recall that in my consideration of meat scientific approaches to taste, the ambiguity of terms like "piggy," "off," and even "strong" suggested that the same terms could be used to describe (possibly identical) tastes that some people found desirable but that others found repellent. The consumers of pasture-raised pork in central North

Carolina confirm some of these disparities, expressed less as positive and negative evaluations of the same flavors than in different characterizations of what is widely agreed to be some very tasty pork. The pig farmers with whom I have worked serve a wide area of central North Carolina. This region is remarkably and increasingly diverse in demographic terms (North Carolina is the fastest-growing state east of the Mississippi River [U.S. Census Bureau n.d.]), and consumers of pastured pork—more commonly called "local pork"—reflect that diversity. Purveyors of such artisanal slow foods are often perceived to be catering to a foodie elite that can afford, for example, pork chops that cost $12 per pound. But it is also clear that consumers have different tastes that shape their purchasing decisions. Recall that the Piedmont runs from the Triad in the West through the Triangle to the East. In very rough terms, the Triad is part of a Southern rust belt, an industrial group of towns that were once dominated by textile and wood-working mills that have in living memory departed in search of cheaper labor in Latin America and East Asia. In contrast, the Triangle is an epicenter of high-tech corporate enterprise including Big Pharma and software engineering, facilitated by its proximity to academic research centers. Among the farmers I know who sell in both regions, the Triangle is seen as a region of avid customers, eager to try new things and willing to pay for them. As one beef farmer put it, "three years ago, when I first started processing cattle, I kept a flank steak for myself figuring it would never sell. I must have had fifteen customers at the Durham Farmers' Market ask me for a flank steak! I haven't eaten one since then." Along the same lines, a pig farmer with the same Triangle clientele told me, "I'd make a fortune if I could figure out how to raise a pig with four bellies" (a sign, as well, of the qualisignificance of belly-providing bacon). These customers also crave the personalized attention and the narrative accounts of heritage[6] along with their farmers' market purchases. In contrast, customers in the Triad are thought of as reluctant to try new things, and it is a hard sell to get them to pay the premium prices that pastured pork commands. As a result, small packs of breakfast sausage are the biggest sellers at the Greensboro farmers' market.

While both sets of customers are, by their own accounts, drawn to the taste of pastured pork, my ethnographic inquiries found that the two groups think of taste in rather different ways. In a customer survey I conducted, Triangle customers described the taste of their preferred pastured pork in terms like these: "The taste is so different, so superior to mass-produced meat products!" "Pork that tastes like pork, not 'the other white meat.'" "The taste—so yummy and different than any other bacon I've ever had." "The taste is superior to all of the commercial pork products I used to buy. In addition, I like knowing where my food comes from, that it was raised with care for both the animal and the environment and in buying it I am supporting values I believe in." And finally, "the meat tastes excellent—but it's not just the sensual flavor of the meat, it's the mental knowledge that what they do is responsible, for the planet, people, and animals." Triad customers much less frequently speak in terms of ethical consumption; rather, they are inclined to appreciate pastured pork for recapturing the tastes they recall from a bygone era: "Tastes like the best meats I have had as a child, that was home grown and free-range." And "the pork tastes the best, like what Grandfather used to have when he had a farm down in Florida where the pigs had lots of pasture." One of the most renowned barbecue pit masters, Ed Mitchell who until recently offered pastured pork at his Raleigh restaurant, sums up the appreciation of its taste this way: "The pork knocked me down. It tasted like the barbecue I remember from the tobacco days; juicy, and full of flavor. I knew that was the pork my grandfather ate all his life. I knew that was the old-fashioned pork we lost when near about everybody went industrial" (quoted in Edge 2005, 54). Here, in short, are tastes both lost and found, an appreciation of innovation, pork unlike any other. Such pork is unique and laden with *distinction* in its methods of "responsible farming" and nonindustrial/commercial qualities; and, at the same time, as farmers stereotype Triad consumers' preferences, it is "pork that tastes like my granddaddy used to raise," redolent of concrete times and places and connections to both kin and personal experience.

As I indicated in my discussion of the iconic status of bacon, these tastes of both innovation and nostalgia are embedded in the fat of the pig. That is, when consumers and chefs extoll the virtues of this simultaneously new and old-fashioned pastured pork, they are inevitably drawn to its fat as evidence of these virtues. Note Ed Mitchell's discussion of the "juicy" pork he prefers, fat that could be found in "the pork my grandfather ate all his life." If taste is a way of evaluating carriers of significance, much of the significance of pork is carried in its fat. Fat exhibits, to return to my original point, qualisigns of ambiguity, for it exemplifies—all at once—a traditional, forgotten experience rooted in kinship and loss and innovation, superiority, and ethical environmental practice.

Conclusion

Let me turn briefly to two examples—each discussed in more depth in other chapters—of attempts to narrate the taste of heritage pork that further clarify this complementary dualism of tastes lost and found. Remember the results of the intriguing evaluation conducted by Talbott, along with Peter Kaminsky of the *New York Times*, to assess and codify the taste of Ossabaw fed on hardwood mast. Their panel reported what is called an "off-flavor," also known as "dark turkey meat" in meat science. To reconcile this apparent discrepancy, Talbott and his coauthors determined that "a new 'On Flavor' classification may be required to distinguish differences in conventional sensory models" (2006, 189–90). The lost taste of mast-fed pork, then, demands new modes of description, and perhaps even new models of taste.

The other example has to do less directly with tasting than with ways of cooking pigs that similarly combines innovation and nostalgia.[7] Renewing food traditions has also renewed interest in dishes that make use of all manner of interesting bits of pig formerly considered "icky." Such snout-to-tail cookery is part and parcel of the agenda of the Slow Food movement and is especially apparent in dishes served in the restaurants across the Piedmont that offer pasture-raised pork. Not always content to serve up Carolina barbecue, local chefs are promoting their skills and tempting their customers with items like grilled pig tails, pork belly confit, and headcheese. Headcheese, in particular, is embedded with traces of paradoxical experiences. Once and sometimes still eaten in North Carolina as "souse," this gelée of pork trimming is recalled as a food eaten in times of hardship or a bit of meat—often eaten at breakfast—providing a hearty energy source for agricultural labors. This ethos of economizing is certainly praised by the Slow Food chefs and many of the consumers who are so taken with snout-to-tail cookery. But, of course, their own experience of consumption—and so, perhaps, of the taste of headcheese—has little to do with hardship, or even with nostalgic recollections of repasts gone by. Most of them describe such dishes as what they call "*real* food," a culinary offering, then, that values authenticity rendered material.

This difference is telling and, I would argue, consistent with the claims made by professional panels about the taste of heritage pork more generally. That is, such foods are modes of renewal and evocations of the past (occasionally, but not always, for those who actually did eat this way in the past) and, simultaneously, innovative techniques of preparation, provisioning, and marketing these tastes. The once lost and now renewed past is offered, in both instances, not simply as a documentary representation, but as an evaluative claim about the past—its complexity, character, and realness—and as a resource for creating the present and future. My argument is that to understand taste as a mode of perception with a privileged relationship to memory is to ask about the character of complex alignments of past, present, and future. In this way, taste is a way of making the world, of evaluating the qualities of the past that are felt to contribute to the present, and of further cultivating those qualities one hopes to secure in the future. Creating history in these perceptual ways requires us to understand the sensory character of the world and our place in it as laden with carriers of significance, mutual attunements beyond stimulus and response. Taste is both of the world and in us; we have taste, and tastes grab us. The particular flavors of pastured pork can reveal how taste offers us a kind of potential, diverse possibilities for aligning historical processes. Pigginess as excess or authenticity is iconic of these possibilities. So, too, are lean loins and fatty bellies and bacon, each of which embodies qualisigns of the very different processes of production through which they come into being. In this regard, they also exhibit the divergent historical potential of taste, as this sensory significance divulges very different orders of labor, ecology, animal welfare, and agriculture more generally. In this way, the qualisigns exhibited by iconic forms conjoin the sensory and the political economic. Tastes in memory are lost and found, heritage and innovation, firmly of time and place as well as unique and unprecedented. This plenipotentiality of pastured pork—life changing and extra fatty— demonstrates how tastes assert the significance of the changing worlds that produce not only pigs but us as the consumers of their pork and the bearers of the tastes by which we engage the worlds we inhabit.

PROFILE: Vimala Rajendran

—

Vimala Rajendran is the chef and proprietor of Vimala's Curryblossom Café in Chapel Hill. She grew up in Bombay, and below she describes her Catholic upbringing in India and its relationship to her commitments today. As a single mother of three, Vimala started cooking community dinners in her Chapel Hill home in 1994. These celebrated meals, cooked by Vimala and a small staff of friends and family members, were meant to serve whoever showed up—often hundreds of people! The proceeds from the donations her guests offered contributed to a wide range of community projects. Vimala drew on this eighteen years of experience to open Vimala's Curryblossom Café in 2010. We spoke in February 2015, and at the conclusion of our discussion she served me a spectacular lunch of uttapam *with barbecue and pork vindaloo.*

BW: It sounds like your Christian background was very important to your cooking. The hospitality and charity that you offer is part of that.

VR: Sure, and also the permissibility and the liberty to eat anything that is available and up for free will access. That's what pork is for me. I know pork is a very controversial meat because of Judaic laws, Islamic laws, and this is how I want to explain how I see pork. I, being a New Testament Christian, am under that liberty. There are examples where Jesus's disciples were chastised for eating the wrong thing. But his answer was, "It's more important what comes out of your mouth."

BW: Was there much access to pork when you were growing up?

VR: We lived in very close quarters with people from Goa and Mangalore. A hundred percent of those people for me were Catholic. The Catholics [in] India were influenced by Portuguese and Spanish culture. I'm originally from Kerala, so my family was Catholic. For the most part, the open-wide European culture which influenced India for 450 years doesn't forbid any meat.

BW: Where were people raising pigs?

VR: When my family was in Kerala, we lived on the backwaters, where there was a combination of saltwater and freshwater. Year round, every day we ate fish. But they ate meat, which was purchased from the market, mostly pork or lamb—or beef—but it was only at the most two times a year. For Easter and Christmas. I laid on eyes on my first pig when I started attending church in Bombay, and I was just three years old. Anywhere around practically every church in Bombay, even if that church is—Bombay has so many Catholic churches. Around practically all of them there are people from Goa or Mangalore, all people who in India are called East Indians. And they are people who are native to Bombay, native in the sense that their languages are Morathi or Konkani. So these East Indians had pigs. Everybody's pigs herded together, and they formed their own pack. And they wandered everywhere together. Everywhere! Into the streets, into the woods, and they

Fig. 5.1 Vimala Rajendran. Photo by J. Caldwell for the Nasher Museum of Art at Duke University. June 28, 2012.

walked all around and they came home to roost. They would go to the next village, but they came home to roost.

I need to talk about pork itself in India, how we went on picnics from this Catholic school. How we hid it from the Muslims—and some of the Muslim kids who were adventurous without telling their parents would eat it and they loved it—and to this day they do! Because in a Catholic school, this is what went on.

The advent of pork for commercial purchase happened right in my lifetime. A brand name called Mafco, which means the government put this together to say, "cook the pork this way, so you don't get tapeworm." We knew in our family, being enlightened about proper food preparation—we would not touch raw pork, we would cook it very well so that we couldn't get sick. So pork was always cooked Goan style.

BW: What is distinctive about Goan style?

VR: There is some palm vinegar, lots of red chilis that were introduced by the Portuguese, and garlic. So vindaloo means vinegar, from wine, and then aloo is actually garlic. A lot of people will misinterpret the name and put potato into their vindaloo in commercial restaurants in the United States and say this just means pork and potato. Potato with any meat is great. It is one way for sustainable meat eating to be encouraged. It makes the meat so delicious. And it stretches the meat. A child can get plenty of potato and two one-inch cubes of pork—that was our portion.

My family didn't have a refrigerator. My mother herself didn't process pork as much as her neighbors did. So my first experience of pork is eating at the home of my neighbors when they had a christening service, or a wedding. So the aroma of pork cooking in the neighborhood and the squeals of the pig came in before I was actually able to put it in my mouth.

BW: So you grew up with pigs.

VR: I've seen them leading intelligent, communal lives. So it was intuitive for me to understand the instant I came to the United States that raising pigs in confinement, without the freedom to dig or forage, is morally and scientifically wrong. When I came to the United States, I came to Michigan. I had enough awareness about fresh and local—organic was not something I even thought about, because I remember that when India started using chemical fertilizers, it was first for wheat growing in Punjab. This was touted to be the new way to have better, bigger yields. The local people, including my family, rejected that. They went for what they called the "real food." They had various names—the real way, the old way, the home way, the village. When I got to Michigan I was interested in purchasing pork, and I don't remember when the connection was made in my mind that the meat that is in Styrofoam trays in a supermarket can come from not so good a source. But I instinctively knew it. So we did go to a farmers' market in Ann Arbor. And there was also something called Eastern Market in Detroit. And I knew that my family's food must come from alternate sources. It was that clear. And I cannot explain how, I just knew it.

I was always a community leader. Even within a few months of my arriving here, I organized the Indian festival, and giving people recipes and saying this is what our feast would be like. And this kind of seems to be the precursor to what I'm doing now—or what I did for eighteen years subsequently leading to the restaurant. Therefore, I must say I had not eaten any pork—not even bacon and sausage. I told myself, "I don't eat that meat." Until I saw an article about Cane Creek Farm in [the] Weaver Street Market newsletter, and the title was, roughly, "Heritage Breed Hogs: Olive Oil on Legs." Perhaps the first word in the article was "Ossabaw Hogs" from Georgia Sea Islands. It did it for me.

BW: This was the first pork that you really ate in the United States?

VR: I started to get pork from Eliza [MacLean of Cane Creek Farm], and I started making it right away into eastern Carolina slow-cooked barbecue and Indian curry.

BW: Was this as part of the community dinners you were doing, as well?

VR: The pulled pork barbeque was always for catering. We catered out of our home. And we catered for conferences, weddings, corporate meetings, and I would slow roast pork in my home oven—and sometimes even with wet wood chips. Just making all that up! And it was totally a home-grown version of pit-cooked barbecue. If I see something or eat something, I can figure it out, and I can make it.

Our community dinners started way before the catering. When I did the community dinners, I simultaneously did church dinners weekly at Chapel Hill Bible Church. And from those times, people were noticing my non-Indian cooking. Mediterranean, African, etc. I must say I have attempted cooking pork in some noneastern Indian styles. Bhutan, Nepal, those areas do cook pork, and I have read up about it, and I have tried to cook it. If I were to commercially serve this, then I want to learn it from the people who actually make it. I wouldn't look up a recipe for Nepalese pork and try to make it and serve it.

BW: So what do you like about pork? As you say, you have this long-term relationship with it, and it's always featured prominently on your menu.

VR: My mom went and spent some time in central India with some of her brothers because she needed medical treatment. Pork happened to be the best and most affordable meat for her brothers to feed her in the ten months that she stayed with them. So she went from weighing about 90 pounds as the mother of four children to a healthy 125 pounds when she came back to Bombay. Those 35 pounds made a huge difference in how she looked and how she felt. She ate pork once or twice a week. She attributed some healing and restorative power to the free-range pork that she ate.

BW: Has barbecue been a popular item on the menu? Do people know they can get it when they come to Curryblossom?

VR: This barbecue plate is a beautiful plate. I don't know of a single restaurant—there are no barbecue restaurants that are serving Cane Creek Farm pork barbecue eastern Carolina style with house-made pickles and the combination of things, all that with Cane Creek Farm pork piled up in such a generous portion. But it's important that we emphasize the fact that my mother had associations of getting healthier through the experience, which was far removed from a scarce ability of meat to having it regularly. And when I saw a headline that said "Olive Oil on Legs," it clicked. So if I ever diet, I know I can have lard and pork. I eat everything in moderation.

For the most part we've only had Cane Creek pork on our menu, and a small amount of Ofuskee Farm's pork. When the *New York Times* came and did an article on Crop Mob (Muhlke 2010), they were at Ofuskee Farm and I was providing food for that crop mob. And Bobby Tucker [of Ofuskee] was providing pork. And he finished them on acorn. And then the meat tastes like maple syrup—unbelievable. Other farmers have approached us about having their pork. I'm very, very loyal to Eliza Mac-Lean and her family. I love the fact that her children and these young up-and-coming farmers who pass through Cane Creek Farm are a great resource and add[ition]s to our agricultural wealth in this region. And they were all trained by Eliza.

Serving this absolutely beautiful, good-for-the-body meat . . . I have trained all of my staff to never ever pick up pork from a factory farm. They learn that from me. That knowledge goes so much farther when one restaurant makes the conscious choice to raise sustainably raised, humanely handled meats.

BW: You've been very active with Crop Mob, yes?

VR: I know some of the founders of Crop Mob. They are still active. It's loosely comprised of young activists who have no access to their own land. But they [don't] have the know-how but are willing to learn. When I had the community dinners at the house, Rob Jones [of Crop Mob] came. And he already had a rule in place for his meat eating. And that is, he wouldn't eat any meat, no matter what the label—if it's Niman Ranch and it says organic, natural pasture-raised—he wouldn't eat it because he hasn't met the farmer. So that kind of affirmed what I was doing. I'm not able to keep up that rule for chickens, because there is too much of a demand for it. We purchase as much local chicken as we can, though.

Here is how obsessive I am about this pork. I have a daughter, Anjali, who is now my pastry chef. When she lived in San Diego [and I went to visit her], I would fill up a suitcase with shrink-wrapped Cane Creek pork—eighty pounds!

BW: So what have you learned since you opened Curryblossom?

VR: What I know is customers get pretty upset if I run out of pork. If I make pork any other way, we cannot have enough pork to satisfy demand. That's amazing. I'm actually excited to have become a prolific consumer of pork in that sense. Because I'm able to get approximately 150 to 200 pounds of pork a week. When we go to some events, it's the first meat to sell out. One bite, and you can see that people can tell the difference. Because [of the way] our bodies are made, we have the fine-tuning to recognize what is good for the body. The taste is *in there* for that very reason. Something that's tasteless . . . I tell you, I saw a piece of factory-farmed pork. I picked it up, and it smelled like a public restroom. There was something about the smell—it smelled like putrefying urine! I have never smelled that on our pork!

Let's go back to pork vindaloo. There's something about pork vindaloo that has a universal appeal. You know people, animals, birds all relate to music no matter where the music is from. I feel so good on the inside, if it had been any other style of curry I don't feel that it would have been as popular as it is. You know, this may be a desirable byproduct of colonialism. Such a practice of cooking meat in a stew, with vinegar, red chilis, and garlic. Garlic and red chilis figure in practically every cuisine in the world because of colonialism. Therefore, there's not a single person who comes in here, if it is permissible for them, that this recipe is not good. I have had so many comments made by people: "What brilliant use of vinegar!" "What perfect texture of the pork!" I want to digress into the matter of cooking the whole hog, which is something people who consume meat from a commercial context do not understand—the rind, and some level of fat, based on the way the hog was raised and the breed, as well as the meat. Those are three separate items that will feature in most whole pieces that come from the outside. Some inside pieces will have muscle only. But rind, fatty tissue, the meat—those three pieces are exactly how pork is cut in India for curries. People need to give that experience a chance. Most people try to take a knife and carve out the fatty tissue and the rind. The fatty tissue is no longer all fat, because we have skimmed that off after slow cooking. That's the only way I've seen pork dishes made in India. We have a kind of ham in India that has the rind, some fat, and a little meat—that's ham. It may be rolled, so it resembles Canadian bacon, so we call it ham. All bacon has the rind. So I've never seen pork not accompanied by rind. And the other way I make pork is pickled. In this case, the slices are very similar to the vindaloo. But the pork pieces are roasted after they're cut into small cubes. And then it preserves in the vinegar.

BW: Do you have a vision for your future?

VR: I'm actually hoping that stories like this will go on to define and recognize the Curryblossom Café in its uniqueness. Its uniqueness being, serving foods not served by other restaurants—especially Indian restaurants do not serve local products. And the next thing for us would be to raise enough money so we can have our own space and building where we can have a teaching space and kitchen, where people can come and learn about this directly from me, and more spreading of knowledge can happen. I hope it is in Carrboro.

BW: Let me ask you a touchy question. Here you are on Franklin Street, and there's a bit of competition from three other Indian restaurants . . .

VR: There's *no* competition—absolutely none. They are [a] very different kind of restaurant. They all fit into the typical expectation that you might expect from an Indian restaurant. They all have fluffy bread, wonderful bread from a tandoor oven. The content of that bread is Cargill flour. We are making our bread with homemade yogurt with fresh milk from local free-roaming cows. And wheat that has been locally grown and milled. There's no matching that. [Other restaurants say] you're doing mother's cooking. Rather than making an extra effort to belong to a sisterhood that seems exclusive, I belong to the motherhood of chefs.

PROFILE: Sam Suchoff

—

Sam Suchoff is the chef and owner of The Pig, a restaurant in Chapel Hill that has been at the forefront of featuring pasture-raised pigs and offering innovative offerings on its menu—like the Vietnamese pork cheek sandwich and a range of smoked and emulsified sausages—that together use every part of the

animal. I met Sam just before he opened The Pig in 2009, when he was working
at various restaurants in Chapel Hill and Carrboro, regularly visiting the Carr-
boro Farmers' Market, and looking to work with niche-market pig farmers in
the area to help develop his ideas for the restaurant. We talked in October 2014
about what had motivated his interest in sustainable foods and pastured pigs,
and what his experience had been like running The Pig.

BW: Tell me your story. How did your concern for local meats develop?

SS: At first I was a vegetarian and then a vegan, and then I realized there were other ways to get involved.

BW: Do you remember what brought about that change?

SS: Cooking. Working. I think it's common for people in the craft of meat cookery. I think it's really alluring. I think that's why it's such a common story. Although I didn't get into it by cooking meat, I got into it cooking at a French restaurant, and then I became the garde-manger and doing the terrines and stuff like that. But it wasn't that I was interested in meat, it was that I was interested in this job.

My parents would go to the farmers' market here, so I was aware of it. It's in the air. I think at the point that I was working in restaurants I was friends with a lot of chefs who were interested in local meats. Garde-manger work kind of dragged me through my next few jobs. And I ended up at the BBQ Joint, where they were making their own sausages and bacon and all that stuff. I could come in and say, "Hey, what do you think about this?" And they'd be like, "All right, let's try it."

For a while, before I started working in kitchens, I got my understanding and connections through the farmers' market. And working through NC Choices I got an awareness of just how many people are out there doing pigs. It's not a niche market. Well, it is a niche market, but the farmers' market is just a niche of what is out there more broadly. There are processors and people hauling stuff back and forth. The farmer brings [the pig] to the slaughterhouse, and their cuts get hauled by this seafood delivery company, for example. I didn't have to create anything; I just had to bring the people together. So I just became aware of all the connections out there through NC Choices. I knew about them through the BBQ Joint, when they would come in to talk to me about some of the stuff I was making, like bologna or hot dogs.

Working through NC Choices I became very aware of the Co-op [the NC Natural Hog Growers Association]. To me, NC Choices was looking

Fig. 5.2 Sam Suchoff.

to have a relationship with the farmer, to find farmers and *be* their connection to customers. And the Co-op has taken the additional step to join together [with NC Choices]. When I opened The Pig, I wasn't aware of how much of the work they'd already done. I was like, "All right, I'm gonna open this place." I kind of thought that what I'd be doing—having relationships with different farmers, and having to do all the scheduling, and all that stuff. But the Co-op is just, "How many pigs do you want a week?" So I started working with the Co-op just after I opened in 2009. At first I was working with some other farmers, but I found the Co-op pretty quickly. They're so easy.

One of the things about the trendiness of the local or Slow Food movement here is this notion that "the farmer can bring you their pork chop." It's a limitation of direct marketing that the Co-op doesn't deal with. I started doing three pigs a week. But this next week I've got ten pigs coming. Ideally, I'd be doing fifteen pigs a week, but twelve pigs a week is probably where we'll be.

BW: How did you go from three to twelve?

SS: I kind of was always aware that you could do whole-hog barbecue, throw the loins in the smoker—that's the least valuable part for barbecue, but it's the most expensive cut. At one point I thought maybe I could trade loins with someone for shoulder. And then I thought I could sell the loins to restaurants, and for a while I was doing that. But once I had time to think about it, and spending fourteen hours a day here, we hit on doing bacon and hot dogs. It became clearer that I could be getting more pigs if I concentrated on these. So I would sell loins to high-end restaurants in town. But then I started this relationship with Weaver Street. They had wanted to do local pork and whole hogs, but they just couldn't use all the parts. People just want to buy pork chops. And I knew that, I knew that I needed to get hooked up with them as a market. I guess up until I really made the deal with them, I thought I might not be big enough to supply them enough. But it works because they have a sausage kitchen, and that allows me to make more hot dogs so that I can supply them with enough volume. The bacon production scaled up first, and the hot dogs were just becoming more popular at the farmers' market. We started doing hot dogs at the market in year one. Until we worked out all the details of them selling hot dogs and bacon and barbecue in their stores, I didn't know I could move through more. And I wouldn't have been able to do enough pigs to supply them. And so it's all tied together.

BW: So why pork? Do people still have an interest in pork? And do you still find it interesting?

SS: Yeah, I think a lot of that inspiration is built on relationships. My relationships with the people I work with. It's not when I make a new product, but it's great when things jibe with me and the Co-op, or making things work with Weaver Street. It's maintaining the relationships. I mean, I love pork, but it's an ingredient, it's taken a smaller and smaller part in mind of what I'm doing.

BW: Do consumers still have an interest?

SS: Yeah, it's busier this year than last, and that's been true every year. But I did not open a *new* restaurant. The BBQ Joint was here before, I didn't build a clientele. It would have been a ton harder, and something I wouldn't have done.

I've never been trying to make "the best barbecue in NC." Although I want to make the best food, and if I'm making barbecue, I want that to be the best. But I'm not concerned with my standing in the barbecue community. For the first couple of years it kind of bothered me. There's this one blogger [who] did something on me, and he really liked what we were doing, but he said, "It's not really a barbecue place." And I was like, "No! I really am!" But it took me a while to realize that a barbecue place has barbecue, cole slaw, cornbread, maybe chicken once a week, and that's all. So it took me a bit to realize that I'm not that, and that's totally fine. And we still sell more barbecue than anything else. Although some weeks it's mac and cheese.

BW: Yeah, because mac and cheese is a vegetable in North Carolina!

SS: And you get two servings [of vegetables] if you put ketchup on it.

BW: What are some challenges you face going forward?

SS: Trusting people and being trusted. 'Cause my relationship with Weaver Street is just that. We have no written agreement. It's precarious. Both sides need the other. Doing the hams is the same. In a year and a half I have to trust that I can find customers for ham eighteen months later. Eighteen thousand pounds of ham is just sitting there curing now. I started really putting them up about sixteen months ago, and those I've sold to a [tapas restaurant in Durham]. It's too expensive for [The Pig]. The idea is to get hooked up with some restaurant group that could distribute it. I made the connection on the hams with Eliza [MacLean of Cane Creek Farm], working with the ham maker in Smithfield.

BW: How did you know that this was going to work?

SS: For the past five plus years charcuterie has been super hot, Southern food has been super hot, and sustainable food has been super hot. So as long as I have these connections that allow me to get the best product for the best price, it should work. And I saw how other restaurants do it. And I thought it would work. Making good food isn't that hard. But it's about the people and the relationships. Being a boss is different for me. I try to create an environment where everyone wants to be here. We all are doing what we want to be doing. And it benefits the person next to us.

BW: Do you have other aspirations?

SS: I want to continue to work with the Co-op and Weaver Street and really create a very inclusive sustainable whole-hog system that gets good food to the most amount of people possible. Not necessarily making the most money at it, but paying people what they're worth. Getting a wholesale line to something bigger, that doesn't interest [me]. I'm fine being this kind of business. Food at that scale doesn't need my help. I want to use every part [of the pig] to its highest value so that you can get pork on everyone's plate.

6

FARM TO FORK, SNOUT TO TAIL

Having moved from butchery and the fabrication of pig parts, each with its particular qualities, through the way that perceptions of taste articulate social and historical modes of consciousness, I turn in this final ethnographic chapter to the reassembly of these parts and tastes in what could be called an ethos-driven cuisine. As was the case with taste, we will find that contemporary cooking, in the Piedmont as well as many other regions across the United States that are committed to the kind of "locavorism" found there, is interested simultaneously in innovation and recollection. How these possibilities are reconfigured and what requalifications are entailed in this culinary program are my central concerns in this chapter. I consider the kinds of alternative totalities that are proposed and enacted in contemporary local food activism. And since each whole is always a relation of parts that can be understood only in terms of the significance that derives from the dynamic organization of the whole (Weiss 1996, 155), these novel totalities are equally composed of reimagined elements (the new parts of new wholes). The totalities considered here instantiate a particular vision of circulation, a model of food as a means of promoting unification and integration in and across different spatial, social, ecological, and culinary domains. The twinned modes of integration I examine, a farm-to-fork producer-consumer nexus and snout-to-tail cookery, each instantiates a complex whole. They do so in parallel, if inverse, fashion. The farm-to-fork spatial process, a theme that is taken up by restaurants, grocery stores, and specialty food purveyors and in a number of events (such as picnics, dinners, and wine tastings) incorporates a range of actors set in motion (and so taking place) and brought together through productive consumption.[1] The snout-to-tail mode of butchery and cookery (Henderson 2004) is also a spatial process, but here the space is an embodied animal—almost always the pig (blessed with snout and tail)—now understood not simply as a source of meat, but as both a once-animate creature with specific life functions (an actual pig) and a field of material forms that offer a range of culinary possibilities (snouts, tails, and all the cuts in between). Neither of the totalities is merely a group of related, substitutable elements, however. Instead, they are distinctive structures, whose distinctiveness lies in both the specificity of the particular parts and the reconfiguration of their relationships to one another. There is both an aesthetic and an ethics at work here, for, as I shall demonstrate, not just any parts will do, and not all relationships are given equal weight. My aim, then, is to think through how and why these wholes are constituted as an appropriate configuration of relations among particular, identifiable parts to understand the forms of value that they generate.

Clearly there is an appeal to totalities, not only in the activities of food activists and farmers but also in the social scientific actors that examine sociocultural phenomena more generally. Why do we find wholes, completion, and integrity compelling in aesthetic as well as analytical terms?[2] We need to recognize the long history of the whole, totality, holism, and structure's assumption of invariant relations among elements—the idea that unity is greater than the sum of its parts—that has marked most of the history of the social sciences to make sense of contemporary interest in partial connections, multiplicity, rupture, and the fragmentary (Haraway 2008; Strathern 2004). All of these singularities carry the weight and plausibility they do precisely because they presume the force of totalization, understood as a kind of mastery or domination (perhaps fictive; undoubtedly contested) that can be productively suspended, interrupted, or interrogated. My approach to the farm-to-fork cookery I describe, then, has reflexive implications for our anthropological assessments as well. In what follows I will, as I have attempted to do throughout this book, demonstrate how the political economic implications of farm-to-fork and snout-to-tail activities are articulated precisely in terms of the concrete qualities that constitute an economy of qualities that incorporates not only things edible but an array of people, animals, objects, and the relations among them that constitute the contemporary American food system and its possible alternatives.

Political Economic and Demographic Realignments

In political economic terms, local food alternatives are routinely advanced as a challenge to received wholes, a disruption of the prevailing forms of totalization manifested most clearly in the agricultural-industrial complex (Niman 2009; Pollan 2007; Schlosser 2001). These challenges nonetheless depend precisely on holism and amalgamation, as analytics and aesthetics, to demonstrate their critiques. Opponents of industrial agriculture decry the damage wrought by food conglomerates, but nonetheless they embrace integration as an esteemed dimension of sociality and action. This embrace can be seen quite clearly in the way that advocates for local food highly value, at the most abstract level, a range of what are deemed connections forged between elements and actors, producers and consumers, terrain and technique, and seasonality and sustenance. As we have seen above, notions of terroir emphasize the ways in which seasonality, animal husbandry, agricultural "tasks" (in Tim Ingold's [2000] sense), and distinctive features of a regional landscape are routinely characterized as modes of connection—a process that I have shown to be central to the ways that place is constituted in this world. My discussion of butchery also emphasized the ways that embodied skills, animal welfare, and specific cuts of meat are all grasped as ways of making a powerful connection— what is described as "a new intimacy" (Moskin 2008) between animals and processors, as well as between chefs and consumers, who increasingly take an interest in participating in these practices. This privileging of linkage and interconnection is vital to contemporary ethics—and contemporary materialism—on a number of levels. It weaves through concerns with sustainability in agriculture and environmental practice; with health, animal welfare, and food security; and with community-building efforts in new food political movements. Such connections are also critical to an overarching motivation (and so a leading value) of the food reform movement—namely, people's desire for authenticity in the foods they eat and the social processes through which this food is produced. I discuss the value of the authentic at length below. What should be clear is that the globalized consolidations of vertically integrated confined animal feeding operations are also a complex set of manifold relations, which (somehow) do not constitute connections to be valued in the same way. Which connections count, then? How should proper connections be forged, and what distinguishes the kinds of complex wholes that locavores aspire to assemble? How do we confront vertical integration with a food ethics of integrity? What kinds of linkages are displaced and which valorized by these projects?

In asking about both displacement and replacement of this kind, we might also note that this new holism and the totalities wrought by it are compelling to a certain kind of community that is itself displaced and replaced. While not a prominent concern (especially in the Piedmont of central North Carolina) among those industrial and agricultural laborers gripped by the ruptures of the present high-industrial moment, con-temporary cosmopolitans have embraced these new modes of totaliza-tion. What I hope to demonstrate, then, is how such highly mobile and well-resourced communities seek to reimagine the spaces they inhabit, cultivating an appreciation of valued connections in a well-integrated and reconfigured domain. In so doing, I will also show how the same processes that have forged industrial agriculture (especially animal production) have promoted the alternative connections that critics of such industrial pro-cesses now also promote.

Working across the diverse sites of farming, marketing, butchery, and restaurant cookery has afforded me a valuable vantage point from which to observe the changing demographics of the Piedmont and so appreciate certain critical political economic dimensions of the newly configured to-talities that constitute the region's efforts to promote an alternative food system. The population of North Carolina is growing faster than that of any other state east of the Mississippi River (U.S. Census Bureau n.d.), and North Carolina has the fastest growing Latino population in the country (Learn NC n.d.). This shifting population has had a wide-ranging but un-even impact on the food systems of the Piedmont. To begin with the de-mographic particulars: many recent arrivals to central North Carolina are drawn by a combination of tax incentives,[3] the educational resources of the three major research universities in the Triangle (the University of North Carolina, Duke University, and North Carolina State University); and the presence of so-called right-to-work laws that weaken unions' abilities to re-cruit workers and bargain with management. This coordination of factors has contributed, for example, to the growth of IBM in the Piedmont, whose campus in Research Triangle Park—an industrial park founded in the late 1950s—employs 11,000 people (although they have been subject to widespread layoffs in recent years), making it the largest of the corporation's operations in the United States. Many of these employees have been relocated from such regions as southern Minnesota, California's Silicon Valley, and New York's Hudson River Valley. This pattern of shifting capital into North Carolina, and the Piedmont in particular, is replicated in industries like pharmaceuticals, software engineering, communications, and electronics that have facilities in the Research Triangle Park.

The influx of a population drawn to high-tech industries (and their relatively higher salaries) and university employment that expanded in the region through the first decade of this century helps define the cosmopolitan community that has attempted to take root in the region. As I showed in chapter 3, many of its members do so, in significant ways, through their commitments to local foods, and so provide a well-resourced and well-educated consumer base for the growth of the burgeoning alternative food movement in the region. That process of finding a place through food is a central focus of this chapter. But at the same time, these demographic shifts have not only generated a powerful clientele for alternative food producers, they have also transformed the character of production itself. This is true in ways that often seem contradictory. The same regulatory environment that motivates shifts in capital in the high-tech (and related) sectors has also led to the expansion of industrial agriculture in the state. As I showed in chapter 1, the legal infrastructure that was enacted in the North Carolina legislature in the 1980s contributed directly to the rapid transformation of the pork industry, which also led to changes in the structures of the financial industry. Indeed, there is reason to assert that that boom in financialized production through contract agriculture contributed to the rise of the banking and insurance industries during the same era. The city of Charlotte, just to the west of the Piedmont, is now home to both Bank of America and Wells Fargo; it is the second largest banking center in the United States, after New York City. The expansion of industrial agriculture has contributed directly to the influx of Latinos to the region, where the meatpacking and processing industry was responsible for the largest share of the growth in North Carolina's Central American and Mexican population from 1993 to 1997 (Duke University Center on Globalization, Governance and Competitiveness n.d.). The food service industry, more generally, in the Piedmont—as in a great many regions of the United States (National Council of La Raza 2011)—employs Latino immigrants in sizable numbers. Indeed, my fieldwork with restaurant staff members across the Piedmont indicates that almost all of the prep work, as well as most of the cooking, is carried out by a Latino (almost exclusively Mexican) labor force in restaurants that explicitly endorse the consumption of local foods.

It's interesting to note, however, that many of these restaurants (in contrast to the meat processing industry) often celebrate their immigrant labor force. Consider Miguel Torres, the chef de cuisine at the James Beard Award–winning locavore Chapel Hill restaurant, Lantern. Torres has been featured in local newspaper accounts that describe his self-taught mastery of restaurant work (Weigl 2011) and further extolled in Slow Food–oriented cookbooks (Reusing 2011; Roahen and Edge 2010). In these mediated representations of Torres's culinary skills, he offers his recipe for *carnitas* (Reusing 2011, 235–36; Roahen and Edge 2010, 143). This is a telling form of representation. While it clearly acknowledges the significance of Mexican craftsmen in the Piedmont's "local food" scene and even reframes the "local" as a place that incorporates Mexican culinary heritage (carnitas, like tamales, are now branded as a Southern food), offering Torres's recipe for a Mexican fiesta dish like carnitas as a demonstration of his contribution to local foods stands in some contrast to the fact that his and his many Mexican coworkers' days are spent cooking Lantern's Beard Award–winning meals that present "a marriage of Asian flavors and North Carolina ingredients" (Lantern n.d.). In other words, the inclusion of the skills of Torres and other Mexican cooks as critical features of the Piedmont's culinary world simultaneously excludes Torres by situating him in an indirect relationship to that locality, as accounts of his expertise in local cuisine represent him primarily as a bearer of Mexican heritage (even as his skills are exhibited in the Asian-fusion cuisine he cooks each day).[4]

The movement of capital produces a widespread displacement and relocation of populations, even across class and racial divisions. This movement, in turn, generates a characteristic social and cultural dynamic in which relationships within and across communities establish modes of belonging that are simultaneously inclusive and exclusive (a widespread feature of neoliberal restructuring around the world; Geschiere and Nyamnjoh 2000; Weiss 2004 and 2009). Erstwhile New York software engineers searching the Durham or Carrboro farmers' markets for artisanal bacon and immigrant line cooks from Celaya, Mexico, are all participants engaged in remaking an alternative, local food system. And they do so in ways that reveal how the cultural forms of such local foods are constituted by practices that valorize certain relationships—or connections—and incorporate certain participants into these new totalities, even as they marginalize the presence of those participants in the totalities.[5] Of course, the political economic implications of this dynamic are many and varied. In what follows I focus on the specific qualities manifested in the connections that constitute pastured pork markets. In this way I aim to show how these esteemed connections—between customers and farmers, between animals and humans, and among the constituent elements of animals (that is, their parts)—are icons of the sociocultural processes of value creation through which they are produced.

Connecting with Carolina Pigs

The Carrboro Farmers' Market where I work celebrates its commitment to connection in its bylaws, which require that farmers or their immediate family members be present at the market to sell their products. The market further requires that farmers actually produce what they sell, a stricture enforced by examining receipts for seeds and feed and the occasional surprise inspection of a farm. All of this is meant to assure, as the presiding officer of the market put it, that "customers make that connection with our producers." Customers confirm this commitment. As one of my survey (discussed in chapter 5) respondents wrote, "I like that every week I can look my farmer in the eye, know her name, and feel good about my purchases." These commitments by farmers and customers to such face-to-face connections are central to the ways that authenticity is materialized in this alternative food system. Both producers and consumers, as we will see, seek to demonstrate that such connections provide the assurance that they are trafficking in "real food." Such food is the product of uncompromising discernment on the part of consumers and of the tactile, hands-on character of labor, personified by "the farmer" at the market. Such direct—indeed, bodily—immediacy and self-evident quality (which is recognized by knowledgeable consumers) are central to the way that authenticity—that is, the realness of this food and of the experience more generally—is constituted by, and works effectively within, this alternative food system.

This kind of commitment to materialized sociality is deeply connected to the demographic transformations described above. Much of the Triangle's population is looking to localize itself precisely through such highly personalized links. More generally, this kind of commitment, and its celebration in such a shifting locale, is part and parcel of what Robert Foster (drawing on Giddens 1991 and Tomlinson 1999) describes as a "dialectical process of disembedding and reembedding" (Foster 2008, 18). Under conditions of postmodernity, systems of abstraction (like industrial production) that amplify social distance and detachment are simultaneously reintegrated into regional lifeworlds (or "appropriated") reflecting the "mutability of local circumstances and engagement" (Giddens 1991, quoted in Foster 2008, 19).

Yet far from a triumph over the disembedding forces of alienation of the sort that anthropologists routinely ascribe to cultural appropriations, these face-to-face connections can in fact be a source of anxiety, as the labor required of farmers at the market and in marketing more generally is a constant topic of discussion among producers. Consider many of the processes involved in farming, marketing, and processing that I have discussed above. Direct marketing has been the preferred method for small farmers to bring their produce to market, but most have discovered that the demands of marketing in terms of the costs of transportation, infrastructure, and especially time often exceed the demands of activities on the farm. Moreover, the apparently straightforward requirement that vendors sell only what they produce turns out to be rather contentious, especially for meat producers. Pigs, for example, are regularly "grown out" by pastured-pork farmers from feeder pigs sold by larger breeders. Moreover, the value-added products—sausages and cured meats—that are a staple for many meat vendors are subject to additional scrutiny. Many meat producers have recounted the challenge of assuring customers—and other vendors—that they can vouch for their products when they have been processed, manufactured, and packaged by a third (and often fourth) party. Such are the carnivorous challenges to a farm-to-fork ethos.[6] These challenges are ameliorated by certain producers who will, on occasion, process their own meat and add their own value, producing what is often called "bootleg sausage." A number of dining establishments that I worked with also acquired some of the pork products they used—usually bacon, but often some other charcuterie—from an unlicensed artisan (often a budding butcher curing meat in his or her home facility) in a kind of contemporary version of bootleg sausage. As the term implies, such unregulated efforts are almost always illegal and necessarily sub rosa, but they also confirm the value of connectedness, as only those in the know—usually through direct, trusted, personal ties to the farmer—can participate in such underground circulation.

The privileged connections of the farmers' market and related venues suggest that there is a kind of enhanced value to the circulations that are forged at various levels among producers, consumers, and the objects—here, the meat—whose transactions constitute these connections. My suggestion is that this enhanced value is widely grasped and described as a quality of authenticity. This authenticity is both an organizing principle of these connections that unites them into a totality and a concrete characteristic that is materially present in the incorporated objects. In this way the kind of value given to the socioeconomic relationships formed between farmers and customers is also present in the meat. The authenticity of the former, we might say, is authenticated by the qualities of the latter. This parallel and the point of correlation between farm-to-fork and snout-to-tail activities were illustrated for me in a not unusual discussion that took place at my neighborhood market. Eliza MacLean and I were chatting with a regular customer of hers, a well-regarded chef at a premier restaurant in the region, when MacLean was approached by another couple who were hoping to begin a culinary tourism service that would take clients to restaurants across the region and to farmers' markets where they could meet and—in their words—"make a connection with local farmers." In the course of this discussion they asked MacLean a very specific question: "What is the message you're trying to get across to customers?" Ever ready with a reply, Eliza answered that her customers "need to know that connection to the animal," and they further need to be aware that there's a "complete disconnect in the confinement operations, where the pigs are treated like car batteries"—each bred to uniform standards under inhumane industrial conditions. At that point the chef added that "from a chef's point of view," he wants people "to see that connection and to make them think about how they use that animal, and what can be wasted and what isn't wasted—and so, how every piece of that life that was sacrificed for us needs to be made use of."

Here is a clear and powerful concatenation of contemporary food activism, combining producers, consumers, farmers, chefs, tourists, towns, markets, animals, humans, the agrarian, and the industrial (although this is less included in the picture than recognized as the standard practice that is negated by pasture raising) into an organized whole, itself a virtual hieroglyph (that is, an icon) of the farm-to-fork principle. What is given value in these accounts are precisely the kinds of privileged connection that are both generated by the transactions among these various actors and also presupposed as a premise of the orientation and motivation of their practices. Why else would a farmer be presumed to have a message—and not just a pork chop—that she wanted to get across to customers, were it not for the prior orientation toward "creating a connection" that underlies these encounters? Note in particular that these privileged connections are not just features of the social relations and transactions described above, as these forms of value are also embedded in the objects themselves—the living, breathing animals raised on pasture as well as "every piece of that life" that becomes the meat that customers consume. In effect, the qualities of integration and linkage (if the porcine adjective can be forgiven) are qualisigns of the modes of sociality and production that are materialized in the pork that consumers desire.

Revaluing Desire and Virtue

In what follows I consider two more complex ethnographic events. The first is an annual fund-raising picnic held in the North Carolina Piedmont fortuitously titled Farm to Fork; the second is one of the butchery programs that was arranged for discerning pork aficionados in a small town in the same region, which I discussed above. My purpose is threefold. First, I want to unpack some of the complex ways in which these modes of totalizing connection are concretely manifested in practice and, more specifically, how they are experienced as features of reality itself—that is, how what we eat has value that makes it part of a wider array of things and people in motion (Farquhar 2006). Second, by describing the concreteness of these qualities, I hope to specify the form of value that circulates through and is objectified in what I have called privileged connections. And finally, I will suggest how this form of value might relate to the wider questions of cosmopolitanism that I spelled out above as a mode of practice and political economy.

The Farm to Fork Picnic is an annual event, a kind of gourmand's state fair—but instead of turkey legs and deep-fried Twinkies on a stick, it combines over two hundred farmers and chefs from across the Piedmont of North Carolina, who offer up seasonal products expertly prepared. Attendees pay over $100 to—well, pig out is too obvious a turn of phrase. In any case, the money supports farm apprenticeship programs in the region. Not surprisingly, pork figures prominently on the menu—as one chef I worked with in 2009 put it, "Hey, it's North Carolina—people expect to have pork at a picnic." What was especially noteworthy about this event was the way the pork was prepared. In May 2010, given the half-dozen pig farmers who participated in the event, only one of the dishes prepared by the eight chefs who offered pork served barbecue, usually a de rigueur component of a Carolina picnic. There were, though, three different preparations of headcheese and two versions of braised pork belly sandwiches. In 2009, a chef I worked with at a pan-Asian restaurant offered braised grilled pig-tails. An illustration of the snout-to-tail aesthetic, and its implications, are exemplified in this encounter at the 2010 picnic, when a customer looked at an offering on a picnic table at the booth of a leading chef in the region (figure 6.1):

CUSTOMER: What is that?

CHEF: It's headcheese.

CUSTOMER (GRIMACING): Ugh.

CHEF: If I would have said pork terrine you would have tried it?

CUSTOMER: If you had said what?

CHEF: It's nothing you've not ever had in a hot dog.

At this point the chef's staff members start to laugh, and the sous chef chimes in, "That's for sure, only it's better."

"If you've ever had a hot dog," continues the chef, "you've had every-thing that's in that. And waaay more!"

The sous chef went on to describe the dish to the next customer: "It's a terrine, or some people call it headcheese. It's made from the jowl of the pig."

"It's a flat hot dog!" one of the staff members pipes up.

So why the prevalence of headcheese? And why not a hot dog? Just to be clear, farmers and chefs in the region produce ample quantities of artisanal sausage (including some of the world's finest hot dogs), some of which was available at the picnic. Yet clearly there is something compel-ling about offering headcheese—that has everything "you've ever had in a hot dog"—in such abundance and with such advocacy at a fund-raiser de-signed to promote local farm products and local chefs' skills. I would note that if headcheese is just like a hot dog, only different, there are a num-ber of things that make up that difference. The sociological indexicality of the foods is a somewhat complicated matter (Bourdieu 1984; Silverstein 2004). While it might seem that the hot dog is the more plebeian of the two, in fact, headcheese is often lauded by the chefs who prepare, and oc-casionally by their patrons who eat, it as an "old-timey" concoction, locally known in North Carolina as souse (from the German *Sülze* by way of local

Fig. 6.1 Preparing headcheese.

people's Pennsylvania Dutch antecedents who brought it, along with most things porcine to the region). And souse is remembered, by those who still remember it, as a meat of hardship, a mixture of accumulated meat trimmings, boiled and congealed in the natural gelatins of animal bone and sinew. It is often eaten, according to the people who recall eating it as souse and not headcheese, not as an appetizer, as a terrine or pâté would be (and as it was served at the picnic), but as a bit of what is called "side meat," a garnish (sometimes fried) for breakfast with grits and eggs. All of which is to say that the social positioning of headcheese is rather complicated. On the one hand, the economizing praxis of the dish—scrap elements prepared for maximum preservation and a nourishing farm breakfast—and the social class fragment with which it is prominently associated suggest a decidedly rural, working-class habitus. Here headcheese seems a classic *"amor fati"* as Pierre Bourdieu describes it, "the choice of destiny, but a forced choice produced by conditions of existence which rule out all alternatives as mere daydreams and leave no choice but the taste for the necessary" (1984, 178).

On the other hand, headcheese has plainly become emblematic of a rather different class fragment, a group of cosmopolitan cognoscenti who can afford to pay substantially for the privilege of sampling a bite of hand-crafted heritage terrine on a cracker. Yet this culinary valorization is not a simple act of sociological distinction, not merely an embodied taste of luxury reserved for the dominant class, as Bourdieu might suggest. I would argue instead that the prominence of headcheese at an event such as the picnic (and on menus across the region, where it is now found with some regularity), is a form of revaluation motivated by producers and consumers—that is, by their tastes—who do not seek to distinguish themselves from plebeian necessity but rather to incorporate the values embedded in "the necessary" (for example, economizing, heartiness, richness, and robustness versus delicacy) into novel modes of gastronomic practice. From this perspective, headcheese is, indeed, just like a hot dog—as long as that hot dog is an emulsified artisanal sausage of grass-fed beef and heritage breed pork fat offered up at $8 a pound. Each preparation is less about making a virtue of necessity than about crafting an aesthetic that appreciates the necessary as virtuous.

This kind of revaluation is widespread among locavores. To assess its significance and specify more concretely what kind of value this revaluation is, it is helpful to look directly at the materiality of the tastes that are desired in this way. Headcheese, to consider this offering again, in its substantive form is, again, just like a hot dog only different, not only in that the dish itself is composed of various tidbits and remnants (like a hot dog), but also in the fact that the form of the preparation draws attention to the fact of this composition. It is plain to see, that is, that headcheese is a collection of odds and ends—of parts—that have been assembled into a totality. In this respect, it is an apt illustration of a commitment to snout-to-tail cookery, a truly iconic dish in the strict Peircean sense, which makes it clear that every element of the once-living animal has been incorporated into the final application. Again, this visible parsimony is presented not because of the constraints of frugality, but to present an interest in caring for each part of the animal—"every piece of that life" as the chef at the farmers' market put it—as a form of inventive virtue, both desirable and caring. The recognition of a regional narrative of hardship and the frank incorporation of visceral pig parts both contribute to an appreciation of headcheese as a real food, an embodiment of the authenticity that animates the wider food movement. Note, as well, that this kind of preparation—in its concrete qualities, its historical recollection of economizing tastes, and its performance within the setting of a fund-raising picnic where it can be offered to a highly discerning (and well-heeled) clientele—also substantiates the dynamic of inclusion and exclusion discussed above. The thrifty culinary practices of rural, working-class communities can be included and even valorized, but only by transformations (even in the simple renaming of souse as headcheese) that decisively exclude working-class participation in the actual eating of the dish, served up on crackers to customers who have paid a tidy sum for the sample.

The Meats of the Matter: The Qualities of Substance

This is how David Chang of Momofuku in New York's East Village begins his recipe for "pig's head torchon": "Pigs have heads. Every one of them does. Farmers do not raise walking pork chops. If you're serious about your meat, you've got to grasp that concept. And if you're serious about sustainability and about honestly raised good meat—which is something that we're deadly serious about at Momofuku *and we try to get more in touch with* each day—you've got to embrace the whole pig" (Chang and Meehan 2009, 201; emphasis added). Here, the cataloging of animal parts draws attention to the whole beast, the living animal, and the connections among its parts that make such committed cookery—committed to taste, animal welfare, sustainability, and community well-being—possible. These same manifold concerns can also account for the prevalence on the menus of fine dining establishments of a host of animal, particularly pig, parts that until recent years might never have been seen there—long braised shanks, the aforementioned tails, an array of porcine offal, and the truly ubiquitous pork belly. As a farmer with whom I work put it, "I'd make a fortune if I could figure out how to raise a pig with four bellies." In fact, her pigs' bellies are regularly sold to restaurants before her animals are even processed. For ingredients like these to receive the attention they do, there must first be an appreciation of the distinctiveness of animal parts that both derive from and contribute to a complex whole. The recognition of this whole-part relationship is also a way of extolling the care (for community, animal life, and taste) that is both embedded in the concrete parts and meant to be characteristic of the cuisine—indeed, of the production and provisioning process as a whole.

In all of these ways, snout-to-tail cookery, with its emphasis on understanding the specific character and qualities of all the various cuts, regions, and purposes of the once-living pig and how to properly prepare them (which in the pork industry is known as "the utilization problem"), is a way of reconfiguring the relationship between the animal as a whole and its body as an assemblage of parts. Note, of course, that all of these preparations are derived from parts (tails, shanks, offal, and bellies) that are characterized as "tough" (see chapter 4), so they require the skills of the butcher or chef who embodies the ethos of connection between the human and nonhuman animal. In all of these ways, highly prized distinctive pork cuts become icons of the sociocultural process that produces them. They are imbued with the qualities of a kind of esteemed connectivity, for they are the revalued elements that make it possible to enact an alternative food system whose members are seeking to energize a social field committed to integration, linkage, and reconnecting parts and wholes, from farm to fork and from snout to tail.

It should also be pointed out that this kind of revaluation runs directly counter to the operational understandings of the meat processing industry during the last century. As Nöelie Vialles puts it in *Animal to Edible*, her study of the French abattoir, "we demand an ellipsis between animal and meat" (1994, 5). This ellipsis is achieved, according to Vialles, by procedures that are designed to "de-animalize" the body of a steer or pig so as to make of the carcass "a foodstuff, a *substance*; all the links that attached it to a once living body [are] severed" (127). This is the feature that distinguishes meat from a living animal: it is a substance that is uniform, homogenized, and devoid of evidence of links.

It should be clear that this demand for an "ellipsis," which I think Vialles astutely identifies and describes, is anathema to contemporary locavores, particularly those interested in pastured pork. In response to my survey question "What do you like best about pastured pork?" one person in September 2010 wrote: "I like the idea that I'm eating meat from an animal that had been treated well and then turned into food, rather than food which just happens to have been attached to an object which unfortunately had to be fed and watered so it would turn into meat." Customers at the farmers' market stand where I work each week routinely express this sentiment. Clearly, such consumers value the presence of the animal and, in some regards, a continuity of the animal's life into the act of consumption, rather than an ellipsis between them. Such preferences are also evident in culinary performances like the butchery program I attended in May 2009. The program, described in chapter 4, was arranged on a strictly charitable basis, as it is illegal to process and distribute meat for sale in the kind of facility where the event was held. Over the course of two nights, participants,[7] each of whom paid $40, were given the opportunity to watch a pig broken down into its component cuts, meats that would then be prepared for a fund-raising picnic later in the week. On the first night, the crowd was also able to help dress a live pig for barbecue (that is, to slaughter the animal and clean its carcass so that it could be slow roasted whole). In addition to emphasizing the seamless connection between the living animal and its ultimate consumption, this event was notable for the way that the pig's parts were made use of. To begin with, the head had already been spoken for—it was meant to be rendered into headcheese, of course. This in itself required special attention, as pigs' heads are not easily procured, for reasons described above. At this event, because the pig was not for sale, the head was saved for one headcheese aficionado; two other participants were disappointed to hear that the head would not be available for them to use. As parts were divided up among the participants for their culinary experiments, it was interesting to see the preferences expressed. Two of the participants, themselves budding farmers and longtime chefs who catered events around town, brought samples of their charcuterie for the group to sample. They took a large jowl home. The bellies were subdivided into enough pieces to provide for everyone who wanted some. I was fortunate to get a jowl on the second night.

Just as interesting was the fact that on one night the full rack of the pig went unclaimed. An export rack is a length of ten pork chops that incorporates the loin and tenderloin cut from the lean and tender lower back of the pig. Consuming it is the very definition of eating "high on the hog," and it is significantly more expensive than any other cut of pork sold at any farmers' market, or grocery store for that matter. But, as I suggested in chapter 4, it was all the organizers could do to cajole someone into preparing it for the fund-raiser. The pork in a rack most closely resembles exactly that deanimated, homogenized "substance" described by Vialles. The pork industry has bred hybrid pigs and promoted the sale of exactly this cut of pork—what the National Pork Producers Council called "the Other White Meat," as I discussed in chapter 5—for the past generation. Leaner than any other cut of the pig, with no connective tissue or other viscera running through it, the loin is—even in a niche-market, heritage breed pig—a uniform slab of meat. It scarcely suggests the animal from which it is removed in name, function, or appearance, unlike the belly, head, jowl, tail, or shank—that is, the cuts that have been revitalized on menus motivated by an interest in snout-to-tail cookery.

In his well-known discussion of "La Pensèe Bourgeoise," Marshall Sahlins describes the "symbolic logic" whereby "edibility is inversely related to humanity" (1976, 175). He writes: "Americans frame a categorical distinction between the 'inner' and 'outer' parts which represents . . . the same principle [of inversion], metaphorically extended. The organic nature of the flesh is at once disguised and its preferability indicated by the general term 'meat' [and] conventions such as 'roast' 'steak' and 'chops'; whereas the internal organs are frankly known as such. The internal and external parts . . . are respectively assimilated to and distinguished from parts of the human body" (175–76). In the contemporary practices I am describing, the logic remains the same, but the signs are exactly reversed. It is precisely because the "frankly known" cuts of pig can be assimilated to the human body that they acquire their edibility. Not, I hasten to add, because we are on the verge of a cannibalistic binge, but because the character of the living animal—whose welfare and material standing are iconic of the wider processes of ecological well-being, healthy eating, artisanal craft, and "honestly raised good meat"—is most plainly expressed in such parts. The totality of the pig includes all aspects of the animal, not just those prominently associated with providing meat, but those associated with sustaining life. It is those parts of the animal—snout to tail—that confirm and contribute to this newly grasped and reconfigured whole that are now highly desirable. Such parts emphasize the way that meat is always embedded in a series of connections at once anatomical, agricultural, sociological, and culinary. The configuration of these parts, then, embodies a contemporary ethics and aesthetics that is simultaneously dependent on a particular materialization. This ethically informed materialism plays on the concrete qualities of animal forms, at times revealing a profound relationship with the vitality and welfare of the animal (a relationship revealed by directly confronting the death of the animal); at times demonstrating the ecological and economizing commitment to eating the totality of the animal; and at times allowing the culinary virtuosity of chefs and foodies attracted to the challenge of making flavorful meals from what were once overlooked, or discarded, forms of flesh to flourish. Each of these material qualities permits the elaboration of values that derive from the concrete configuration of part-whole relationships. Such connections are both ethical and aesthetic commitments whose form is determined by the quality of these connections, now understood with respect to food in particular as forms of virtue, caring, and desire.

Circulation, Exclusion, and Revitalization

It is interesting to contrast this current fascination with the partible pig with Deborah Gewertz and Frederick Errington's (2010) exegesis of "cheap meat" in the South Pacific. New Zealanders, prohibited from exporting whole lamb carcasses to the United Kingdom, have broken down their ovine offerings into expensive legs and racks for European and American markets and the "cheap meats"—especially fatty lamb flaps bound for Papua New Guinea. The trade with Papua New Guinea has not been straightforward and is rife with ambivalence. Papuans have welcomed a cheap source of succulent, savory, if fatty meat and an opportunity to expand their economic prospects though the resale of cooked flaps even as they acknowledge the detrimental effects of this meat on their health and the insult to their national character and standing in the wider world. As one snack stand owner put it, lamb flaps are "waste-products being sold to us" (95).

How can we account for this apparent discrepancy between lamb flaps that circulate as an omen of diabetes and the emblem of second-class citizenship across Papua New Guinea and the pork bellies and jowls that promise restored well-being for farmers, diners, and pigs alike across the Carolina Piedmont? New Zealander meat traders working in the Pacific Islands find that they are severely limited in their ability to sell even to a market where fatty meat is consumed. Gewertz and Errington write that traders "would like to be able to work with their clients to develop their market—to encourage greater sophistication in their customers and expand their sales from flaps to necks, chops, and legs (if not racks!). In so doing, traders and clients would develop ongoing relationships—mutual commitments that transcend, at least somewhat, the precise price of a product at a particular moment" (2010, 68–69). What such ambivalence indicates is that the partibility of animals stands in relationship to a wider whole. In the Carolina Piedmont the farm-to-fork and snout-to-tail orientation of local food consumers situates these parts within a set of concerns that works to demonstrate how these parts fit together into a wider pattern—of well-being, sustainability, vitality, and so on. Yet it is precisely the way lamb parts fit together in the Pacific Island trade—with flaps for Papua New Guinea and legs for Britain—that materializes and confirms what everybody already knew, even prior to the recent circulation of "cheap meat"—namely, the marginal standing of Papuans relative to New Zealand and, indeed, the wider world.[8] The disembedding of meat production in the region is reembedded in Papuans' experience in ways that heighten their sense of exclusion. Yet in both the Pacific and the Piedmont, it is the character of the connections that determines the configuration of the totality and the value of its constituent parts. Clearly, not all connections are created—or enacted—equally.

How, then, might we characterize the connections that are so central to the contemporary reconfigurations of totalities in the realm of food in the Piedmont and other regions that celebrate a farm-to-fork ethos? As I asked above, which connections count? How are proper connections forged? The connections of farm-to-fork and snout-to-tail practices are clearly multidimensional. These practices insist that there are linkages at a series of levels that are, on the one hand, intrinsic to food provisioning and preparation and, on the other hand, need to be carefully cultivated through committed social action. Thus, pigs themselves offer a veritable font of connections: living, breathing animals whose well-being, growth, and even fat-producing physiology is at once a biological process (certified by animal welfare guidelines) and an ecological boon, as pigs rototill the pastures they inhabit, offering nutrients to the soils and the species that share their paddocks in the very model of sustainability. At the same time, the same pig literally embodies connections in the quirky parts it possesses. These parts permit the culinary expression of two critical and related forms of connection: a commitment to creative parsimony, using every last bit of the animal as a whole; and a recognition that this economizing use of distinctive parts is informed by a taste for the necessary and so pays its respects to culinary techniques that are being recuperated from less distinguished cuisines.

All of the dimensions of the pig and its pork are present in the central themes I have articulated in this book. The pigs themselves are being modified in keeping with this commitment to recovering such tastes and cuisines, as pastured-pork farmers revitalize older breeds and crosses of animals—Berkshires and Tamworths and Gloucestershire Old Spots—that both adapt better to outdoor living and provide well-marbled, unashamedly fatty meat reminiscent, as many farmers' market customers put it, of "the way that pork used to taste." Those pigs that are thought suited to recapturing ancient techniques of swine husbandry and the forgotten gustatory pleasures they provide are aptly known as heritage breeds.

These breeds not only permit the restoration of the cultural modes of raising and eating animals, but they also "make a statement in favor of genetic diversity in agriculture," as "each breed has unique genetics, offering variety and biodiversity to our food and biological systems" (American Livestock Breed Conservancy E-News 2010). Connections across space and over time—including ecological commitments to sustainable well-cared-for animals and culinary commitments to recalling lost foodways and animal breeds—are, thus, fixed in these pigs.

Real Pigs

This potent combination of connections—in animal vitality and culinary revitalization, genetic diversity and cultural heritage—can be summarized as a commitment to "authenticity," a term I have used to characterize many of the sociocultural processes described in this book. This is a term that is widely and regularly used by farmers, breeders, chefs, and consumers to describe their preferences for pastured pork. "A chef who's cooked 2,000 sheep should kill at least one, otherwise *you're a fake*," notes the celebrated Jamie Oliver on his Channel 4 television show (quoted in Robertson 2005). "Real food—the sort of food our great grandmothers would recognize as food—stands in need of defense" from the food industry and nutritional science, writes Michael Pollan (2009, 4). When I asked Eliza MacLean what she thinks most moves her customers to buy the un-car-battery-like pigs she raises, she tells me, "I'm authentic. I control the entire process from genetics to slaughter." The seamless connection among all dimensions of production—not a process generated by an industrial division of specialized, repetitive tasks, but one carried out by the direct application of unmediated, skilled labor—is critical to confirming the authenticity of this process. This tactile labor is extolled, for example, in the discussions that farmers routinely have with one another at markets about the kinds of physical tasks they perform. Livestock farmers, for example, inevitably discuss the challenges of coordinating all of the tasks they perform: moving animals, building fences, corralling animals for slaughter, and the grueling work of driving animals to processing facilities.[9] What makes such work evidence of authenticity is the fact that it is all (theoretically and often actually) carried out by the farmers themselves, whose daily activities demand the ability to engage in this diverse array of skilled tasks. Such capacities for real work are seen in no less trivial ways in the pictures of farmers out in their fields, among their flocks, and adorned in overalls and baseball caps that grace the websites, menus, and entryways of many Piedmont restaurants. These farmers and chefs also know their customers well: my 2010 survey confirmed this. In answer to my question "What do you like best about pastured pork?" one respondent wrote, with perfect economy of language, "Authenticity."

Real, living animals are cared for as animals should be cared for, allowed to express all of the physiological and anatomical characteristics appropriate to them, and processed into a product whose vital qualities are present in each and every part of the animal taken as a whole. Discerning consumers can also partake of these qualities, confirming the character of these pig parts through their direct, face-to-face encounters with the farmers that provide assurance of the virtue of the transaction. In all of these respects, and at multiple levels, esteemed connections are forged, integration is materialized, and the disruptions of the agricultural-industrial complex are reconfigured. The central quality of this reconfiguration is authenticity, whose form is materialized in the modes of connectivity—among producers and consumers and within the parts of the animals themselves—through which it circulates. Authenticity is a value that serves both to motivate consumers and producers who aspire, as one Piedmont farmer put it to me recently, "to live an authentic life." This authenticity is characterized by an unmediated link to animal life, as well as a grounding in an imagined historical connection with recuperated cuisines and tastes. It is enacted in the performance of frugality, subverting distinction through a celebration of the necessary—now revalued not as a form of restraint but as a mode of thoughtful and innovative culinary and gustatory practice. Real pigs are at once a natural and historical alibi for (often imbued with heritage) and an embodiment of these authentic ambitions.

Conclusion

In all of these ways, farm-to-fork and snout-to-tail practices aim to reconfigure a dynamic totality—at once cultural and natural, social and zoological—composed of iconic parts whose dense and multiple connections allow participants in these totalities to experience authenticity, understood at once as an objective feature of productive life and a subjectively cultivated taste and appreciation for good things. I am an eager and hungry advocate of these connections, and it is not hard to see how a highly mobile community, migrating into the Piedmont at an accelerated rate, might imagine a heritage for itself that is embedded in regional cookery and agriculture and old-fashioned tastes composed of the rustic pieces of pigs whose names and lineage evoke English yeoman farmers, Spanish galleons, and Hungarian peasants. Critiques of foodie sensibilities as elitist and hierarchical are legion, especially within the food activist community itself. But it should come as no surprise to find that many people—even consumers—who have been inspired to reclaim and elevate the plebeian tastes of homespun cooking also hope to expand the appeal and availability of such local foods. Grants have been procured across the Piedmont, for example, that provide matching funds for patrons to use Electronic Benefits Transfer credits—benefits from the Supplemental Nutrition Assistance Program (SNAP), formerly known as food stamps—at farmers' markets, just as recipients of coupons from the Special Supplemental Nutrition Program for Women, Infants, and Children (commonly referred to as WIC) are targeted at a national level by the Farmers' Market Nutrition Program. These efforts aim to reach consumers—like the migrants from Central America and Mexico already mentioned. And there have also been projects intended to help underresourced and minority farmers in the region produce and market their crops and meats as local foods.

As the Niman project (discussed in chapter 1) and its results suggest, these efforts have had a mixed success, at best.[10] At the same time, the overall demographic and economic changes in the Piedmont make it unclear to what extent the kinds of connections I have been describing as foundational to these new social wholes can be made fully available to everyone in any community. Efforts to expand pastured-pork production in North Carolina, and specifically to target minority farmers, are ongoing. As I have shown, very few African American livestock producers sell their meat at farmers' markets in the Triangle. Moreover, Mexican and Central American immigrants have been targeted as consumers by innovative marketing programs, but even though many of the immigrants come from rural, agricultural regions in their home country, very few of them work as farmers or even farm labor on the small, sustainable farms where pastured animals are raised in the Piedmont. The economic inclusion of consumers with sufficient, if subsidized, funds can be cultivated, and programs to help producers who comply with consumer expectations of animal welfare and ecological sustainability can be implemented. But much of the work in this reconfigured economy is done through the revaluation of experience, bodies, and memories—in the forms of heritage breeds, recuperated cuisines, and performed frugality—and in forms and practices that are often not even legible as such to underresourced communities. We might ask: What happens when a taste of necessity is not only desired, but felt to be necessary? Or what happens when your family has struggled to raise and slaughter a few pigs for winter meat over many generations, without benefit of any recognizable heritage? As Foster has shown, a network of perspectives among distributed local social relations is crucial to the way producers and consumers collaborate to generate the value of commodities. At the same time, it is precisely through such networks that some participants become aware of the ways in which their perspectives on themselves are shaped by others' misrecognition of them—and so come to devalue their own perspectives (Foster 2008, 30–31). To be sure, cosmopolitan locavores are conscious of and concerned about the barriers to full inclusion in their activities. Yet the efforts made to expand participation may provide access to this new economy at the cost of satisfying the expectations of those hoping to render authentic value from the lives of others.

CONCLUSION

Authentic Connections

Consider how both Joel Salatin, the farmer-activist celebrated in Michael Pollan's *The Omnivore's Dilemma* (2007), and Eliza MacLean describe their own husbandry practices in terms of porcine possibilities. Salatin notes: "Plants and animals should be provided a habitat that allows them to express their physiological distinctiveness. Respecting and honoring the pigness of the pig is a foundation for societal health" (Polyface 2008). MacLean says much the same about her herd: "All they know in their life is pigness—they get to root, wallow, and naturally breed" (Weigl 2008, D1).

This "pigness" highlights the notion that pigs have their own unique, irreducible qualities that are central to their well-being and to the husbandry practices through which they are raised. This conception also entails the understanding that pigness can also be subverted or thwarted. It is an ever-present potential, but it has to be permitted to fully express itself. In this way, it is both in the pigs and a quality that shapes good husbandry. Moreover, if it is properly attended to, a variety of pigness is available to the consumer of the pork that comes from such pigs. One chef who offers pasture-raised pork told me, echoing the gustatory lingo of contemporary discernment: "A lot of people still want that [flavor]. It tastes like something. It tastes a little bit more like an animal, a little bit barnyard." Pigness is central to "real pigs" as I have described them throughout this work; it is an authentic feature of the animal that guides proper (also described as "authentic") farm management and pig husbandry.

I have also suggested that qualities like pigness are grasped as both intrinsic features of the world (in the pig, needing to get out) and as value orientations, or motivations that guide various actors' practices. In this sense, pigness has the doubled character that John and Jean Comaroff (2009) associate with much contemporary cultural production. It is both a given dimension of the real and a product that is created through concerted social activity. Pigness, I would argue, is just one example of a wider range of similar concepts and values that guides much of the world of pastured pork, understandings that I would collectively call authenticity. The desire for authenticity is something I have traced across a series of domains, including husbandry practices that encourage farmworkers to "think like the animal," conservation initiatives driven by heritage, butchery techniques that try to find uses for every piece of the carcass, and culinary methods that seek to revitalize regional tastes. Authenticity is an underlying preoccupation that, I would suggest, places these diverse practices within a common framework, but it is also an overt ideological commitment. Innumerable chefs, farmers, pork consumers, activists, butchers, and others explicitly describe their activities as authentic, assert that they are striving for authenticity, or claim that they most admire those actors who share a commitment to being authentic. In this conclusion I want to address these commitments directly. Having shown throughout this book how such assertions are deployed, I want to think about what they might mean (that is, how they are understood to make sense); what implications they have for wider social and historical processes; and what, reflexively, claims about being authentic mean for the people that make them, as well as for observers like me who are attentive to such claims. The realness of real pigs is worth a moment's reflection.

There are a cluster of ways that authenticity is framed, both in the critiques of the term and in the world of food. In food-related practices, an appeal to some form of historical legacy or heritage is often at issue. As we have seen, this is a concern that is germane to the production of some pasture-raised pork, but I would also suggest it has a somewhat limited relevance in this field for reasons I suggest below. Far more important, though, are claims about authenticity that relate to what I will call coordinated actions. For example, allowing pigs to make their own wallows or build their own nests for farrowing with straw and other materials (provided by the farmer) is a kind of authentic practice constituted by the attentive practices of the farmer and the aptitude of the pigs. Their actions are coordinated in a way that permits the authentic character of the pig's life—its pigness—to be manifest. Similarly, using techniques to cure hams taken from pigs that have the proper physiological attributes (the product of niche evolution, good husbandry, careful breeding) can produce "funky" or "barnyard-y" tastes that many would call an authentic jamon or prosciutto. Here, the product can be called authentic (without in any way implying that it actually comes from Spain or the Mediterranean), and so can the activities—the artisanship—that create the food. This notion of coordination is, I will argue, central to what is going on in claims about authenticity and being authentic. It is the way in which practices are coordinated that is ultimately being assessed in assertions of authenticity, and thus authentic forms and products can be seen as icons of the actions that generate them when those actions are carried out in authentic ways.

A good deal of social theory, and anthropology in particular, can be said to derive from a quest for the authentic. Many commentators have noted that such founding Enlightenment figures as Rousseau and Herder are central to contemporary anthropological inquiry (Fillitz and Saris 2012; Lindholm 2008) and that their claims about the general will or the genius of a people as ineffable yet critical characteristics of social communities can be traced through phenomenologically oriented anthropologies that develop understandings of *Geist* from Hegel through Dilthey, and certainly Heidegger's exposition of *Dasein*. Often, though, the assessment of how this quality is pursued or recognized is either conflated with the phenomenon itself, or naturalized as a sui generis concern. Charles Lindholm's recent account, for example, holds that "authenticity gathers people together in collectives that are felt to be real, essential, and vital, providing participants with meaning, unity, and a surpassing sense of belonging" (2008, 1), and—while his work offers a broad overview of a host of arenas (from Israeli politics to the slow food movement) in which the authentic is pursued—his assumption is that this "surpassing sense of belonging" is ineluctable. This is akin to the assertion that foodways are expressions of cultural identities, as though identities—like a "sense of belonging"— were irreducible goods whose desirability is self-evident.

Arguments that would historicize these kinds of projects often turn out to be not that far removed from such essentializing claims. To say, for example, that authenticity and the inauthentic emerge together with the founding of modernity as communal ties dissolve and then reform in the wake of rupture and deterritorialization, or that capitalism dialectically projects the authentic as an ideological mode of resolving the enduring alienation it generates, has a certain ring to it. I am tempted by the notion that the very structures of contract and financialization that facilitated the megaconsolidation of confinement pigs in North Carolina are products of the same process that led to the radical demographic transformation of the state, as legislative actions eased the regulatory environment, which encouraged corporations to move their headquarters and labor force to Research Triangle Park and Charlotte. In this way, the degradations of the food system also created the wealthy, deracinated consumers in search of local food with which to reterritorialize themselves in their new Piedmont homes. There is a certain compelling logic to this historical argument. But in the final analysis, I think this leaves too much of the inevitability of the authentic in place, as though the perils of a range of detrimental experiences—from precarious migrant labor to the ennui of cosmopolitan grocery stores—were all resolvable by reversion to some putatively prior and primary condition. What could such a condition possibly look like? And what privileges the specific qualities (depth, craft, and so on) that characterize this value?

At the same time, I am loath to follow the lead of so much contemporary theorizing that would turn the pursuit of authenticity into an exercise in inventing tradition (Hobsbawm and Ranger 2012). Such assessments tend to turn claims of authenticity into simple instrumental measures whereby actors seek to advance a given political project or sustain a tenuous status quo. While there is little doubt that such invention is an ongoing practice—for example, in the ways that restaurants fabricate genealogies for some of the dishes they offer (such as serving polenta in an Italian restaurant as "Mediterranean grits") to present themselves as supporters of local food or guardians of regional heritage (such as presenting headcheese as a traditional North Carolina dish, as I described in chapter 6)—the utilitarian motives for such invention (for example, self-interest and desire for status, prestige, class position, and so on) are, again, simply presumed to orchestrate these actions. It is also the case that many people in the world of pastured pork are wary of exactly this sort of instrumentalism and fear that appeals to terroir, heritage, or artisanship are little more than expert (or crass) marketing tools. But again, if these terms have this potential, why should an appeal to them (and not some others—like cosmopolitan, sophisticated, and elite—that also characterize this movement) be understood to be effective? What is the appeal of the authentic?

To address this problem I will return to the model that I have been making use of throughout this book. The world of niche-market meats operates as an economy of qualities that develops through a network of often dispersed perspectives. In this sense, it is critical to focus on more than the discursive claims about authenticity, to focus on the concrete activities through which authenticity is held to be materialized. This requires that we look at the specific qualities that are extolled as evidence of the authentic and consider how these qualities work together to confirm something like a plausible reality. What are these specific qualities? How are they registered in social and cultural forms? How and when do they come together in a coherent, if never completely seamless, whole?

I have traced a series of requalifications across a field of related practices, a series that works to draw out different dimensions of the process of making real pigs and pastured pork. For example, terroir or simply place can articulate a sense of the proper fit among landscapes, human tasks, and animal physiology. A breed can embody a temporal sense of depth, as well as purity and distinction. A pork chop can be well marbled and "funky" and have a unique flavor, or a shank can be transformed into something unctuous and melting from a tough, lively muscle of a well-tended pig. All of these qualities are perceived in the material features of the productive process itself. They are real things in the world that function as icons of the authentic character of pig husbandry, breeding, cookery, and so on. Each of these authentic material forms also has its social correlate. The farmer's attention to pig performance is drawn out through selection. The market encounter formulates and enacts trust and integrity through the face-to-face encounter between farmer and customer. The butcher and chef offer their hand-crafted artisanship, which they reveal through the care of their labor, its tactile characteristics (recall the butcher's kit, the tough cuts of the animal, and its offal), their attention to (which may mean innovation within) a regional culinary legacy, and the ways they perform their relations with place and face-to-face integrity by highlighting the farmers they work with in their public presentations. All of these qualities are both the outcome of coordinated actions and a method for coordinating action; and collectively they articulate an authenticity, a unique realness that both emerges within and motivates the ongoing making of pastured pork.[1]

What makes these qualities of evocative places, vital animals, redolent fat, and face-to-face integrity icons of authenticity? All of these, I suggest, share characteristics that are relevant to the phenomenology as well as the political economy of the world of real pigs. They can each be perceived as authentic because they are felt to have an immediacy and irrefutability. They offer a tangible presence of something undeniably real. This may sound like pop metaphysics, but in fact people in these networks routinely discuss exactly these qualities. Here is MacLean, again, commenting on her farming and marketing: "It's a great word of mouth game. Generally being able to tell the stories of why and how we do things is inspirational to people. They feel the connection, they want to hear the stories, and it works. And it sustains us" ("Audio Slide Show: Ossabaw Pigs" 2008). It is this notion of connection that is thoroughly pervasive among partisans of the alternative food movement and the pastured-pork advocates among them. Once I noticed the term I found it everywhere.[2] Such connections reveal the imminently social and intersubjecive character of authenticity. To be authentic requires making a connection. Connections further suggest the coordinated dimensions of the authentic as a phenomenon and an experience that conveys a way of bringing together elements—the pigness that is expressed when porcine creatures are husbanded properly and the character in a tough pork shank from a well-raised pig, butchered by a craftsman and skillfully cooked—that allows for a disclosure of the real thing.

These connections suggest that directness and immediacy are what make them effective. The face-to-face encounter as a source of integrity, the chef's celebration of his or her ties to farmers, the methods of direct marketing, the "word of mouth" storytelling—these are all extolled as irreducibly valuable connections. So are the acts of slaughtering and butchering a hog, and then using all of the animal as a totality. Again, these acts are explicitly grasped as forms of intimate connection that eschew the mediation of third parties in production, or distribution, or exchange. Indeed, I would suggest that, in many ways, this is the central dimension of connection that is valued: connection is felt by many to embody a kind of antimediation, as though a vital presence in agricultural growth, animal activity, or even vibrant flavor is available to us if we can only get direct, immediate access to the source. People in this book's profiles make exactly these kinds of assertions again and again.[3]

There are, though, a number of ways in which these connections cannot be made, and these gaps in the circuit are also telling. As much as authenticity is valued in the practices I describe, they are not readily knowable through standard forms of authentication. That is, ways of confirming provenance, origin, or historical depth are rather less to the fore, especially in the Piedmont and with respect to meat, than they might be, especially with respect to other systems of food denomination (Trubek and Bowen 2008). As I have indicated, many food activists in the region are skeptical about notions like terroir, not because they doubt whether such a phenomenon actually exists but because they are dubious about translating the conditions in which it is usually found into the very different historical contexts of North Carolina (see Paxson 2010 on attempts to "reverse engineer" terroir in the cheese industry). It has been notoriously difficult to launch systems of denomination in the South in the way that primarily European models of quality have worked. Heritage breeds are recognized and valued in the world of pastured pork, but as I have suggested, even these breeds are dependent on the presence of hybrid animals to sustain these bloodlines through cross-breeding programs that create wider markets for the specialty animals. Connection, I would therefore argue, is less about an unbroken line of continuity that grounds a community of actors and material forms to a specific locale for the *longue durée*—the kind of specificity of technique, territory, and taste that denomination is associated with in Appellation d'Origine Contrôlée, for example (Trubek and Bowen 2008)—than it is about an unmediated transparency, a direct intersubjective encounter that is not subject to denomination precisely because it is unmarked. It is apparently unmediated and unadulterated.

These qualities of unmediated (or antimediated) presence that are found in authentic connections brings us to some notoriously thorny political questions that pertain to these alternative food system movements. Are they intrinsically elitist? Do they exploit class inequalities even as they denounce corporate hegemony in the U.S. food system (Gray 2013; Guthman 2007)? Are systems of ethical consumption ever adequate to address the political challenges on which they claim to act, or are they merely another neoliberal example of the way that identity politics generates higher profits (West 2012)? I make no definitive claims about these matters, but I think my claims about authenticity and connection offer a useful vantage point from which to pose the questions. To be sure, the advocates I have worked with in farmers' markets, agricultural extension, and food aggregators, as well as a great many chefs, are seriously committed to reforming what they see as a degrading and exploitative food system. The Carrboro Farmers' Market, for example, has taken a number of initiatives to make its food available to underresourced consumers, who constitute a significant part of the population even in Carrboro and Chapel Hill, the relatively affluent home to the vast majority of the market's customers. The market was among the first in the state to develop programs to allow recipients of Electronic Benefits Transfer credits and Special Supplemental Nutrition Program for Women, Infants, and Children benefits to use those funds for making purchases at the market, often adding value to these funds through supplementary programs. Other markets have sought ways to offer better transportation to markets or delivery methods so that local food could be made available to a wider customer base. Of course, it could be argued that such efforts are self-interested, but, in fact, they have probably cost markets more time and money than they have brought into the markets in sales (Farmers Market Coalition 2014). The number of sales from these programs has been quite small, but the programs are evidence of a commitment to reach underresourced consumers.

The political opinions of small farmers are well known to be quite diverse. I have had conversations with anarchist-inspired vendors whose views on the undue regulatory burden on market activity corresponds almost exactly to those held by members of the Tea Party—which includes a small but not insignificant number of farmers, even in communities as reportedly progressive as Carrboro and Durham. Furthermore, as Heather Paxson (2012) also shows for dairy farmers in Vermont, the social class of niche-meat producers varies widely: producers include both trust-fund kids and wealthy software moguls who have decided to spend some of their fortune on farming; family farmers working land that has been in their families for, in some cases, centuries; and small farmers who make most of their money in so-called public jobs—that is, off-farm employment that allows these men and women to earn a somewhat stable income while they raise a very few animals per year. The abuses of farm labor that Margaret Gray describes across New York State (albeit in farms with larger acreage [2013, 152]) are not found, in my experience, on livestock farms in the Piedmont—although they are clearly pressing concerns even in the smaller processing facilities that are found there. What is far more common in the Piedmont are internships in which (mostly young) laborers, often hoping to get into farming themselves, do farm work for very little remuneration.[4] One could argue that this is akin to the growth of internships in corporate culture, but the outrage about exploitation should be tempered by the recognition that—unlike Wall Street firms—most livestock farms in the Piedmont are barely (if at all) profitable (as Jennifer Curtis and John O'Sullivan make clear in their profiles). Certainly Gray's call for renewed scholarship to address the connections among immigration, labor practices, and food (150) is warranted, and a system of labor certification like that being developed by the Rural Advancement Foundation International makes a great deal of sense. Still, the abuses of labor in small livestock farms do not seem the most pressing concern—although, as I have indicated above, it is surprising and somewhat disturbing to hear so many pork customers routinely ask about the welfare of a farm's pigs without once asking about the conditions of the laborers who work on these farms.

The food movements that gave rise to the world of pastured pork are certainly seeking alternatives to the corporate agriculture that has come to dominate the U.S. food system so thoroughly. These efforts are often driven by a sense of the social and environmental injustice of corporate agriculture (though there is certainly a vein of right-wing activism that sees it as simply an extension of government overreach) and by a desire to make the food system more equitable and, perhaps especially, more inclusive. Having said this, I think it is also important to point out that it is a very tall order to expect these activities to successfully overcome the power of the dominant systems. It is foolhardy to think that ethical consumption can seriously threaten their domination, but it is perhaps cruel to hold it accountable for failing to do so. Nonetheless, I would like to suggest that the alternative food movement exemplified by the niche market in meat is embedded in some of the same social and cultural processes that have given rise to corporate agriculture, and these processes are worth some consideration. In emphasizing the qualities of authenticity and connection, I suggested that immediacy and direct, tactile presence are highly valued by this food movement. Note, for example, how connection is experienced in a way that makes it unmarked, which emphasizes not a specific history or legacy or practice of making relationships, but a sense of an unadulterated presence. It is not difficult to see how appeals to exactly this kind of unmarked presence represent a kind of racialized claim. That is, asserting that connections should be unmediated can be a discursive strategy for displacing or misrecognizing all of the ways in which connections are not and can never be simply honest and direct. We might say that the normative colorless character of these perspectives need not announce its racial implications (indeed, it never does). Nonetheless, those implications prove to be highly effective at validating certain types of connections while obscuring others. Connection, I would submit, is simply a feature of any sociocultural practice. It is a necessary and unavoidable dimension of being-in-the-world. Even radical alienation generates certain historical modes of connection. The commodity form may obscure and misrepresent sociality, but it is a means of creating the characteristic social connections of capitalism (Marx 1977, 163–69).

While authenticity and connection and their ineffable qualities of vitality, integrity, and depth certainly can serve as a counter to the threats of corporate domination, it is clearly the case that precisely the same qualities have been used for centuries to ensure the continuation of systems of hierarchy and exclusion. Efforts to promote hand-crafted artisanship or face-to-face interactions deploy (if perhaps unwittingly) the same ideologies that have served for so long to undermine the productivity of those who were not only rarely permitted to engage in these connections, but whose contributions to them took the form of practices that were unrecognizable by the beneficiaries of the connections. The fact that so few—indeed, virtually none—African American or Latino farmers market their produce, and especially their pork, directly—although many participants in these practices extoll direct marketing for its capacity to create the connections that are imbued with these valuable qualities—suggests that commitments to connection can also enforce forms of exclusion. Trust, integrity, and character have all worked to create social exclusion and institutionalize domination in the Piedmont itself, even with the end of legal discrimination. They, too, are part of that something extra that distinguishes certain connections and not others.

This is also part of what makes a company like Firsthand Foods so interesting and important to these networks. As an aggregator, Firsthand makes it possible for farmers who do not have access to the consumer base that most producers who use direct marketing do—because they have very limited production, are far from significant population centers, or (as Pierre Bourdieu might say) lack the cultural capital needed (in my terms, they are not perceived to have the qualities that facilitate connections)—to get a good price for the pigs they raise. At the same time, it is entirely predictable, for the many reasons I have discussed, to find that efforts to cooperate among the various farmers who participate in this kind of collective marketing model are so often riven by concerns about racial inequality and favoritism, as John O'Sullivan notes in his profile.

Can authenticity facilitate a more equitable transformation? Advocates in pursuit of the authentic overtly attack the ethos and methods of an industrial system, but they often do so in terms that do not fully recognize the people caught up in it. Like connection, there is little reason to embrace the authentic as a boundary object; authenticity is not a privileged quality. Like embodied engagement, it can be a dimension of experience that is present even in the industrial financialized contract system of confinement agriculture.[5] Furthermore, claims about the authentic may not only overlook the caring, ethical concerns of some actors, but they may also work as a way to obscure the terms in which full participation is legitimated. As MacLean says in her profile, "Along came NC Choices, but the black farmers didn't want to have anything to do with that. They didn't want to be a part of what they thought was a little 'club.'" While the values of authenticity may work to integrate the economy of qualities I have described, they may also work to make the conditions for engaging in that economy seem daunting or threatening. It is no surprise, given these conditions, that the presence of people of color remains notably limited in farmers' markets, farm-to-table restaurants, and the like either as producers, consumers, or other types of participants, even though there are sincere efforts to make these venues more inclusive. As many graduates of North Carolina Agricultural and Technical State University told me, the local food movement often seems to promote making black folks farm like their grandparents did—and while Pollan may encourage us to avoid foods that our great-grandmother would not recognize (2009, 128), not everyone's great-grandparents had access to the same privileges.

If these efforts to promote pasture-raised pork make use of a liberatory language that contains echoes of a language of oppression, they would not be the first efforts by a social movement to do so (Povinelli 2002). I really do not mean to denigrate participants in the pastured-pork niche market that I describe in this book. They are subject to the same historical forces that have produced enduring structures of inequality that are pervasive in U.S. society. This is a testament to just how invidious those forces are, and how they can influence even the best intentioned and most self-aware people. It is, moreover, quite unreasonable to expect that this community could overcome these forces simply through its best and most concerted efforts. I have tried to show in this book that the qualities of vitality, integrity, and immediacy (among others) that animate this movement make for a compelling network of perspectives, one that can seem uniquely real to its partisans. It is not contradictory to point out that these same qualities also generate certain blind spots. It is worth taking this critical, reflexive view of this economy of qualities, the discourses and practices that constitute it, to suggest possible refinements to generate new possibilities for how a different kind of alternative politics might develop in time. My hope is not just to develop a more inclusive framework, a multicultural program that makes an equal place for everyone at the table. Instead I think we might imagine a different table altogether, one at which everyone participates—now as an advocate, now as a diner, now as a craftsman, and always as both a host and a guest. Moreover, what comes to this table—however innovative and inclusive it might be—clearly reflects a much wider array of relations and, indeed, of connections, conceived of rather differently than they tend to be in the world I have described here. We need to seek those wider perspectives and networks across a breadth of activities and communities. The food system (if such a coherent entity can ever be said to exist) cannot be an exclusive focus of concerted action, and ethical consumption is unlikely to produce anything beyond a highly personal politics. I am uncertain what form this table might take, and how accommodating it might be, but the efforts of those engaged in the niche market I have described suggest that innovation at least remains possible.

NOTES

Preface

1. See, in particular, my discussion of heritage breeds in chapter 4.
2. A number of recent popular cookbooks and food writers extoll the virtues of "real food" (Planck 2007). See also Mark Bittman's "simple message," "Eat Real Food" (2014).

Introduction

1. I discuss this point more fully in chapter 5.
2. As I show below, it is a term that multiple actors engaged in the world of promoting pasture-raised pigs use to describe these animals, as well as their own activities.
3. The tendency to categorize industrial agricultural products as commodity crops, for example, tends to neglect the fact that alternative, niche, or artisanal products are, of course, also commodities. This characterization can distort both political economic and sociocultural analyses. It should be clear that many anthropologists, historians, and others that I cite here have been attentive to these political economic concerns.
4. See, for example, his assertion of a distinction between "outside" and "inside" meanings (Mintz 1985, 167).
5. To use his word, they form a "habitus."
6. In my view, it is certainly Bourdieu's tendency to focus on sociality and the instrumentality of material forms—as in his problematic assessment of the gift as self-interest deferred—that leads many to see his work as ahistorical and mechanistic.

7. My work on the Haya lived world (Weiss 1996) was very much indebted to Munn's framework. There are a few points I would like to add to the way I formulated my approach to quality and qualisigns there (1996, 152–55) that reflect some contemporary insights. To begin with, a focus on quality allows us to address perception itself as a mode of evaluation. That is, our sensuous grasp of experience, the very substance of consciousness, is shot through with judgments, points of view, and appraisals. This is not at all to say that perceptions are merely subjective; rather, they necessarily emerge in the encounter between subjects and their worlds and are often grasped as autonomous features of the world itself. Qualities are, as Peirce suggests, potentials of things (1932; see also Keane 2003, 415; Manning 2012, 12).

8. I offer evidence of this kind of circuit of qualifications in many of the following chapters.

9. This overt emphasis on connection is especially evident in many of the profiles featured in this book. See also Schneidermann (2014) for a related example of what she calls "connectionwork" in the entirely unrelated field of pop music in urban Uganda.

10. At the time that I was working there, Cane Creek was in a partnership with its geographical neighbor Braeburn Farms, a farm dedicated to beef production.

11. Over 700 farmers across the state have a meat handler's license (see Sarah Blacklin's profile). This is an indirect measure of the number of farmers who are directly marketing their products at farmers' markets.

12. In the end, as I argue below, these diverse values are rendered more compatible than contradictory, but farmers' markets stage the performance of these alternative values in ideological ways that emphasize their disjuncture (through sociability, personalized encounters, idiosyncratic products, and transactions as opposed to standardization and so forth) more than their complementarity.

13. I discuss this extensively in chapter 2.

14. Operation Spring Plant, for example, works with African American and limited-resource farmers-in-training, as well as offering legal services to farmers seeking to address the long-standing devastating loss of black-owned farms promoted through discriminatory lending policies of the U.S. Department of Agriculture.

15. I have only anecdotal evidence—drawn, however, from over six years of working in a very prominent farmers' market—but that suggests that less than 1 percent of the customers for pastured pork in the area are African American.

16. See the profile of Jennifer Curtis below for a fuller discussion of this process.

17. Many of them were unwilling to talk with me because of the difficult regulatory conflicts this kind of practice entails.

18. See the profile of John O'Sullivan below for a further discussion of such operations.

19. Boars often live long lives that do not end in slaughter, but even they are kept as livestock only to facilitate the production of future generations of pigs that can provide pork products.
20. My essay "Eating Ursula" (Weiss 2014) addresses one such life and character in a bit more detail and also grapples with these wider questions.
21. Mike Jones told me that he gave up working in confinement facilities because he saw and felt the destructive consequences of these operations on the lives of pigs—as well as on his own life.

1. Pigs on the Ground

1. Oral History Interview with John Raymond Shute, June 25, 1982. Interview B-0054-1. Southern Oral History Program Collection (#4007) in the Southern Oral History Program Collection, Southern Historical Collection, Wilson Library, University of North Carolina at Chapel Hill. Published by Documenting the American South, accessed December 19, 2013, http://docsouth.unc.edu/sohp/B-0054-1/B-0054-1.html.
2. I discuss processing in more detail below.
3. "Smithfield 2013 Integrated Report," accessed December 7, 2015, http://www.smithfieldfoods.com/pdf/past-reports/smithfield-integrated-report2013.pdf.
4. For such analyses, see Morgan 1998 and Niman 2009. For a striking ethnographic account of industrial pig production, see Blanchette 2013.
5. This process of consolidation has only accelerated in the past twenty years. Indeed, North Carolina has over 10.1 million pigs, which is more than its 9.4 million humans.
6. The account I offer here is derived in large part from the Pulitzer Prize–winning series "Boss Hog: The Power of Pork," which ran in the *Raleigh News and Observer* in February 1995 (Stith, Warrick, and Sill 1995).
7. Murphy was a Democrat and the leading supporter of Jim Hunt, the Democratic governor of North Carolina in this era. Lauch Faircloth, a one-term U.S. senator from the state, switched his party affiliation after forty years as a Democrat to run and win his Senate seat as a Republican. He began his career as a hog farmer in Sampson County, and while serving as the state's secretary of commerce under Hunt, Faircloth supported the legislation sponsored by Murphy.
8. "Wendell H. Murphy, a former state senator who is now the nation's largest producer of hogs, said in an interview this month that 'lagoons will seal themselves,' and that there is 'not one shred, not one piece of evidence anywhere in this nation that any groundwater is being contaminated by a hog lagoon'" (Stith, Warrick, and Sill 1995).
9. All of that was entirely legal in North Carolina at the time. There were no regulations to enforce ethical practices to ensure that legislators could not actively pursue legislation that would be of direct financial benefit to themselves ("Hog-Tied on Ethics" 1995).

10. "Jim Graham, state agriculture commissioner, predicts that tobacco, cotton and other commodities will soon follow hogs as part of the march toward corporate ownership. 'Whether I like it or whether I don't like it, that's the way it's going,' he said" (Stith, Warrick, and Sill 1995).

11. That is, premium cuts of meat like pork chops or loins were badly butchered, cutting their value to the farmer in half in many instances.

12. Jennifer Curtis addresses this point directly in her profile below.

13. I discuss the process of branding in chapter 3.

14. The Carrboro Farmers' Market, for example, requires that all of its vendors produce what they sell within fifty miles of the market.

15. John O'Sullivan, who also worked at A&T in this period, discusses these events in his profile below, as does Eliza MacLean in hers (she worked for Talbott in the early 2000s).

16. Peter Kaminsky describes Talbott's—and his own—pursuit of these European tastes and practices in *Pig Perfect* (2005).

17. Niman worked to develop a network of smaller processors in North Carolina to serve its farmers.

18. Eliza MacLean's profile describes these resources in more detail.

19. Members of the Golden LEAF Foundation's board are appointed by the governor of North Carolina.

20. For example, I heard reports of farmers fearing snakes in the woods.

21. MacLean was a competitive ultramarathoner in the 1990s (Dellwo n.d.).

22. The mission of A&T with respect to sustainable agriculture is problematic, according to former employees and students I worked with. I discuss this further in chapter 1 and conclusion.

23. A farm and livestock aggregator (aggregation is a process discussed further in the profile of Jennifer Curtis), in Fairview, North Carolina, just southeast of Asheville.

24. A cow-calf operation is a method of raising beef cattle. Farmers or ranchers maintain a permanent herd of cows (in North Carolina, these herds may be smaller than a few dozen cows) and produce calves for later sale, often to feedlots in places like Nebraska and Colorado.

25. Farmers in North Carolina refer to jobs that someone takes that are not on the family farm as "public jobs."

26. O'Sullivan has taught in the Semester at Sea program with the University of Virginia, where he both taught about sustainability and learned from the communities visited by the program.

27. NC Growing Together (Center for Environmental Farming Systems n.d.).

28. The W. K. Kellogg Foundation (n.d.) has been instrumental in funding sustainable agriculture projects in North Carolina and elsewhere.

29. Ed Mitchell is discussed in chapter 5.

30. Small regional processors.

31. As noted in chapter 1, Hurricanes Fran and Floyd hit North Carolina in 1996 and 1999, respectively, causing tremendous devastation.

32. Nancy Cramer, says O'Sullivan, is "the director of CEFS and the inspiration for CEFS and the way it is open to listening but holding to its own values and principles—as well as being an excellent proposal writer!"

2. Pigs in a Local Place

1. Both North Carolina and Iowa, the two leading producers of pork in the United States, are seeing a rapid growth in pasture-raised pork production. This growth suggests that a familiarity with industrialization and a long-standing interest in consuming pork (and presumably similar agricultural products), can stimulate the development of local economic activities.

2. The Ossabaw Island Hog is one of the central characters in this book. I focus on the development of this breed as a sociocultural project in chapter 3.

3. Although Lefebvre writes about the "production of space," I refer to "place" throughout this chapter. Places are typically characterized by the presence of concrete qualities, and Lefebvre's model incorporates an understanding of how the production of space imbues spaces with experiential features.

4. For a discussion of the contrast between "space" and "place," see Casey 1998.

5. "Connection" is a key word whose value in the network of perspectives I examine here is discussed in much more detail throughout this book.

6. Sponsored by the Carolina Farm Stewardship Association and the Center for Environmental Farming Systems, respectively.

7. Most of those farmers are new to raising hogs outdoors, and to animal husbandry practices more generally, and have less experience than MacLean in dealing with restaurants interested in distinct flavor profiles.

8. These skills also have a political economic point of reference. MacLean contrasts her skilled management techniques with confinement operations where, in her view, no skill is required because "pigs are raised like car batteries." Another farmer who once worked in confinement said the work "turned me into a machine" through constant grueling power-washing that did not develop husbandry skills or even increase his physical strength but rather "broke down my body."

9. North Carolina had the fastest growing population in the United States east of the Mississippi River at the time of the 2010 census and much of the in-migration is concentrated in the Piedmont.

10. My thanks to Alex Blanchette for pointing out the many other ways that pigs can be, and are, consumed.

11. The reorganization of pig breeding and the selection of market pigs to meet consumer interests is a feature of production that every pig farmer I have spoken with has acknowledged. This consumer-driven production—called "market response agriculture" in the agricultural community—has led many farmers to transform their operations, from what they feed pigs to how they select breeding stocks.

12. As I noted in the introduction, this book does not fully take up the question of the animal as it has been developing in a very broad and stimulating

literature across the posthumanistic social sciences (Despret 2004; Haraway 2007; Kirksey 2014; Wolfe 2003). My discussion here, though, strongly affirms the notion that multispecies relationships generate forms of mutual "worlding" (Haraway 2007), and that locavores' tastes are very much the product of such processes.

13. "Discernment" has parallels with Pierre Bourdieu's (1984) understandings of "distinction" but is not identical to it. There are consumers for whom the taste of niche-market pork embodies their distinguished class standing, but there are any number of consumers of this same pork who speak of it as "just like my grandfather's pigs used to taste" and so see their tastes as a mode of affiliation with tastes that counter hierarchies of class distinction. Such tastes are not simply dominated by a dominant aesthetic (41). This reveals the ways that Bourdieu's sociocentric analysis fails to incorporate a concern for the materiality of the objects he describes, which remain essentially empty forms animated by class judgments. The taste of pork is not so easily neutralized.

14. See the conclusion of this chapter for a discussion of who constitutes this public.

15. I would not say that the presence of industrial pork "creates" the Piedmont's (or Iowa's) interest in local food, but I do think that the prominence of pork production in the Piedmont creates an awareness of pork that allows it to become a central, even exemplary, local food.

16. These dimensions of making pigs local are the focus of my ongoing research.

17. A pseudonym.

18. A pseudonym.

19. A nonprofit (Rural Center n.d.).

20. This refers to the value-added elements of processing (for example, making sausages) as well as distribution issues.

21. Coddling moth is the most common apple pest. The moths lay their larvae in apples and produce the proverbial worm in the apple.

22. That is, literally, as a disposal system for animal waste.

23. A pseudonym.

24. A system that follows an animal from the field through processing so that each cut of meat sold can be traced to the animal from which it was taken.

25. Selling savory foods as opposed to pie, ice cream, or other dessert items.

26. Primal cuts are discussed in chapter 4.

27. A retail subscription service, similar to community-supported agriculture, in which subscribers receive monthly supplies of various meat cuts at a discounted price.

28. How to breed for meat quality from selected male animals.

3. Heritage, Hybrids, Breeds, and Brands

1. Somehow (White 2011, 104).

2. White notes that the lines of Asian and European swine were separated nine thousand years ago, only to be reunited in the eighteenth century (2011, 94).

3. Interestingly, the British Pig Association also recognizes the Hampshire and Large White—which in the United States today are almost exclusively considered conventional breeds that contribute to the biosocial development of industrial hogs—as Pedigree Breeds.

4. James Neel's hypothesis of a genetic basis for diabetes rooted in an evolutionary adaptation advantageous to hunter-gatherer populations (the source of his infamous collaborations with Napoleon Chagnon), which has proved to be quite controversial in the anthropological and epidemiological literature, has been central to the development of animal models designed to study the group of disorders described as metabolic syndrome (Neel 1962).

5. And in South Carolina by Emile deFelice of Caw Caw Creek Farm.

6. Moize has a degree in anthropology from the University of North Carolina at Greensboro.

7. This is another example of the way that human-animal relationships figure in a mutual process of worlding (Haraway 2008; Kirksey 2014).

8. I am tremendously indebted to Gillian Feeley-Harnik for encouraging me to think through these dimensions of performance in greater detail.

9. As shown in Weiss 2010.

10. My thanks to Gillian Feeley-Harnik for making me think more deeply about Ursula's perspectives.

11. Today the Farmer's Hybrid Company is out of business and offers no more stock. Niman says it raises pigs that are a cross of Durocs, Berkshires, and Chester Whites.

12. There is nothing about this assertion that runs counter to the notion that a breed embodies a distinctive genetic legacy that might be preserved as critical to biodiversity, as the Livestock Conservancy aspires to do. I simply want to point out that epistemologically and practically, crossing genetic content is central to engendering particular types of inheritance.

13. Crop Mobs began in central North Carolina in 2008 as a form of mutual aid. A mob consists of a group of workers, some aspiring farmers, some families that support local food, and other activists who come together to work on a particular farm, usually on a specific project (for example, fencing, weeding, or turning soil), and typically in exchange for a meal. They make a point of not exchanging money in the process.

14. Breeze Farms is an incubator farm program in Hurdle Mills, North Carolina, just north of Hillsborough. It is funded by the Orange County Economic Development Office and Orange County Cooperative Extension and is designed to train new farmers in sustainable agricultural practices and give them experience and insights into farming as an agricultural and business activity.

15. Willing Workers on (or World Wide Opportunities on) Organic Farms (WWOOF) is a network of organizations that places volunteers on farms (usually organic, though organic certification is not a requirement) around the world.

16. Cover crops are plants grown after a field has been harvested as a way to prevent soil erosion, produce organic fertilizer, and often to extract unwanted

excess nutrients from soil so that a production crop can be cultivated after the cover crop is removed or plowed into the field.

17. We were eating barbeque during this interview.

18. "Chores" is the commonplace term for daily feeding and watering of animals.

19. The store has invested in a mobile butchery trailer that can be used at farmers' markets and other direct-marketing events.

20. Rose's Meat Market and Sweet Shop is a butchery that opened in Durham in 2013.

21. Primal cuts are discussed in chapter 4.

22. A payment due thirty days after receipt of goods, as opposed to payment upon receipt.

4. Pigs in Parts

1. For a cinematic presentation of the themes of this chapter, see "Dario Cecchini" n.d.

2. For example, the Grrl's Meat Camps organized by Kari Underly (see http://grrlsmeatcamp.com/). See also Hanel 2013; Inge 2014; and Paynter 2013.

3. In one case, a head had been put aside for an audience member who requested it, but that was an exception.

4. A pseudonym.

5. A pseudonym.

6. I am indebted to Chris Nelson for his astute observations on this point.

7. A pseudonym.

8. There is a point to be made here about the prevalence of tattoos as part of the embodied apparel of a significant percentage of butchers, a demonstration of their own bodies as fleshly—both subject to and in command of unmediated, tactile, forceful penetration. That point will have to wait for another work. But for nice illustrations of my point, see "Green Ink Cock and Pig Head Tattoos on Feet" n.d.

9. For an excellent discussion of this classical example, see Palmié 2013.

10. This understanding is developed further in my considerations of authenticity in chapter 6.

11. In many First Nations' cosmologies, the body of the animal is merely the outer manifestation of the spirit of the animal, and the debt to the animal is repaid by offering up both its meat and skin at a potlatch, which liberates the animal spirit to be reborn. This certainly demonstrates a form of generalized reciprocity, moral obligation, and the sociality of animals, but it is not clear how human life or substance is gifted in these exchanges. Hence, I find the idea of reciprocity less compelling than the notion of moral obligation.

12. The tremendous popular support that Temple Grandin has received for designing slaughterhouses that are humane illustrates this kind of conflation of animal welfare with a good death.

13. As I indicated above, farmers' market customers inquire about the feed and care of the pigs on the farms where I work but virtually never ask about the farmworkers.

14. And the wider commitments to niche-market meats of which they are a part.

15. Especially in a state like North Carolina, whose politicians today seem particularly indifferent to concerted popular action.

5. A Taste for Fat

1. In 1987, when the campaign began, the *New York Times* reported, "Chicken lovers are the main target since the experts say that this year, for the first time, chicken will push pork out of second place in consumer hearts and threaten beef" (Dougherty 1987).

2. Recall Julie Guthman's (2007) critique of Michael Pollan and others on this point, discussed in the introduction.

3. See, for example, Pollan's account of a fast-food meal (2006, 109).

4. Stephen Shapin notes that "compared to the language pertaining to vision, we do not possess a rich vocabulary for describing tastes" (2005, 4).

5. My thanks to Margaret Weiner for encouraging me to examine this contrast between loins and bacon or bellies.

6. Like the ones I recounted in chapter 3.

7. I discuss this in much greater depth in chapter 6.

6. Farm to Fork, Snout to Tail

1. So pervasive is this farm-to-fork model that a Google search for the phrase produced 2,780,000 results.

2. Virtually every social scientific perspective in the twentieth century, in approaches as varied as Saussurian linguistics, Durkheimian sociology, British functional-structuralism, and Gestalt psychology, emphasizes the necessity of holism and totalities for analytical coherence (Durkheim 1950; Lévi-Strauss 1966; Radcliffe-Brown 1952; Saussure 1917).

3. An example is the recruitment of Dell Computers to the Triad through the offer of $260 million in state and county tax breaks ("Dell to Close N.C. Plant, Eliminate 905 Jobs" 2009).

4. Torres is uniformly respected by his colleagues and employers and by farmers and diners in Chapel Hill. My assessment of these public representations is meant to demonstrate that media accounts are structured in a way that is consistent with the kinds of demographic and neoliberal shifts at work in North Carolina.

5. I am grateful to Laura Lewis for helping me clarify my thinking about this process.

6. For a widely circulated, pitch-perfect rendering of this ethos and its anxieties, see this excerpt from *Portlandia*, titled "Is it Local?," https://www.youtube.com/watch?v=WAlWrT5P2VI, accessed December 8, 2015.

7. The participants at this butchery event were more economically diverse than the attendees of the picnic. The group on both nights of the butchery event was largely, but not exclusively, male. The butchery group was also notably younger than the picnic group—in part a reflection of the fact that the organizers of the event were young men working with local farmers. A few chefs and farmers attended, hoping to enhance their working skills, as well as offer their wares (as I discuss below).

8. I recently found that lamb belly is being cured by American home curers interested in precisely the snout-to-tail practices I have been describing (Royer 2011). This demonstrates the way that the circulation of lamb flaps in Papua New Guinea is evidence of the way the partibility of lamb confirms Papuans' understandings of their marginality relative to a wider whole. It is not to dismiss the materiality of a fatty cut, but rather to confirm that the qualisigns of taste—a taste for fatty stews, as opposed to cured, desiccated meat—contributes to the sociocultural and political economic sense of marginalization.

9. This is a particularly common topic of discussion, given the narrow range of options for small-scale animal processing in North Carolina and, indeed, most of the country.

10. I am grateful, again, to Laura Lewis for discussions on this point.

Conclusion

1. This formulation is meant to recall Pierre Bourdieu's habitus (1984) as a structuring structure.

2. It is by no means exclusively a value that people associate with food—all manner of activities can be grasped as sources of connection—but I do think it is a privileged concern in food activist circles.

3. See especially Ross Flynn talking about his connections to his suppliers and his customers and Will Cramer describing the connections of the farmers' market as central to his ethos.

4. Will Cramer, profiled above, exemplifies this kind of career trajectory.

5. Indeed, Alex Blanchette's extraordinary ethnography in a massive confinement facility in the Midwest pays special attention to the way that animal handlers on the floors of these facilities show great concern and compassion in their care of sickly piglets. These workers engage in a tactile interaction motivated by the welfare of these animals—prompting some managers to state (with some concern) that "they're invested emotionally into those pigs" (Blanchette n.d., 240).

REFERENCES

Agamben, Giorgio. 2003. *The Open: Man and Animal*. Translated by Kevin Attell. Stanford, CA: Stanford University Press.

American Livestock Breed Conservancy. 2010. "Breed Information—ALBC Conservation Priority List." Accessed September 30, 2015. http://hosted-po.vresp.com/369883/9c0eb50314/ARCHIVE.

Anderson, Virginia DeJohn. 2006. *Creatures of Empire: How Domestic Animals Transformed Early America*. New York: Oxford University Press.

Appadurai, Arjun. 1981. "Gastro-Politics in Hindu South Asia." *American Ethnologist* 8 (3): 494–512.

Aristotle. 1986. *De Anima (On the Soul)*. Translated by Hugh Lawson-Tancred. London: Penguin.

Arvidsson, Adam. 2006. *Brands: Meaning and Value in Media Culture*. London: Psychology Press.

"Audio Slide Show: Ossabaw Pigs." 2008. *Raleigh News and Observer*, August 7. http://www.newsobserver.com/entertainment/article10366919.html. Accessed September 30, 2008.

Barham, Elizabeth. 2003. "Translating Terroir: The Global Challenge of French AOC Labeling." *Journal of Rural Studies* 19 (1): 127–38.

Behr, Edward. 1999. "The Lost Taste of Pork: Finding a Place for the Iowa Family Farm." *Art of Eating*, no. 51: 1–20.

Berry, Wendell. 1990. *What are People For? Essays*. San Francisco: North Point.

Bittman, Mark. 2011. "Is 'Eat Real Food' Unthinkable?" *New York Times* Opinion Section, February 8. Accessed August 17, 2012. http://opinionator.blogs.nytimes.com/2011/02/08/is-eat-real-food-unthinkable/?_r=0.

———. 2014. "What Causes Weight Gain." *New York Times*, June 10. Accessed September 5, 2015. http://www.nytimes.com/2014/06/11/opinion/what-causes-weight-gain.html.

Blanchette, Alexander David. 2013. *Conceiving Porkopolis: The Production of Life on the American "Factory" Farm*. PhD diss., Department of Anthropology, University of Chicago.

Bourdieu, Pierre. 1984. *Distinction: A Social Critique of the Judgement of Taste*. Translated by Richard Nice. London: Routledge.

Boyd, William, and Michael Watts. 1997. "Agro-Industrial Just-in-Time: The Chicken Industry and Postwar American Capitalism." In *Globalising Food: Agrarian Questions and Global Restructuring*, edited by David Goodman and Michael Watts, 193–225. London: Routledge.

Buckser, Andrew. 1999. "Keeping Kosher: Eating and Social Identity among the Jews of Denmark." *Ethnology* 38 (3): 191–209.

Butcher's Grip. 2010. "Yes You Can." December 6. Accessed January 12, 2011. http://thebutcherandlarder.com/yes-you-can.

Callon, Michel, Cécile Méadel, and Vololona Rabeharisoa. 2002. "The Economy of Qualities." *Economy and Society* 31 (2): 194–217.

Casey, Edward. 1998. *The Fate of Place: A Philosophical History*. Berkeley: University of California Press.

Center for Environmental Farming Systems. n.d. "NC Growing Together." Accessed July 21, 2012. http://www.cefs.ncsu.edu/whatwedo/foodsystems/ncgt.html.

Chang, David, and Peter Meehan. 2009. *Momofuku*. New York: Clarkson Potter.

Chumley, Lily Hope, and Nicholas Harkness. 2013. "Introduction: Qualia." *Anthropological Theory* 13, nos. 1–2 (2013): 3–11.

"CME: Decline in Hog Prices." 2014. The Pig Site. November 5. Accessed August 13, 2014. http://www.thepigsite.com/swinenews/38155/cme-decline-in-hog-prices.

Comaroff, John L., and Jean Comaroff. 1990. "Goodly Beasts, Beastly Goods: Cattle and Commodities in a South African Context." *American Ethnologist* 17 (2): 195–216.

———. 2009. *Ethnicity, Inc.* Chicago: University of Chicago Press.

Curtis, Jennifer, et al. 2010. "From Farm to Fork: A Guide to Building North Carolina's Sustainable Local Food Economy." Center for Environmental Farming Systems. Accessed September 6, 2015. http://www.cefs.ncsu.edu/resources/stateactionguide2010.pdf.

"Dario Cecchini: 'Carne E Spirito.'" n.d. Vimeo. Accessed August 17, 2013. http://vimeo.com/74282454.

"Dell to Close N.C. Plant, Eliminate 905 Jobs." 2009. WRAL.com. October 7. Accessed November 17, 2011. http://www.wral.com/business/story/6156112/.

Dellwo, Lisa M. n.d. "Eliza MacLean." Nicholas School of the Environment, Duke University. Accessed September 6, 2015. https://nicholas.duke.edu/people/alumni/eliza-maclean.

Derry, Margaret E. 2003. *Bred for Perfection: Shorthorn Cattle, Collies, and Arabian Horses since 1800*. Baltimore, MD: Johns Hopkins University Press.

Despret, V. 2004. "The Body We Care For: Figures of Anthropo-zoo-genesis." *Body and Society* 10 (2–3): 111–34.

Dickerman, Sara. 2006. "Some Pig: The Development of the Piggy Confessional." Slate, December 14. Accessed March 20, 2010. http://www.slate.com/articles /life/food/2006/12/some_pig.html.

Dougherty, Philip H. 1987. "Dressing Pork for Success." *New York Times*, January 15. Accessed January 15, 2012. http://www.nytimes.com/1987/01/15/business /advertising-dressing-pork-for-success.html.

Douglas, Mary. 2012. "The Abominations of Leviticus." In *Food and Culture: A Reader*, third edition. Edited by Carol Counihan and Penny Van Eterik, 48–58. New York: Routledge.

Dover, Michael, and Lee M. Talbot. 1987. *To Feed the Earth: Agroecology for Sustainable Development*. Washington: World Resources Institute.

Dransfield, Eric. 2008. "The Taste of Fat." *Meat Science* 80 (1): 37–42.

Duke University Center on Globalization, Governance and Competitiveness. n.d. "North Carolina in the Global Economy." Accessed September 6, 2015. http://www.soc.duke.edu/NC_GlobalEconomy/hog/overview.shtml.

Durkheim, Emile. 1950. *The Rules of Sociological Method*. Translated by Sarah A. Solovay and John H. Mueller. Glencoe, IL: Free Press.

Edge, John T. 2005. "Redesigning the Pig." *Gourmet*, July, 49–54.

Estabrook, Barry. 2015. *Pig Tales: An Omnivore's Quest for Sustainable Meat*. New York: W. W. Norton.

Factory Farm Map. n.d. "North Carolina Facts." Accessed September 6, 2015. http://www.factoryfarmmap.org/states/nc/.

Farmers Market Coalition. 2014. "Carrboro Prototype." July 21. Accessed August 12, 2014. http://farmersmarketcoalition.org/programs/farmers-market -metrics/winooskisummary_page_2/#main.

Farquhar, Judith. 2002. *Appetites: Food and Sex in Postsocialist China*. Durham, NC: Duke University Press.

———. 2006. "Food, Eating, and the Good Life." In *Handbook of Material Culture*, edited by Chris Tilley et al., 145–60. London: Sage.

Fearnley-Whittingstall, H. 2004. *The River Cottage Meat Book*. London: Hodder and Stoughton.

Feeley-Harnik, Gillian. 2007. "'An Experiment on a Gigantic Scale': Darwin and the Domestication of Pigeons." In *Where the Wild Things Are Now: Domestication Reconsidered*, edited by Rebecca Cassidy and Molly Mullin, 147–82. New York: Berg.

Fehérváry, Krisztina. 2009. "Goods and States: The Political Logic of State-Socialist Material Culture." *Comparative Studies in Society and History* 51 (2): 426–59.

———. 2013. *Politics in Color and Concrete: Socialist Materialities and the Middle Class in Hungary*. Bloomington: Indiana University Press, 2013.

Fennema, Owen. 1996. *Food Chemistry*. 3rd ed. London: CRC.

Fillitz, Thomas, and A. Jamie Saris, eds. 2012. *Debating Authenticity: Concepts of Modernity in Anthropological Perspective*. Oxford: Berghahn.

Finz, Stacy. 2009. "Niman Ranch Founder Challenges New Owners." SFGate, February 22. Accessed June 24, 2014. http://www.sfgate.com/news/article/Niman-Ranch-founder-challenges-new-owners-3249982.php.

Foer, Jonathan Safran. 2010. *Eating Animals*. New York: Penguin.

Foster, Robert. 2008. *Coca-Globalization: Following Soft Drinks from New York to New Guinea*. New York: Palgrave Macmillan.

Gell, Alfred. 1977. "Magic, Perfume, Dream." In *Symbols and Sentiments: Cross-Cultural Studies in Symbolism*, edited by Ioan Myrddin Lewis, 25–38. London: Academic.

Geschiere, Peter, and Frances Nyamnjoh. 2000. "Capitalism and Autochthony: The Seesaw of Mobility and Belonging." *Public Culture* 12 (2): 432–52.

Gewertz, Deborah, and Frederick Errington. 2010. *Cheap Meat: Flap Food Nations in the Pacific Islands*. Berkeley: University of California Press.

Giddens, Anthony. 1991. *Modernity and Self-Identity: Self and Society in the Late Modern Age*. Stanford, CA: Stanford University Press.

Goffman, Erving. 1959. *The Presentation of Self in Everyday Life*. New York: Anchor.

Grasseni, Cristina. 2004. "Skilled Vision. An Apprenticeship in Breeding Aesthetics." *Social Anthropology* 12 (1): 41–55.

Gray, Margaret. 2013. *Labor and the Locavore: The Making of a Comprehensive Food Ethic*. Berkeley: University of California Press.

"Green Ink Cock and Pig Head Tattoos on Feet." n.d. Tattoostime.com. Accessed July 11, 2013. http://www.tattoostime.com/tattoos/pig/page/18/.

Grey, Mark A. 2000. "The Industrial Food Stream and Its Alternatives in the United States: An Introduction." *Human Organization* 59 (2): 143–50.

Gundaker, Grey, and Judith McWillie. 2005. *No Space Hidden: The Spirit of African American Yard Work*. Knoxville: University of Tennessee Press.

Guthman, Julie. 2007. "Can't Stomach It: How Michael Pollan et al. Made Me Want to Eat Cheetos." *Gastronimica* 7 (3): 75–79.

Hanel, Marnie. 2013. "The Proper Way to Eat a Pig." *New York Times Magazine*, April 4. Accessed September 9, 2015. http://www.nytimes.com/2013/04/07/magazine/the-proper-way-to-eat-a-pig.html?pagewanted=all.

Hannerz, Ulf. 1992. *Cultural Complexity: Studies in the Social Organization of Meaning*. New York: Columbia University Press.

Haraway, Donna. 2008. *When Species Meet*. Minneapolis: University of Minnesota Press.

Heidegger, Martin. 1962. *Being and Time*. Translated by John Macquarrie and Edward Robinson. New York: Harper.

Henderson, Fergus. 2004. *The Whole Beast: Nose to Tail Eating*. London: Ecco.

Hobsbawm, Eric, and Terence Ranger, eds. 2012. *The Invention of Tradition*. Cambridge: Cambridge University Press.

"Hog-Tied on Ethics." 1995. Editorial. *Raleigh News and Observer*, February 23.

Holtzman, Jon D. 2006. "Food and Memory." *Annual Review of Anthropology* 35: 361–78.

———. 2009. *Uncertain Tastes: Memory, Ambivalence, and the Politics of Eating in Samburu Northern Kenya*. Berkeley: University of California Press.

Hubert, Henri, and Marcel Mauss. 1964. *Sacrifice: Its Nature and Function*. Translated by William D. Halls. Chicago: University of Chicago Press.

"Huge Spill of Hog Waste Fuels an Old Debate in North Carolina." 1995. *New York Times*, June 25.

"Hurricane Floyd: Economic Impact." n.d. RENCI East Carolina Regional Engagement Center. Accessed July 17, 2013. https://www.ecu.edu/renci /StormsToLife/Floyd/economic.html.

Hymes, Del. 1974. "Ways of Speaking." In *Explorations in the Ethnography of Speaking*, edited by Richard Bauman and Joel Sherzer, 433–51. London: Cambridge University Press.

Inge, Leonida. 2014. "Female Butchers Are Slicing through the Meat World's Glass Ceiling." NPR, December 7. Accessed September 9, 2015. http://www .npr.org/blogs/thesalt/2014/12/07/366642071/women-butchers-are-slicing -through-the-meat-worlds-glass-ceiling.

Ingold, Tim. 2000. *Perception of the Environment: Essays in Livelihood, Dwelling and Skill*. London: Routledge.

Iowa State University. 2004. "Hog Reference List." Accessed May 15, 2010. http://econ2.econ.iastate.edu/faculty/lawrence/PorkStat/porkstat.htm.

Johnson, B. J., P. T. Anderson, J. C. Meiske, and W. R. Dayton. 1996. "Effect of a Combined Trenbalone Acetate and Estradiol Implant on Feedlot Performance, Carcass Characteristics and Carcass Composition of Feedlot Steers." *Journal of Animal Science* 74:2, 363–71.

Kaminsky, Peter. 2005. *Pig Perfect: Encounters with Remarkable Swine and Some Great Ways to Cook Them*. New York: Hyperion.

Keane, Webb. 2003. "Semiotics and the Social Analysis of Material Things." *Language and Communication* 23 (3–4): 409–25.

Kenner, Robert, dir. 2009. *Food Inc.* New York: Magnolia Home Entertainment. DVD.

Kingsolver, Barbara. 2008. *Animal, Vegetable, Mineral: A Year of Food Life*. New York: Harper Perennial.

Kirksey, Eben, ed. 2014. *The Multispecies Salon*. Durham, NC: Duke University Press.

Kloppenburg, Jack, Jr., et al. 2000. "Tasting Food, Tasting Sustainability: Defining the Attributes of an Alternative Food System with Competent, Ordinary People." *Human Organization* 59 (2): 177–86.

Knowlton, Andrew. 2008. "America's Foodiest Small Town." *Bon Appétit*, August 8. Accessed September 6, 2015. http://www.bonappetit.com/entertaining-style /holidays/article/america-s-foodiest-small-town.

Kohn, Eduardo. 2013. *How Forests Think: Toward an Anthropology beyond the Human*. Berkeley: University of California Press.

Korsmeyer, Carolyn. 1999. *Making Sense of Taste: Food & Philosophy*. Ithaca, NY: Cornell University Press.

Krisel, Jonathan. 2011. "Farm." *Portlandia*, season 1, episode 1.

Land Loss Prevention Project. n.d. "Our Mission." Accessed September 6, 2015. http://landloss.org/.

Lantern. n.d. Home page. Accessed April 17, 2009. http://lanternrestaurant.com /about.html.

Latour, Bruno. 2012. *We Have Never Been Modern*. Cambridge, MA: Harvard University Press.

Leach, Edmund Ronald. 1964. "Anthropological Aspects of Language: Animal Categories and Verbal Abuse." In *New Directions in the Study of Language*, edited by Eric H. Lenneberg, 23–63. Cambridge, MA: MIT Press.

Learn NC. n.d.a. "3.6. Key Industries: Hog Farming." Accessed June 12, 2012. http://www.learnnc.org/lp/editions/nchist-recent/6257.

———. n.d.b. "6.3 Latino Immigration." Accessed December 17, 2012. http:// www.learnnc.org/lp/editions/nchist-recent/6182.

Lefebvre, Henri. 1991. *The Production of Space*. Translated by Donald Nicholson-Smith. New York: Wiley-Blackwell.

Lévi-Strauss, Claude. 1966. *The Savage Mind*. Chicago: University of Chicago Press.

Lienhardt, Godfrey. 1961. *Divinity and Experience: The Religion of the Dinka*. New York: Oxford University Press.

Lindholm, Charles. 2008. *Culture and Authenticity*. Malden, MA: Wiley-Blackwell.

Livestock Conservancy. n.d. "Conservation Priority List." Accessed March 6, 2014. http://www.livestockconservancy.org/index.php/heritage/internal /conservation-priority-list.

———. 2015. "Our Mission." Accessed September 8, 2015. http://www.livestock conservancy.org/.

Local Harvest. n.d. "Slow Food USA's Ark of Taste." Accessed September 5, 2015. http://www.localharvest.org/ark-of-taste.jsp.

Lock, Margaret M. 2002. *Twice Dead: Organ Transplants and the Reinvention of Death*. Berkeley: University of California Press.

Loisy, Alfred. 1920. *Essai historique sur le sacrifice*. Paris: Émile Nourry.

Manning, Paul. 2010. "The Semiotics of Brand." *Annual Review of Anthropology* 39: 33–49.

———. 2012. *Semiotics of Drink and Drinking*. New York: Bloomsbury.

Marx, Karl. 1968. *Economic and Philosophic Manuscripts of 1844*. Translated by Martin Milligan. New York: Prometheus.

———. 1977. *Capital*. Vol. 1. Translated by Ben Fowkes. New York: Vintage.

Mauss, Marcel. 1954. *The Gift: Forms and Functions of Exchange in Archaic Societies*. Translated by Ian Cunison. New York and London: W. W. Norton.

Mazzarella, William. 2003. *Shoveling Smoke: Advertising and Globalization in Contemporary India*. Durham, NC: Duke University Press.

Meinert, Lene, et al. 2008. "Eating Quality of Pork from Pure Breeds and DLY Studied by Focus Group Research and Meat Quality Analyses." *Meat Science* 80 (2): 304–14.

Meinert, Lene, Kaja Tikk, Meelis Tikk, Per B. Brockhoff, Camilla Bejerholm, and Margit D. Aaslyng. 2008. "Flavour Formation in Pork Semimembranosus: Combination of Pan-Temperature and Raw Meat Quality." *Meat Science* 80 (2): 249–58.

Meneley, Anne. 2008. "Oleo-Signs and Quali-Signs: The Qualities of Olive Oil." *Ethnos* 73:3, 303–26.

Merleau-Ponty, Maurice. 1962. *The Phenomenology of Perception.* Translated by Colin Smith. London: Routledge and Kegan Paul.

Mintz, Sidney W. 1986. *Sweetness and Power: The Place of Sugar in Modern History.* New York: Viking.

Mintz, Sidney W., and Christine M. Du Bois. 2002. "The Anthropology of Food and Eating." *Annual Review of Anthropology* 31: 99–119.

Moeller, S. J., R. K. Miller, K. K. Edwards, H. N. Zerby, K. E. Logan, T. L. Aldredge, C. A. Stahl, M. Boggess, and J. M. Box-Steffensmeier. 2010. "Consumer Perceptions of Pork Eating Quality as Affected by Pork Quality Attributes and End-Point Cooked Temperature." *Meat Science* 84 (1): 14–22.

Moore, Robert E. 2003. "From Genericide to Viral Marketing: on 'Brand.'" *Language and Communication* 23 (3): 331–57.

Morgan, Robert. 1998. "Legal and Political Injustices of Industrial Swine Production in North Carolina." In *Pigs, Profits and Rural Communities,* edited by Kendall M. Thu and E. Paul Durrenberger, 138–44. Albany: State University of New York Press.

Morrow, Morgan. 2005. "Marketing 'Niche Pork.'" Accessed October 27, 2015. http://www.thepigsite.com/articles/1522/marketing-niche-pork/.

Moskin, Julia. 2008. "Chefs' New Goal: Looking Dinner in the Eye." *New York Times,* January 16. Accessed September 10, 2015. http://www.nytimes.com/2008/01/16/dining/16anim.html?8br.

Muhlke, Christine. 2010. "Field Report: Plow Shares." *New York Times,* February 24. Accessed September 12, 2015. http://www.nytimes.com/2010/02/28/magazine/28food-t-000.html?_r=0.

Munn, Nancy. 1977. "The Spatiotemporal Transformations of Gawa Canoes." *Journal de la Société des Océanistes* 33 (54): 39–53.

———. 1986. *The Fame of Gawa: A Symbolic Study of Value Transformation in a Massim Papua New Guinea Society.* Cambridge: Cambridge University Press.

———. 1996. "Excluded Spaces: The Figure in the Australian Aboriginal Landscape." *Critical Inquiry,* 446–65.

Nadasdy, Paul. 2007. "The Gift in the Animal: The Ontology of Hunting and Human-Animal Sociality." *American Ethnologist* 34 (1): 25–43.

National Council of La Raza. 2011. "Feeding the Economic Recovery: Latinos in the Food Services Sector." Accessed September 12, 2015. http://issuu.com/nclr/docs/employment_report_may_2011.

National Pork Producers Council. 2012. "Pork Quality Standards." Des Moines, IA: National Pork Producers Council.

Neel, James V. 1962. "Diabetes Mellitus: A 'Thrifty' Genotype Rendered Detrimental by 'Progress'?" *American Journal of Human Genetics* 14 (4): 353–62.

Nestle, Marion. 2013. *Food Politics: How the Food Industry Influences Nutrition and Health.* Vol. 3. Berkeley: University of California Press.

Niman, Nicolette Hahn. 2009. *Righteous Porkchop: Finding a Life and Good Food beyond Factory Farms.* New York: William Morrow.

O'Laughlin, Marina. 2010. "London's Sandwich Bars: A Tasty Slice of Culinary Life." *London Times Metro*, July 20. Accessed August 20, 2012. http://metro.co .uk/2010/07/20/londons-sandwich-bars-a-tasty-slice-of-culinary-life-453473/.

Operation Spring Plant. n.d. Home page. Accessed April 17, 2014. http:// operationspringplant.blogspot.com/.

"The Ossabaw Pig." n.d. Ossabaw Island. Accessed July 22, 2009. http://www .ossabawisland.org/indexa.php?docid=274.

"Ossabaw Swine Resource." n.d. Indiana Clinical and Translational Science Institute. Accessed July 17, 2011. https://www.indianactsi.org/servicecores?view =core&cid=57.

Pachirat, Timothy. 2011. *Every Twelve Seconds: Industrialized Slaughter and the Politics of Sight.* New Haven, CT: Yale University Press.

Page, Brian. 1997. "Restructuring Pork Production, Remaking Rural Iowa." In *Globalising Food: Agrarian Questions and Global Restructuring*, edited by David Goodman and Michael Watts, 133–57. London: Routledge.

Palmié, Stephan. 2013. "Mixed Blessings and Sorrowful Mysteries." *Current Anthropology* 54 (4): 463–82.

Patel, Raj. 2007. *Stuffed and Starved: The Hidden Battle for the World Food System.* London: Portobello Books.

Paxson, Heather. 2010. "Locating Value in Artisan Cheese: Reverse Engineering *Terroir* for New World Landscapes." *American Anthropologist* 112 (3): 444–57.

———. 2012. *The Life of Cheese: Crafting Food and Value in America.* Berkeley: University of California Press.

Paynter, Ben. 2013. "Bacon, and How It Came to Be." *New York Times*, January 28. Accessed September 9, 2015. http://www.nytimes.com/2013/01/30 /dining/in-kansas-city-a-butcher-shop-teaches-the-butchers-art.html?_r=0.

Peirce, Charles Sanders. 1932. Collected Papers of Charles Sanders Peirce, vols. I and II. Edited by Charles Hartshorne and Paul Weiss. Cambridge, MA: Harvard University Press.

Petrini, Carlo. 2006. *Slow Food Nation: Why Our Food Should Be Good, Clean, and Fair.* New York: Rizzoli Ex Libris.

Pilcher, Jeffrey M. 1998. *Que vivan los tamales! Food and the Making of Mexican Identity.* Albuquerque: University of New Mexico Press.

Planck, N. 2007. *Real food: what to eat and why.* New York: Bloomsbury Publishing USA.

Pollan, Michael. 2007. *The Omnivore's Dilemma: A Natural History of Four Meals*. New York: Penguin.

———. 2009. *In Defense of Food: An Eater's Manifesto*. New York: Penguin.

Polyface. 2008. "Polyface Guiding Principles." Accessed October 25, 2015. http://www.polyfacefarms.com/principles/.

Portlandia. 2011. "Is It Local?" IFC, January 25. http://www.youtube.com/watch?v=12LBICPEK6w, March 3, 2100.

Povinelli, Elizabeth A. 2002. *The Cunning of Recognition: Indigenous Alterities and the Making of Australian Multiculturalism*. Durham, NC: Duke University Press.

Prothero, Donald R., and Paul C. Sereno. 1982. "Allometry and Paleoecology of Medial Miocene Dwarf Rhinoceroses from the Texas Gulf Coastal Plain." *Paleobiology* 8 (1): 16–30.

Putnam, Heath. 2009. "The Unfortunate Demise of the Ossabaw." Wooly Pigs. January 16. Accessed March 10, 2010. http://woolypigs.blogspot.com/2009/01/unfortunate-demise-of-ossabaw.html.

Randall, Kate. 1999. "North Carolina Hurricane Flooding—The Manmade Component of a Natural Disaster." World Socialist Web Site, September 28. Accessed September 6, 2015. http://www.wsws.org/en/articles/1999/09/nc-s28.html.

Rappaport, Roy. 1968. *Pigs for the Ancestors: Ritual in the Ecology of a New Guinea People*. New Haven, CT: Yale University Press.

Reusing, Andrea. 2011. *Cooking in the Moment: A Year of Seasonal Recipes*. New York: Clarkson Potter.

Roahen, Sara, and John T. Edge, eds. 2010. *The Southern Foodways Alliance Community Cookbook*. Athens: University of Georgia Press.

Robertson, Cameron. 2005. "Jamie Oliver: The Silencer of the Lamb; Campaigners Slam Chef for Slaughtering Animal on TV." Accessed October 27, 2015. http://www.thefreelibrary.com/JAMIE+OLIVER%3a+THE+SILENCER+OF+THE+LAMB%3b+Campaigners+slam+chef+for . . . -a0138558579.

Royer, Blake. 2011. "Lamb Pancetta: Charcutepalooza February Challenge; Plus, a Killer Recipe to Use It In." Paupered Chef, February 15. Accessed September 12, 2015. http://thepauperedchef.com/article/lamb-pancetta-charcutepalooza-february-challenge.

Rural Advancement Foundation International. n.d. "Agricultural Justice Project." Accessed September 6, 2015. http://rafiusa.org/agricultural-justice-project/.

Rural Center. n.d. Home page. Accessed September 6, 2015. http://www.ncruralcenter.org/.

Sahlins, Marshall. 1976. *Culture and Practical Reason*. Chicago: University of Chicago Press.

Saussure, Ferdinand de. 1917. *Cours de linguistique générale*. Paris: Payot.

Schlosser, Eric. 2001. *Fast-Food Nation: The Dark Side of the All-American Meal*. New York: Perennial.

Schneidermann, Nanna. 2014. "Connectionwork—Making a Name in Uganda's Music Industry." PhD diss., Aarhus University.

Seremetakis, C. Nadia. 1994. "The Memory of the Senses." In *The Senses Still: Perception and Memory as Material Culture in Modernity*, edited by C. Nadia Seremetakis. Boulder, CO: Westview.

Severson, Kim. 2008. "With Goat, a Rancher Breaks Away from the Herd." *New York Times*, October 14. Accessed September 6, 2015. http://www.nytimes.com /2008/10/15/dining/15goat.html?_r=0.

Sewell, Bradford H., and Robin M. Whyatt. 1989. "Intolerable Risk: Pesticides in Our Children's Food—Summary." Natural Resources Defense Council. February 27. Accessed September 6, 2015. http://docs.nrdc.org/health/files/hea _11052401a.pdf.

Shapin, Stephen. 2005. "Hedonistic Fruit Bombs." *London Review of Books*, February 3, 30–32.

———. n.d. "Changing Tastes: How Foods Tasted in the Early Modern Period and How They Came to Taste Differently Later." Unpublished manuscript.

Silverstein, Michael. 2004. " 'Cultural' Concepts and the Language-Culture Nexus." *Current Anthropology* 45 (5): 621–52.

———. 2006. "Old Wine, New Ethnographic Lexicography." *Annual Review of Anthropology* 35: 481–96.

Smith, W. Robertson. 1972. *The Religion of the Semites: The Fundamental Institutions*. 1st Schocken paperback ed. New York: Schocken.

Soler, Jean. 1997. "The Semiotics of Food in the Bible." In *Food and Culture: A Reader*, first edition. Edited by Carol Counihan and Penny Van Eterik, 55–66. New York: Routledge.

Søltoft-Jensen, A. J. 2010. "Organic Feed Results in Tough Pork Chops!" Report of Danish Meat Research Institute, Danish Agriculture and Food Council, København, Denmark.

Southern Foodways Alliance. n.d. "About Us." Accessed December 15, 2012. https://www.southernfoodways.org/about-us/.

Stallybrass, Peter, and Allon White. 1986. *The Politics and Poetics of Transgression*. Ithaca, NY: Cornell University Press.

Stith, Pat, Joby Warrick, and Melanie Sill. 1995. "Boss Hog: The Power of Pork." *Raleigh News and Observer*, February 19–25.

Stoller, Paul. 1989. *The Taste of Ethnographic Things: The Senses in Anthropology*. Philadelphia: University of Pennsylvania Press.

Strathern, Marilyn. 2004. *Partial Connections*. Walnut Creek, CA: AltaMira.

Sturek, Michael, et al. 2007. "Ossabaw Island Miniature Swine: Cardiometabolic Syndrome Assessment." In *Swine in the Laboratory: Surgery, Anesthesia, Imaging, and Experimental Techniques*, edited by M. Michael Swindle, 397–402. 2nd ed. Boca Raton, FL: CRC.

Sula, Mike. 2009. "The Charcuterie Underground." *Chicago Reader*, November 26. Accessed September 30, 2015. http://www.chicagoreader.com/chicago

/the-charcuterie-underground-outlaw-bacon-curers-and-sausage-grinders
/Content?oid=1241681.

Sutton, David E. 2001. *Remembrance of Repasts: An Anthropology of Food and Memory*. Oxford: Berg.

———. 2010. "Food and the Senses." *Annual Review of Anthropology* 39: 209–23.

Talbott, Charles, et al. 2006. "Enhancing Pork Flavor and Fat Quality with Swine Raised in Sylvan Systems: Potential Niche-Market Application for the Ossabaw Hog." *Renewable Agriculture and Food Systems* 21 (3): 183–91.

"Taste Test: British Charcuterie." 2010. *The Guardian* Food Section, December 9. Accessed August 23, 2012. http://www.theguardian.com/lifeandstyle/2010 /dec/09/taste-test-british-charcuterie.

Tomlinson, John. 1999. *Globalization and Culture*. Chicago: University of Chicago Press.

Trubek, Amy B. 2008. *The Taste of Place: A Cultural Journey into Terroir*. Berkeley: University of California Press.

Trubek, Amy B., and Sarah Bowen. 2008. "Creating the Taste of Place in the United States: Can We Learn from the French?" *GeoJournal* 73 (1): 23–30.

Tsing, Anna Lowenhaupt. 2005. *Friction: An Ethnography of Global Connection*. Princeton, NJ: Princeton University Press.

Turner, Terence S. 1968. "Parsons' Concept of 'Generalized Media of Social Interaction' and Its Relevance for Social Anthropology." *Sociological Inquiry* 38 (2): 121–34.

U.S. Census Bureau. n.d. "2010 Census Data." Accessed December 10, 2011. http://www.census.gov/2010census/data/index.php.

Valeri, Valerio. 1985. *Kingship and Sacrifice: Ritual and Society in Ancient Hawaii*. Chicago: University of Chicago Press

Vialles, Nöelie. 1994. *Animal to Edible*. Cambridge: Cambridge University Press.

W. K. Kellogg Foundation. n.d. Home page. Accessed September 6, 2015. http:// www.wkkf.org/.

Walton, John R. 1986. "Pedigree and the National Cattle Herd Circa 1750–1950." *Agricultural History Review* 34 (2): 149–70.

Warrick, Joby, and Pat Stith. 1995a. "Corporate Takeover." *Raleigh News and Observer*, February 21.

———. 1995b. "Money Talks: The Smell of Money." *Raleigh News and Observer*, February 24.

Watson, Lyall. 2004. *The Whole Hog: Exploring the Extraordinary Potential of Pigs*. Washington: Smithsonian Books.

Weigl, Andrea. 2008. "Rooting for Locavores." *Raleigh News and Observer*, August 10, D1.

———. 2011. "Behind Every Successful Chef . . ." Sustainable Grub, May 27. Accessed September 12, 2015. http://sustainablegrub.wordpress.com/2011/05/27 /behind-every-successful-chef/.

Weil, Kari. 2010. "A Report on the Animal Turn." *differences* 21 (2): 1–23.

Weiss, Brad. 1996. *The Making and Unmaking of the Haya Lived World: Consumption, Commoditization, and Everyday Practice*. Durham, NC: Duke University Press.

———, ed. 2004. *Producing African Futures: Ritual and Reproduction in a Neoliberal Age*. Leiden: Brill.

———. 2009. *Street Dreams and Hip Hop Barbershops: Global Fantasy in Urban Tanzania*. Bloomington: Indiana University Press.

———. 2014. "Eating Ursula." *Gastronomica* 14 (4): 17–25.

Weiss, Ezra. 2010. "Cane Creek 12/2010." December 20. Accessed December 8, 2015. https://picasaweb.google.com/1bradweiss/CaneCreek122010?authkey=GvisRgCNLQiLCA1-nYiQE#slideshow/5555367375168499058.

West, Paige. 2012. *From Modern Production to Imagined Primitive: The Social World of Coffee from Papua New Guinea*. Durham, NC: Duke University Press.

White, Sam. 2011. "From Globalized Pig Breeds to Capitalist Pigs: A Study in Animal Cultures and Evolutionary History." *Environmental History* 16 (1): 94–120.

Williams, Raymond. 1985. *Keywords: A Vocabulary of Culture and Society*. Oxford: Oxford University Press.

Wolfe, Cary. 2003. *Animal Rites: American Culture, the Discourse of Species, and Posthumanist Theory*. Chicago: University of Chicago Press.

INDEX

artisanal production, 3, 10, 18, 116, 199

artisans, artisanship, 156, 178, 197, 245, 246, 252

Art of Eating (journal), 33, 43

authenticity, 3–4, 17, 46, 50, 136, 243, 204, 245, 246; in alternative foods system, 225; bloodline preservation and, 118; butchery and, 164; commitment to, 238; connection and, 248, 249, 251, 252; headcheese and, 231–32; icons of, 247; materialization of, 247; of pastured pork, 239, 244; pigness and, 243–45, 248; value of, 227, 241. *See also* real food; real pigs

bacon, 23, 82, 120, 135, 198–99, 215, 263n5; fat bellies and, 202; hogs for, 120; iconic status of, 203; qualisigns of, 205; as quick cooking, 171; in restaurants, 226. *See also* fat

Bakewell, Robert, 107–8

barbecue: in North Carolina, 62, 67, 204, 209, 210, 216, 228; pit masters, 203; whole-hog, 170–71, 215, 234

BBQ Joint (restaurant), 213, 216

beef and beef industry, 103, 104, 206, 256n10. *See also* cattle and cattle farming

Behr, Edward, 200

Beranger, Jeannette, 115, 116, 118–19

Berkshire breed, 73, 108, 115, 116, 126, 130, 261n11; performance of, 131; pork of, 132, 171, 174; revitalization of, 237

Berry, Wendell, 63, 69, 80, 122

biodiversity, 238, 261n12

Blacklin, Sarah, *87*, 172; profile of, 86–94

Bladen County, 23, *25*, 28

Blanchette, Alex, 171, 259n10, 264n5

Bon Appétit (magazine), 39

Bourdieu, Pierre, 80, 126, 252, 255n6, 260n13; on habitus, 6, 230–31, 264n1

Braeburn Farms, 40, 45, 46, 147, 153, 256n10; beef from, 182, 184

braising, 171, 229, 232

branding, brands, 17; antibrand, 131–35; breeds as, 135; building of, 102; Firsthand Foods, 104; management of, 133

breeds and breeding of pigs, 11, 37–38, 73, 78, 107–16, 247, 261n3; antibrand and, 131–35; Asian, 107, 108, 114, 260n2; Berkshire hybrids, 124; bloodline preservation in, 116, 117, 118, 122, 138; as brands, 133, 135;

in Britain, 108, 261n3; Chester Whites, 130, 261n11; Crossabaws, 128; Durocs, 73, 108, 130, 133, 261n11; English, 107–8, 118; Eurasian, 43; European, 118, 260n2; genetic diversity and, 117, 238; genotypes and, 114; Gloucestershire Old Spots, 78, 108, 124, 126, 144, 237; Guineas, 42, 115; Hampshires, 108, 115, 116, 130, 132, 133, 261n3; hybridity and hybrids, 125–31, 136–37, 160, 249; Iberian pata negras, 200–201; Ibéricos, 71, 73–74, 111, 120, 127, 201; Large Whites, 261n3; Mangalitsas, 117; multidimensionality of, 109; Ossabaw Crosses, 72, 73, 78, 79, 81, 129; Pedigree Breeds, 108, 261n3; phenotypes, 114, 132; Pietrains, 115, 116; Poland Chinas, 130; process of, 77–78; Red Wattles, 126; reorganization of, 259n11; selective, 8, 108, 112, 119, 125, 131, 133; Spanish black foots, x; Suffolks, 108; Tamworths, 42, 78, 108, 144, 237; variables in, 123; Yorkshires, 108, 130. *See also* Berkshire breed; heritage breeds; Farmer's Hybrids; Ossabaw Island Hogs

Breeze Farms, 139, 141, 261n14

Brown, Drew, 88, 102

Business Alliance for Sustainable Entrepreneurship, 101

butchery, 22, 23, 88, 147–53, 159, 173, 174, 258n11; artisanal, 156, 178; authenticity and, 164; dressing of pigs, 159, 160; gender and, 92–93, 172; humaneness in, 156; kit, 164–65, *166*, 247; licenses for, 31–32, 40, 88, 256n11; participation in, 156; performance of, 17, 157, *157*–59, 171–73, 179; programs, 158–59, 168, 176, 178, 179, 228, 234, 264n7; respect, 175; skills, 165, 169; snout-to-tail, 151, 219–41; techniques, 244; as value added, 148. *See also names of individual butchers*

Cabarrus County, 22

California, vii, viii, x, 33, 37, 130, 161, 200

Callaghan, Kevin, *181*; profile of, 180–86

Callahan, Fred, 100–101

Cane Creek Farm, 11, 40, 45, 147, 199, 216, 256n10; breeding herd, 73, 78; Farmer's Hybrids, 128; marketing events, 71–79; Ossabaws, 71, 74, 113; pigs, 1–2, 62, 123; pork from, 82, 210, *211*; publicity, 208–9

capital, 101–2, 223, 224; cultural, 252

carcass, 167; breaking down, 158, 163, 168, 169; de-animalization, 233–34; lamb, 236; as meat, 158–64; primals, 103, 152, 165, 168–71. *See also* butchery and butchering, butchers

Carolina Farm Stewardship Association (CFSA), 14, 42, 45, 259n6

Carolina Meat Conference, 15, 88

Carrboro, 86, 180, 212, 249, 250

Carrboro Farmers' Market, 45, 47, 50, 60, 123, 127, 180, 199, 213, 224; Blacklin and, 86, 87; local foods, ix, 258n14; MacLean and Cane Creek Farm products, viii, 12, 40, 72, 199; regulations, 68, 225; socializing, 69; WIC benefits, 249–50

cattle and cattle farming, 53, 97–98, 120, 123, 202, 258n24. *See also* beef and beef industry

Center for Environmental Farming Systems (CEFS), 15, 35, 70, 102, 259n6; NC Choices and, 89, 98, 99; O'Sullivan and, 47, 55–56, 259n32

Center for Sustainable Entrepreneurship, 101

Chang, David, 232

Chapel Hill, viii, 21, 39, 147, 209, 249; farmers' markets, 32, 139, 145; Franklin Street, 212; restaurants, 205, 212, 224; UNC, 86, 96, 101, 185, 222

charcuterie, 158, 174, 196, 216, 226, 234

Charlotte, 22, 185, 223, 246

cheese, 65, 191

chefs, 12, 13, 135, 150, 180, 212; awards for, 12, 39; as butchers, 158; in Chapel Hill, 205, 212, 224; as end consumer, 119; Farm to Fork Picnic, 81–82; farmers' markets, 146; Firsthand Foods, 102; food reform and, 249; marketing events, 72; philosophy, 227; pork and, 1–2, 33, 45, 79, 113; relationship with animal, 174; skills, 229; Slow Food and, 204. *See also* restaurants; *names of individual chefs*

Cherry Farm, 56

Chez Panisse (restaurant), 33, 200

chicken and poultry, 183, 184, 187, 188, 263n1; free-range, 195; industry, 27; local, 210; raising, 139, 140, 141–42

China, 28, 107, 190–91. *See also* breeds and breeding of pigs: Asian

circulation, 236–38

class: divisions, 224, 249, 260n13; food and, 85, 230–31; inequalities, 249; middle, 61; pork production and, 3; relations, 6, 29; struggle, 5; working, 4, 6–7, 230, 232

Coastal Plain, 21, 22, 24, 29, 32, 37

colonialism, 113, 211; colonial narrative and, 77, 81

Comaroff, Jean, 110, 244

Comaroff, John, 110, 244

commodities, 6, 8, 17–18, 122; agriculture and, 65, 117, 255n3, 257n10

community, 151–52, 178, 261n13

community-supported agriculture (CSA), 141, 152

confined animal feeding operations (CAFOs), 25, 85, 130, 178, 259n8, 264n5; consolidation, 246; contract system and, 253; environment and, 26–27, 29; problems with, 56, 59, 198, 200, 208, 227; Talbott and, 32–33, 199; vertical integration, 221; vitality and, 173

connection, connections, 17, 156, 177, 183, 221, 225; among animal parts, 232, 233; authenticity and, 249, 251, 252; food and, 186; locavores and, 155; multidimensional, 237; networks and, 10, 259n3; pastured pork and, 239; pig people, 213; privileged, 228; in profiles, 256n9; stories and, 248; value, 222, 226–27; virtues, 179

connoisseurship, connoisseurs, 155–56, 175, 178, 201

consistency, 89–90, 100

consumption, consumers, 9, 12, 18, 135; brands, 133; butchering and, 160–61; commodity supply chains, 6; convenience and, 142; education, 158; ethical, 249, 251, 254; farmers connected to, 69; networks, 34; of pork, 79, 202; preferences, 193, 202–3

Cook, Leah, 87

Co-op, The. *See* NC Natural Hog Growers Association (The Co-op)

Cooper, John, 28

cooperative extension, 15, 44, 53, 55, 91, 132, 261n14

co-ops, 104

cosmopolitans, 6, 9, 61, 138, 180, 222, 223, 231, 241, 246

Cramer, Nancy, 98, 259n32

hog industry (*continued*)
in North Carolina, 26–30; in United States,
197–98. *See also* confined animal feeding operations; industrial hog farming;
industrial pork production; pig farming,
farmers; pigs and hogs
hogs. *See* pigs and hogs
holism, 220, 221, 222, 263n2. *See also* totalization, totalities
Holtzman, Jon, 190
hot dogs, 213, 215, 229, 231
human-animal relations, 173–78; edibility, 235;
hunting, 173–74, 175; vitality and, 165, 175
Hummel, Sam, 139, 141, 144, 145, 146
Hurdle Mills, 261n14
hurricanes, 29, 42, 56, 98, 258n31
Hymes, Del, 19

icons, 7–8, 17, 177, 225, 227, 235, 245, 247;
agricultural, 61; of authenticity, 247;
brands as, 133–34; discernment, 82; fatty
pork and bacon as, 197, 199, 203; Peircean,
199, 231; pigginess, 205; pork cuts, 233;
whole animal, 164. *See also* qualisigns
India, 205, 206–8, 211
industrial agriculture, 173, 197–98, 255n3;
African Americans and, 14, 36; critics of,
198, 221, 222; degrading conditions, 15, 39,
59, 61, 62, 85; Latinos and, 223; small farmers harmed by, 138, 147. *See also* industrial
hog farming; industrial pork production
industrial food system, x, xi, 1, 5, 60, 135–36,
177
industrial hog farming, 23, 120; contract
production system, 27–28, 29, 199;
evolutionary history of, 107; global
market, 108; heritage vs., 117. *See also*
hog industry
industrialization, 63, 65, 85, 156
industrial pork production, 59, 61, 171,
197–98; environmental degradation,
199; heritage breeds vs., 135; local food
and, 260n15; meat science's ties to,
193; National Pork Producers Council,
197–98; taste of meat, 198. *See also* pork
production
Ingold, Tim, 125
innovation, 84, 86, 203, 204, 219, 247, 254;
in pasture-raised pig farming, 34–38
insular dwarfism, 111

integration, 30, 228, 233, 239. *See also* vertical
integration
integrity, 252, 253
Iowa, 2, 55, 59, 99, 130; Niman project, 37, 45;
pasture-raised pigs in, 33, 34, 200, 259n1
Islam, pork and, 206, 207
Italy, 54, 67, 156; slow food movement,
87–88

James Beard Foundation, 39, 67, 224
Johnston County, 25, 43
Jones, Mike, 33, 43, 55, 132–33
Jones, Rob, 210
Judaism, pork and, 206

Kaminsky, Peter, 127, 204; *Pig Perfect*, 112–13,
258n16
Kinston, 24
knowledge, 9–10
Korsmeyer, Carolyn, 188
Ku Klux Klan, 53

labor, 11; exploitation, 61, 65, 198
lagoons, 29, 56, 97, 257n8
lamb, 186, 206, 236–37, 264n8
Lantern (restaurant), 12–13, 45, 67, 82–83,
224
lard, 22, 120, 195
Latinos, 61, 222, 223–24, 252
Lefebvre, Henri, 63, 65–66, 68, 259n3
Left Bank Butchery, 147
Lewis, Laura, 263n5, 264n10
Lienhardt, Godfrey, 177
Lindholm, Charles, 245
linkage, 228, 233
Livestock Conservancy, 11, 15, 115–16,
125–28, 132, 261n12. *See also* American
Livestock Breed Conservancy
livestock farming, farmers, 11, 14, 25, 109
local, locality, 84, 91, 117, 155
local foods, viii, 1, 3, 10, 60, 63, 65, 80, 99,
258n14, 260n15; cosmopolitans, 223; definition of, ix; immigrants and, 224; local
meat, 156, 202, 213; place and, 77; politics
of, 85, 219; promotion of, 61; restaurants,
67, 182, 185; sociospatial relations, 85; system, 18, 52, 224; taste, 71; trendiness, 214.
See also locavorism, locavores; terroir
locavorism, locavores, 61, 65, 85, 219;
cosmopolitans, 241; pastured pork, 197,

233; connection and, 155; revaluation, 231; tastes, 260n12

loins, 73, 135, 165, 169, 234, 263n5; leanness, 205; premium cuts, 258n11; smoked, 215; tenderness, 169; white meat, 187, 198

mac and cheese, 216

MacLean, Eliza, 11, 38, *41*, 55, 62, 71, 83, 113, 127, 216, 238, 258n21, 259n7; on connection, 227, 248; on industrial hog farming, 259n8; at marketing event, 72–79; as mentor, 210; on Ossabaws 70, 72–73; on pigness, 243; pigs of, 1–2, 209; profile of, 40–46

Magnolia Grill, 45

Manning, Paul, 134

Maple Springs Garden, 86, 87

markets: agriculture, 259n11; demand, 46; economics, 51; heritage breeds, 132; pricing, 46; selective breeding, 108

marketing: breeding and, 116; Cane Creek Farm pork, 62, 71–79; independent, 31; niche markets, 39; as postproduction, 89; skill, 81; tools, 246; value-added dimension, 127. *See also* direct marketing; farmers' markets

Marx, Karl, 176, 190, 252

mast, as feed, 70, 78, 107, 204

materialization, materiality, 221, 235, 255n6; authenticity, 225, 247; brands, 134; breeds, 110, 131; integration, 239; Ossabaw Island Hogs, 201; primals, 171

Matkins, 145

Mauss, Marcel, 175

McKissick, Casey, 88, 89

meat: carcass, 158–64; cheap, 236, 237; ellipsis between animal and, 233–34; ethics, 175; pork, 187, 197–98; processing, 136, 148–49, 226, 233; quality, 132; respect for, 173–78; side, 230; tenderness, 169, 171; toughness, 169, 171, 172; science, 17, 71, 189, 192, 193, 196, 200; transition of animal to, 160; understanding of, 159. *See also* butchery and butchering, butchers; niche-market meats; *specific types of meat*

Meat Box, 104

media, 39, 96, 174, 263n4. *See also titles of magazines and newspapers*

memory, taste and, 189–91

methodology, 15, 18; fieldwork, 11–13; network of perspectives, 10–11; pseudonyms,

16; sites of research, 11, 12–13, 19, 61. *See also* profiles

Mexicans, 223, 224, 240. *See also* Latinos

Midwest, 44, 130

Mintz, Sidney, *Sweetness and Power*, 4–5, 6

Mitchell, Ed, 55, 203

model, in sentiment, 177–78

Moize, Steve, 115, 119, 120, 122, 139–40, 261n6

Momofuku, 232

morality, morals, 177, 262n11

Mountain Agriculture Project (MAP), 53

Munn, Nancy, 7–8, 256n7

Murphy, Wendell H., 26–27, 35–36

Murphy Family Farms, 26, 28

Nadasdy, Paul, 173–74

Nash County, 15

National Institutes of Health, 74, 112–13

National Pork Producers Council, 187; "Other White Meat" campaign, 197–98, 234

Natural Food Holdings, 38

Natural Resource Defense Council (NRDC), 94, 95

nature, 2, 8, 60

NC Choices, 35, 44, 56–57, 90, 94, 213–14, 253; Blacklin, 86, 87, 88–89, 98; mission, 91, 99

NC Growing Together (NCGT), 52, 258n27

NC Natural Hog Growers Association (The Co-op), 38–39, 51, 55, 104, 213–14, 217

Neal, Sheila, 87

Neil, Bill, 185

neoliberalism, 224, 249, 263n4

networks, 10, 11, 34, 62, 93; of perspectives, 9, 12, 131–32, 133, 135, 247, 253, 259n5

Neuse River, 56

New Deal, 52

New River, 29

News and Observer (Raleigh), 98

New South, 179

New York, 141, 147, 232, 250

New York Times, 39, 113, 204, 210, 263n1

New Zealand, lamb trade, 236–37

niche markets, 91, 117, 132, 134, 135, 179, 213; as alternative, 89, 108, 255n3; heritage breeds, 201

niche-market meats, 5, 38, 91, 250, 251, 260n13; butchers and, 174; discernment, 82; marketing, 173; network of perspectives, 247; pasture-raised pork, 14, 15, 19,

Special Supplemental Nutrition Program for Women, Infants, and Children (WIC), 240, 249–50

standards: butchers, 148; meat quality, 34, 37, 70–71

Stanly County, 22

stewardship, environmental, 178

strawberries, 67, 68

structural constraint, in pasture-raised pig farming, 34–38

subsistence farming, 22–23, 25

Suchoff, Sam, 123, 171, *214*; profile of, 212–17

sugar production, 4

Supplemental Nutrition Assistance Program (SNAP), 240

supply chains, 90, 101, 103

sustainability, 10, 11, 42, 60, 139, 140, 240, 221, 232, 258n26; CEFS, 100; contested term, 63–64; Europe, 72; local food economy, 99, 216; Kellogg Foundation, 258n28; locavores, 61; North Carolina A&T, 47, 258n22; unpredictability, 142

Sustainable Agriculture Research and Education (SARE), 34–35, 39, 43, 54

Sutton, David, 190

Sweden, 2

sweet potatoes, 97, 98

Swine Initiative (American Livestock Breed Conservancy), 115

Sydnor, Charles ("Doc"), 40, 45, 153

Sydnor, Eliza, 147, 152

symbolic action and symbols, 177, 188. *See also* icons

Talbott, Charles (Chuck), 34, 70, 98, 204, 258n16; North Carolina A&T, 32–35, 42–43, 54; Ossabaws, 37–38, 43–44, 199–200; Small-Scale Hog Producer project, 112–13

Tanzania, vii, 191, 256n7

taste, 6, 17, 70–71, 188, 200, 241, 260n13, 264n8; anthropological approaches, 189–91; attuned engagement, 194; definitions, 192; industrial pork production, 198; mode of perception, 205; new models, 204; panels testing for, 196; place, 60, 63, 64, 68, 80, 86, 155, 197; political, 189; recuperation, 201–2; region, 3, 72; vocabulary, 263n4. *See also* fat; flavor; terroir

taste buds, 192

technology, 180

tenderness of meat, 169, 171. *See also* toughness of meat

Tennessee Valley Authority (TVA), 53

Terra Madre (conference), 87–88

terroir, 17, 59, 84, 189, 221, 246, 247, 249; definition, 60, 64; Piedmont historicity, 79, 197–201; term, 63–64

ticks, 193–94

tobacco and tobacco farmers, 52, 53, 258n10; community of practice, 54; tobacco buyout, 35, 43, 51, 200

Tobacco Trust Fund, 101

Torres, Miguel, 224, 263n4

totalization, totalities, 163, 219–20, 221, 222, 228, 235, 239, 263n2

toughness of meat, 169, 171, 172, 233, 248. *See also* tenderness of meat

tractors, 141, 142

transparency, in butchering, 156

Triad, 11, 21, 22, 39, 202, 203, 263n3

Triangle, viii, 11, 22, 38, 104, 202; cosmopolitan mobility, 138; defined, 21; farmers' markets, 39; niche-market pork, 60; pastured-pork consumers, 202–3; research universities, 222; restaurants, 39, 139

Trubek, Amy, 64

Tucker, Bobby, 144

Twain, Mark, 67

typification, 109

Tyson Foods Inc., 27

umami, 189

United States: heritage breeds, x; hog industry, 197–98; hog producers, 26; pork consumption, 197

United States Department of Agriculture (USDA), 54, 160; discriminatory lending practices, 36, 61; Economic Research Service, 197; National Resource Conservation Service, 98; SARE program, 34–35; Southern Risk Management and Education Center, 90

United States Environmental Protection Agency, 27

University of California, Berkeley, 41

University of California, Davis, 40, 41

University of California, Los Angeles, 47

University of North Carolina, Asheville, 86